Key Issues

HUME ON NATURAL RELIGION

To Barbara, Justine, Tzvi,
and to my parents Fay and Dave Tweyman

Key Issues

HUME ON NATURAL RELIGION

Edited and Introduced by
STANLEY TWEYMAN
York University, Toronto

Series Editor
ANDREW PYLE
University of Bristol

THOEMMES PRESS

© Thoemmes Press 1996

Published in 1996 by
Thoemmes Press
11 Great George Street
Bristol BS1 5RR, England

US office: Distribution and Marketing
22883 Quicksilver Drive
Dulles, Virginia 20166, USA

ISBN
Paper : 1 85506 450 2
Cloth : 1 85506 451 0

Hume on Natural Religion
Key Issues No. 12

British Library Cataloguing-in-Publication Data

A catalogue record of this title is available
from the British Library

Printed in Great Britain by Antony Rowe Ltd., Chippenham

CONTENTS

NATURAL HISTORY OF RELIGION

INTRODUCTION

This is the second of two volumes dealing with some of the most important secondary literature on David Hume's writings on religion. Volume one addresses Hume's essay 'Of Miracles'; the present volume is concerned with Hume's books *Dialogues Concerning Natural Religion* and *The Natural History of Religion*, and his essays 'On the Immortality of the Soul', 'Of a Particular Providence and of a Future State', and 'On Suicide'. I have also included material of interest, written both by Hume and by others, on 'The Life and Writings of David Hume'. The contents in this volume originally appeared between 1757 and 1907, a period of 150 years. The essays, book chapters, and book reviews included in this volume reveal a period which is, in the main, hostile to Hume's views and to Hume's arguments on religion. Hume is regarded by many as an atheist, an enemy of religion, and as an opponent of the Christian religion. It is this latter consideration – the perception that Hume was an ardent opponent of Christianity – that led Adam Smith to distance himself from the *Dialogues Concerning Natural Religion* and, therefore, to refuse Hume's request that he ensure the publication of this book after Hume's death.

The readings reveal that many regarded Hume as holding negative views toward religion, and then seeking to construct arguments which support this anti-religion bias. It is important to point out that, in various places, Hume goes to great lengths to insist that this is not his manner of doing philosophy, and that his philosophy (from the standpoint of what in Section XII of the first *Enquiry* he calls 'mitigated scepticism') requires that 'in general, there is a degree of doubt, and caution, and modesty, which, in all kinds of scrutiny and decision, ought for ever to accompany a just reasoner' (paragraph 129). In an earlier passage in the first *Enquiry* (the opening paragraph of Section V, Part I), Hume writes:

> The passion for philosophy, like that for religion, seems liable to this inconvenience, that, though it aims at the correction of our manners, and extirpation of our vices, it may only serve, by imprudent management, to foster a predominant inclination, and to push the mind, with more determined resolution, towards that side which already draws too much, by the bias and propensity of the natural temper. It is certain that, while we aspire to the magnanimous firmness of the philosophic sage, and endeavour to confine our pleasures altogether within our own minds, we may, at last, render our philosophy like that of Epictetus, and other Stoics, only a more refined system of selfishness, and reason ourselves out of all virtue as well as social enjoyment. While we study with attention the vanity of human life, and turn all our thoughts towards the empty and transitory nature of riches and honours, we are, perhaps, all the while flattering our natural indolence, which, hating the bustle of the world, and drudgery of business, seeks a pretence of reason to give itself a full and uncontrolled indulgence.

This is philosophy approached from the standpoint of the dogmatist: '... while they see objects only on one side, and have no idea of any counterpoising argument, they throw themselves precipitately into the principles, to which they are inclined; nor have they any indulgence for those who entertain opposite sentiments' (paragraph 129).

The starting point of philosophy for the mitigated sceptic is developed immediately following the passage quoted above:

> There is, however, one species of philosophy which seems little liable to this inconvenience, and that because it strikes in with no disorderly passion of the human mind, nor can mingle itself with any natural affection or propensity; and that is the Academic or Sceptical philosophy. The academics always talk of doubt and suspense of judgement, of danger in hasty determinations, of confining to very

narrow bounds the enquiries of the understanding, and of renouncing all speculations which lie not within the limits of common life and practice. Nothing, therefore, can be more contrary than such a philosophy to the supine indolence of the mind, its rash arrogance, its lofty pretensions, and its superstitious credulity. Every passion is mortified by it, except the love of truth; and that passion never is, nor can be, carried to too high a degree. It is surprising, therefore, that this philosophy, which, in almost every instance, must be harmless and innocent, should be the subject of so much groundless reproach and obloquy. But, perhaps, the very circumstance which renders it so innocent is what chiefly exposes it to the public hatred and resentment. By flattering no irregular passion, it gains few partizans. By opposing so many vices and follies, it raises to itself abundance of enemies, who stigmatize it as libertine, profane, and irreligious.

From this passage we learn, therefore, that (1) Hume anticipated, in general, the negative response which his writings on religion would generate; and (2) he recognized, as it were a priori, that his writings on religion would not be understood by most of his readers who would adopt this dogmatical position.

In Hume's *Dialogues Concerning Natural Religion*, Cleanthes is the one who personifies (at different points in the text) both standpoints in philosophy discussed by Hume in these passages. At the end of Part One of the *Dialogues*, prior to presenting his Argument from Design, Cleanthes explains:

It is very natural, said CLEANTHES, for men to embrace those principles, by which they find they can best defend their doctrines; nor need we have any recourse to priestcraft to account for so reasonable an expedient. And surely, nothing can afford a stronger presumption, that any set of principles are true, and ought to be embraced, that to observe, that they tend to the confirmation of true religion, and serve to confound the cavils of atheists, libertines, and freethinkers of all denominations.

Here we find Cleanthes the dogmatist, urging that the

Argument from Design is to be accepted because it confirms 'true religion'. On the other hand, when, at the beginning of Part 9 of the *Dialogues*, Demea urges acceptance of his a priori argument for God's existence because it proves the 'infinity of the divine attributes' and the 'unity of the divine nature', Cleanthes interjects:

> You seem to reason, DEMEA, interposed CLEANTHES, as if those advantages and conveniences in the abstract argument were full proofs of its solidarity. But it is first proper in my opinion, to determine what argument of this nature you choose to insist on; and we shall afterwards, from itself, better than from its useful consequences, endeavour to determine what value we ought to put upon it.

Obviously, there has been a change in Cleanthes between Part 2 and Part 9 from dogmatism to mitigated scepticism (which I develop in my *Scepticism and Belief in Hume's Dialogues Concerning Natural Religion*, 1986). It is also obvious that, however this change in Cleanthes has been brought about, Hume regards his critics as never having gone beyond the stage of the dogmatist. But the irony in this moment in the history of philosophy is clear: Hume, the philosopher who took great pains to prepare the mind for the study of philosophy, and who claims to be proceeding by no passion but the love of truth, is repeatedly accused of doing philosophy in order to promote his own prejudices regarding religion.

My efforts in this project, as always, are dedicated to my parents, Fay and Dave Tweyman, my wife Barbara, and our children Justine and Tzvi, and my brother Martin.

Stanley Tweyman
Glendon College, York University
Toronto, Ontario, 1996

OTHER BOOKS BY STANLEY TWEYMAN ON THE PHILOSOPHY OF DAVID HUME

Reason and Conduct in Hume and His Predecessors, Martinus Nijhoff (Kluwer), The Hague, 1974

Scepticism and Belief in Hume's Dialogues Concerning Natural Religion, Martinus Nijhoff (Kluwer), The Hague, 1989

Descartes and Hume: Selected Topics, Caravan books, Delmar, New York, 1989

David Hume: Dialogues concerning Natural Religion, In Focus, a new edition edited and with an Introduction by Stanley Tweyman, Routledge, London and New York, 1991

David Hume: Critical Assessments, a six-volume work, edited by Stanley Tweyman, containing 191 papers on various aspects of Hume's Philosophy, Routledge, London and New York, 1995

Essays on the Philosophy of David Hume: Natural Religion, Natural Belief, and Ontology, Caravan Books, Delmar, New York, 1996

Hume on Miracles, edited and with an Introduction by Stanley Tweyman, Thoemmes Press, 1996

I. The Life and Writings
of David Hume

THE LIFE OF DAVID HUME, ESQ.
David Hume

MR. HUME, a few months before his death, wrote the following short account of his own Life; and, in a codicil to his
will, desired that it might be prefixed to the next edition of
his Works. That edition cannot be published for a considerable time. The Editor, in the mean while, in order to serve
the purchasers of the former editions; and, at the same time,
to gratify the impatience of the public curiosity; has thought
proper to publish it separately, without altering even the title
or superscription, which was written in Mr. Hume's own
hand on the cover of the manuscript.

My own Life

IT is difficult for a man to speak long of himself without
vanity; therefore, I shall be short. It may be thought an
instance of vanity that I pretend at all to write my life; but
this Narrative shall contain little more than the History of
my Writings; as, indeed, almost all my life has been spent in
literary pursuits and occupations. The first success of most
of my writings was not such as to be an object of vanity.

I was born the 26th of April 1711, old style, at Edinburgh. I was of a good family, both by father and mother:
my father's family is a branch of the Earl of Home's, or
Hume's; and my ancestors had been proprietors of the estate,
which my brother possesses, for several generations. My
mother was daughter of Sir David Falconer, President of
the College of Justice: the title of Lord Halkerton came by
succession to her brother.

My family, however, was not rich, and being myself a
younger brother, my patrimony, according to the mode of my
country, was of course very slender. My father, who passed
for a man of parts, died when I was an infant, leaving me,
with an elder brother and a sister, under the care of our
mother, a woman of singular merit, who, though young and

handsome, devoted herself entirely to the rearing and educat-
ing of her children. I passed through the ordinary course of
education with success, and was seized very early with a
passion for literature, which has been the ruling passion of
my life, and the great source of my enjoyments. My studious
disposition, my sobriety, and my industry, gave my family a
notion that the law was a proper profession for me; but I
found an unsurmountable aversion to every thing but the
pursuits of philosophy and general learning; and while they
fancied I was poring upon Voet and Vinnius, Cicero and
Virgil were the authors which I was secretly devouring.

My very slender fortune, however, being unsuitable to this
plan of life, and my health being a little broken by my ardent
application, I was tempted, or rather forced, to make a very
feeble trial for entering into a more active scene of life. In
1734, I went to Bristol, with some recommendations to eminent merchants, but in a few months found that scene totally
unsuitable to me. I went over to France, with a view of
prosecuting my studies in a country retreat; and I there laid
that plan of life, which I have steadily and successfully pursued. I resolved to make a very rigid frugality supply my
deficiency of fortune, to maintain unimpaired my independency, and to regard every object as contemptible, except the
improvement of my talents in literature.

During my retreat in France, first at Reims, but chiefly at
La Fleche, in Anjou, I composed my *Treatise of Human
Nature*. After passing three years very agreeably in that
country, I came over to London in 1737. In the end of 1738,
I published my Treatise, and immediately went down to my
mother and my brother, who lived at his country-house, and
was employing himself very judiciously and successfully in
the improvement of his fortune.

Never literary attempt was more unfortunate than my
Treatise of Human Nature. It fell *dead-born from the press*,
without reaching such distinction, as even to excite a murmur
among the zealots. But being naturally of a cheerful and
sanguine temper, I very soon recovered the blow, and prosecuted with great ardour my studies in the country. In 1742,
I printed at Edinburgh the first part of my Essays: the work
was favourably received, and soon made me entirely forget
my former disappointment. I continued with my mother
and brother in the country, and in that time recovered the

knowledge of the Greek language, which I had too much neglected in my early youth.

In 1745, I received a letter from the Marquis of Annandale, inviting me to come and live with him in England; I found also, that the friends and family of that young nobleman were desirous of putting him under my care and direction, for the state of his mind and health required it. – I lived with him a twelvemonth. My appointments during that time made a considerable accession to my small fortune. I then received an invitation from General St. Clair to attend him as a secretary to his expedition, which was at first meant against Canada, but ended in an incursion on the coast of France. Next year, to wit, 1747, I received an invitation from the General to attend him in the same station in his military embassy to the courts of Vienna and Turin. I then wore the uniform of an officer, and was introduced at these courts as aid-de-camp to the general, along with Sir Harry Erskine and Captain Grant, now General Grant. These two years were almost the only interruptions which my studies have received during the course of my life: I passed them agreeably, and in good company; and my appointments, with my frugality, had made me reach a fortune, which I called independent, though most of my friends were inclined to smile when I said so; in short, I was now master of near a thousand pounds.

I had always entertained a notion, that my want of success in publishing the Treatise of Human Nature, had proceeded more from the manner than the matter, and that I had been guilty of a very usual indiscretion, in going to the press too early. I, therefore, cast the first part of that work anew in the Enquiry concerning Human Understanding, which was published while I was at Turin. But this piece was at first little more successful than the Treatise of Human Nature. On my return from Italy, I had the mortification to find all England in a ferment, on account of Dr. Middleton's Free Enquiry, while my performance was entirely overlooked and neglected. A new edition, which had been published at London of my Essays, moral and political, met not with a much better reception.

Such is the force of natural temper, that these disappointments made little or no impression on me. I went down in 1749, and lived two years with my brother at his country-house, for my mother was now dead. I there composed the second part of my Essays, which I called Political Discourses, and also my Enquiry concerning the Principles of Morals, which is another part of my treatise that I cast anew. Meanwhile, my bookseller, A. Millar, informed me, that my former publications (all but the unfortunate Treatise) were beginning to be the subject of conversation; that the sale of them was gradually increasing, and that new editions were demanded. Answers by Reverends, and Right Reverends, came out two or three in a year; and I found, by Dr. Warburton's railing, that the books were beginning to be esteemed in good company. However, I had fixed a resolution, which I inflexibly maintained, never to reply to any body; and not being very irascible in my temper, I have easily kept myself clear of all literary squabbles. These symptoms of a rising reputation gave me encouragement, as I was ever more disposed to see the favourable than unfavourable side of things; a turn of mind which it is more happy to possess, than to be born to an estate of ten thousand a year.

In 1751, I removed from the country to the town, the true scene for a man of letters. In 1752, were published at Edinburgh, where I then lived, my Political Discourses, the only work of mine that was successful on the first publication. It was well received abroad and at home. In the same year was published at London, my Enquiry concerning the Principles of Morals; which, in my own opinion (who ought not to judge on that subject), is of all my writings, historical, philosophical, or literary, incomparably the best. It came unnoticed and unobserved into the world.

In 1752, the Faculty of Advocates chose me their Librarian, an office from which I receive little or no emolument, but which gave me the command of a large library. I then formed the plan of writing the History of England; but being frightened with the notion of continuing a narrative through a period of 1700 years, I commenced with the accession of the House of Stuart, an epoch when, I thought, the misrepresentations of faction began chiefly to take place. I was, I own, sanguine in my expectations of the success of this work. I thought that I was the only historian, that had at once neglected present power, interest, and authority, and the cry of popular prejudices; and as the subject was suited to every capacity, I expected proportional applause. But miserable was my disappointment: I was assailed by one cry of reproach, disapprobation, and even detestation; English, Scotch, and Irish, Whig and Tory, churchman and sectary, freethinker and religionist, patriot and courtier, united in their rage against the man, who had presumed to shed a generous tear for the fate of Charles I. and the Earl of Strafford; and after the first ebullitions of their fury were over, what was still more mortifying, the book seemed to sink into oblivion. Mr. Millar told me, that in a twelvemonth he sold only forty-five copies of it. I scarcely, indeed, heard of one man in the three kingdoms, considerable for rank or letters, that could endure the book. I must only except the primate of England, Dr. Herring, and the primate of Ireland, Dr. Stone, which seem two odd exceptions. These dignified prelates separately sent me messages not to be discouraged.

I was, however, I confess, discouraged; and had not the war been at that time breaking out between France and England, I had certainly retired to some provincial town of the former kingdom, have changed my name, and never more have returned to my native country. But as this scheme was not now practicable, and the subsequent volume was considerably advanced, I resolved to pick up courage and to persevere.

In this interval, I published at London my Natural History of Religion, along with some other small pieces: its public entry was rather obscure, except only that Dr. Hurd wrote a pamphlet against it, with all the illiberal petulance, arrogance, and scurrility, which distinguish the Warburtonian school. This pamphlet gave me some consolation for the otherwise indifferent reception of my performance.

In 1756, two years after the fall of the first volume, was published the second volume of my History, containing the period from the death of Charles I. till the Revolution. This performance happened to give less displeasure to the Whigs, and was better received. It not only rose itself, but helped to buoy up its unfortunate brother.

But though I had been taught by experience, that the Whig party were in possession of bestowing all places, both in the state and in literature, I was so little inclined to yield to their senseless clamour, that in above a hundred alterations, which farther study, reading, or reflection engaged me to make in the reigns of the two first Stuarts, I have made all of them invariably to the Tory side. It is ridiculous to consider the

English constitution before that period as a regular plan of liberty.

In 1759, I published my History of the House of Tudor. The clamour against this performance was almost equal to that against the History of the two first Stuarts. The reign of Elizabeth was particularly obnoxious. But I was now callous against the impressions of public folly, and continued very peaceably and contentedly in my retreat at Edinburgh, to finish, in two volumes, the more early part of the English History, which I gave to the public in 1761, with tolerable, and but tolerable success.

But, notwithstanding this variety of winds and seasons, to which my writings had been exposed, they had still been making such advances, that the copy-money given me by the booksellers, much exceeded any thing formerly known in England; I was become not only independent, but opulent. I retired to my native country of Scotland, determined never more to set my foot out of it; and retaining the satisfaction of never having preferred a request to one great man, or even making advances of friendship to any of them. As I was now turned of fifty, I thought of passing all the rest of my life in this philosophical manner, when I received, in 1763, an invitation from the Earl of Hertford, with whom I was not in the least acquainted, to attend him on his embassy to Paris, with a near prospect of being appointed secretary to the embassy; and, in the meanwhile, of performing the functions of that office. This offer, however inviting, I at first declined, both because I was reluctant to begin connexions with the great, and because I was afraid that the civilities and gay company of Paris, would prove disagreeable to a person of my age and humour: but on his lordship's repeating the invitation, I accepted of it. I have every reason, both of pleasure and interest, to think myself happy in my connexions with that nobleman, as well as afterwards with his brother, General Conway.

Those who have not seen the strange effects of modes, will never imagine the reception I met with at Paris, from men and women of all ranks and stations. The more I resiled from their excessive civilities, the more I was loaded with them. There is, however, a real satisfaction in living at Paris, from the great number of sensible, knowing, and polite company with which that city abounds above all places in the universe. I thought once of settling there for life.

I was appointed secretary to the embassy; and, in summer 1765, Lord Hertford left me, being appointed Lord Lieutenant of Ireland. I was *charge d'affaires* till the arrival of the Duke of Richmond, towards the end of the year. In the beginning of 1766, I left Paris, and next summer went to Edinburgh, with the same view as formerly, of burying myself in a philosophical retreat. I returned to that place, not richer, but with much more money, and a much larger income, by means of Lord Hertford's friendship, than I left it; and I was desirous of trying what superfluity could produce, as I had formerly made an experiment of a competency. But, in 1767, I received from Mr. Conway an invitation to be Under-secretary; and this invitation, both the character of the person, and my connexions with Lord Hertford, prevented me from declining. I returned to Edinburgh in 1769, very opulent (for I possessed a revenue of 1000 l. a year), healthy, and though somewhat stricken in years, with the prospect of enjoying long my ease, and of seeing the increase of my reputation.

In spring 1775, I was struck with a disorder in my bowels, which at first gave me no alarm, but has since, as I apprehend it, become mortal and incurable. I now reckon upon a speedy dissolution. I have suffered very little pain from my disorder; and what is more strange, have, notwithstanding the great decline of my person, never suffered a moment's abatement of my spirits; insomuch, that were I to name the period of my life, which I should most choose to pass over again, I might be tempted to point to this later period. I possess the same ardour as ever in study, and the same gaiety in company. I consider, besides, that a man of sixty-five, by dying, cuts off only a few years of infirmities; and though I see many symptoms of my literary reputation's breaking out at last with additional lustre, I knew that I could have but few years to enjoy it. It is difficult to be more detached from life than I am at present.

To conclude historically with my own character. I am, or rather was (for that is the style I must now use in speaking of myself, which emboldens me the more to speak my sentiments); I was, I say, a man of mild dispositions, of command of temper, of an open, social, and cheerful humour, capable of attachment, but little susceptible of enmity, and of great moderation in all my passions.   Even my love of literary fame, my ruling passion, never soured my temper, notwithstanding my frequent disappointments.   My company was not unacceptable to the young and careless, as well as to the studious and literary; and as I took a particular pleasure in the company of modest women, I had no reason to be displeased with the reception I met with from them.   In a word, though most men any wise eminent, have found reason to complain of calumny, I never was touched, or even attacked by her baleful tooth: and though I wantonly exposed myself to the rage of both civil and religious factions, they seemed to be disarmed in my behalf of their wonted fury. My friends never had occasion to vindicate any one circumstance of my character and conduct: not but that the zealots, we may well suppose, would have been glad to invent and propagate any story to my disadvantage, but they could never find any which they thought would wear the face of probability.   I cannot say there is no vanity in making this funeral oration of myself, but I hope it is not a misplaced one; and this is a matter of fact which is easily cleared and ascertained.

April 18, 1776.

LETTER FROM ADAM SMITH, LL.D.
TO WILLIAM STRAHAN, ESQ.
Adam Smith

Kirkaldy, Fifeshire, Nov. 9, 1776.

Dear Sir,

IT is with a real, though a very melancholy pleasure, that I sit down to give you some account of the behaviour of our late excellent friend, Mr. Hume, during his last illness.

Though, in his own judgment, his disease was mortal and incurable, yet he allowed himself to be prevailed upon, by the entreaty of his friends, to try what might be the effects of a long journey. A few days before he set out, he wrote that account of his own life, which, together with his other papers, he has left to your care. My account, therefore, shall begin where his ends.

He set out for London towards the end of April, and at Morpeth met with Mr. John Home and myself, who had both come down from London on purpose to see him, expecting to have found him at Edinburgh. Mr. Home returned with him, and attended him during the whole of his stay in England, with that care and attention which might be expected from a temper so perfectly friendly and affectionate. As I had written to my mother that she might expect me in Scotland, I was under the necessity of continuing my journey. His disease seemed to yield to exercise and change of air, and when he arrived in London, he was apparently in much better health than when he left Edinburgh. He was advised to go to Bath to drink the waters, which appeared for some time to have so good an effect upon him, that even he himself began to entertain, what he was not apt to do, a better opinion of his own health. His symptoms, however, soon returned with their usual violence, and from that moment he gave up all thoughts of recovery, but submitted with the utmost cheerfulness, and the most perfect complacency and resignation. Upon his return to Edinburgh, though he found himself much weaker, yet his cheerfulness never abated, and he continued to divert himself, as usual, with correcting his own works for a new edition, with reading books of amusement, with the conversation of his friends; and, sometimes in the evening, with a party at his favourite game of whist. His cheerfulness was so great, and his conversation and amusements run so much in their usual strain, that, notwithstanding all bad symptoms, many people could not believe he was dying.

> "I shall tell your friend, Colonel Edmondstone," said Doctor Dundas to him one day, "that I left you much better, and in a fair way of recovery." "Doctor," said he, "as I believe you would not chuse to tell anything but the truth, you had better tell him, that I am dying as fast as my enemies, if I have any, could wish, and as easily and cheerfully as my best friends could desire."

Colonel Edmondstone soon afterwards came to see him, and take leave of him; and on his way home, he could not forbear writing him a letter bidding him once more an eternal adieu, and applying to him, as to a dying man, the beautiful French verses in which the Abbe Chaulieu, in expectation of his own death, laments his approaching separation from his friend, the Marquis de la Fare. Mr. Hume's magnanimity and firmness were such, that his most affectionate friends knew, that they hazarded nothing in talking or writing to him as to a dying man, and that so far from being hurt by this frankness, he was rather pleased and flattered by it. I happened to come into his room while he was reading this letter, which he had just received, and which he immediately showed me. I told him, that though I was sensible how very much he was weakened, and that appearances were in many respects very bad, yet his cheerfulness was still so great, the spirit of life seemed still to be so very strong in him, that I could not help entertaining some faint hopes. He answered,

> "Your hopes are groundless. An habitual diarrhœa of more than a year's standing, would be a very bad disease at any age: at my age it is a mortal one. When I lie down in the evening, I feel myself weaker than when I rose in the morning; and when I rise in the morning, weaker than when I lay down in the evening. I am sensible, besides,

that some of my vital parts are affected, so that I must soon die."

"Well," said I, "if it must be so, you have at least the satisfaction of leaving all your friends, your brother's family in particular, in great prosperity."

He said that he felt that satisfaction so sensibly, that when he was reading a few days before, Lucian's Dialogues of the Dead, among all the excuses which are alleged to Charon for not entering readily into his boat, he could not find one that fitted him; he had no house to finish, he had no daughter to provide for, he had no enemies upon whom he wished to revenge himself.

"I could not well imagine," said he, "what excuse I could make to Charon in order to obtain a little delay. I have done every thing of consequence which I ever meant to do, and I could at no time expect to leave my relations and friends in a better situation than that in which I am now likely to leave them; I, therefore, have all reason to die contended."

He then diverted himself with inventing several jocular excuses, which he supposed he might make to Charon, and with imagining the very surly answers which it might suit the character of Charon to return to them.

"Upon further consideration," said he, "I thought I might say to him, Good Charon, I have been correcting my works for a new edition. Allow me a little time, that I may see how the Public receives the alterations."

But Charon would answer,

"When you have seen the effect of these, you will be for making other alterations. There will be no end of such excuses; so, honest friend, please step into the boat."

But I might still urge,

"Have a little patience, good Charon, I have been endeavouring to open the eyes of the Public. If I live a few years longer, I may have the satisfaction of seeing the downfal of some of the prevailing systems of superstition."

But Charon would then lose all temper and decency.

"You loitering rogue, that will not happen these many hundred years. Do you fancy I will grant you a lease for so long a term? Get into the boat this instant, you lazy loitering rogue."

But, though Mr. Hume always talked of his approaching dissolution with great cheerfulness, he never affected to make any parade of his magnanimity. He never mentioned the subject but when the conversation naturally led to it, and never dwelt longer upon it than the course of the conversation happened to require: it was a subject indeed which occurred pretty frequently, in consequence of the inquiries which his friends, who came to see him, naturally made concerning the state of his health. The conversation which I mentioned above, and which passed on Thursday the 8th of August, was the last, except one, that I ever had with him. He had now become so very weak, that the company of his most intimate friends fatigued him; for his cheerfulness was still so great, his complaisance and social disposition were still so entire, that when any friend was with him, he could not help talking more, and with greater exertion, than suited the weakness of his body. At his own desire, therefore, I agreed to leave Edinburgh, where I was staying partly upon his account, and returned to my mother's house here, at Kirkaldy, upon condition that he would send for me whenever he wished to see me; the physician who saw him most frequently, Doctor Black, undertaking, in the mean time, to write me occasionally an account of the state of his health.

On the 22nd of August, the Doctor wrote me the following letter:

"Since my last, Mr. Hume has passed his time pretty easily, but is much weaker. He sits up, goes down stairs once a day, and amuses himself with reading, but seldom sees any body. He finds that even the conversation of his most intimate friends fatigues and oppresses him; and it is happy that he does not need it, for he is quite free from anxiety, impatience, or low spirits, and passes his time very well with the assistance of amusing books."

I received the day after a letter from Mr. Hume himself, of which the following is an extract.

Edinburgh, 23rd August, 1776.

"My Dearest Friend,

I am obliged to make use of my nephew's hand in writing to you, as I do not rise today.

I go very fast to decline, and last night had a small fever, which I hoped might put a quicker period to this tedious illness, but unluckily it has, in a great measure, gone off. I cannot submit to your coming over here on my account, as it is possible for me to see you so small a part of the day, but Doctor Black can better inform you concerning the degree of strength which may from time to time remain with me. Adieu, &c."

Three days after I received the following letter from Doctor Black.

Edinburgh, Monday, 26th August, 1776.

"Dear Sir,

Yesterday about four o'clock afternoon, Mr. Hume expired. The near approach of his death became evident in the night between Thursday and Friday, when his disease became excessive, and soon weakened him so much, that he could no longer rise out of his bed. He continued to the last perfectly sensible, and free from much pain or feelings of distress. He never dropped the smallest expression of impatience; but when he had occasion to speak to the people about him, always did it with affection and tenderness. I thought it improper to write to bring you over, especially as I heard that he had dictated a letter to you desiring you not to come. When he became very weak, it cost him an effort to speak, and he died in such a happy composure of mind, that nothing could exceed it."

Thus died our most excellent, and never to be forgotten friend; concerning whose philosophical opinions men will, no doubt, judge variously, every one approving, or condemning them, according as they happen to coincide or disagree with his own; but concerning whose character and conduct there can scarce be a difference of opinion. His temper, indeed, seemed to be more happily balanced, if I may be allowed such an expression, than that perhaps of any other man I have ever known. Even in the lowest state of his fortune, his great and necessary frugality never hindered him from exercising, upon proper occasions, acts both of charity and generosity. It was a frugality founded, not upon avarice, but upon the love of independency. The extreme gentleness of his nature never weakened either the firmness of his mind, or the steadiness of his resolutions. His constant pleasantry was the genuine effusion of good-nature and good-humour, tempered with delicacy and modesty, and without even the slightest tincture of malignity, so frequently the disagreeable source of what is called wit in other men. It never was the meaning of his raillery to mortify; and therefore, far from offending, it seldom failed to please and delight, even those who were the objects of it. To his friends, who were frequently the objects of it, there was not perhaps any one of all his great and amiable qualities, which contributed more to endear his conversation. And that gaiety of temper, so agreeable in society, but which is so often accompanied with frivolous and superficial qualities, was in him certainly attended with the most severe application, the most extensive learning, the greatest depth of thought, and a capacity in every respect the most comprehensive. Upon the whole, I have always considered him, both in his lifetime and since his death, as approaching as nearly to the idea of a perfectly wise and virtuous man, as perhaps the nature of human frailty will permit.

I ever am, dear Sir,
Most affectionately your's,

ADAM SMITH

SUPPLEMENT TO THE LIFE
OF DAVID HUME, ESQ.
David Hume

THERE can be no stronger proof of the high estimation in which Mr. Hume was held, and of his being considered as an extraordinary character, than the eager, yet, perhaps, idle curiosity, which the public entertained to learn the most minute circumstances respecting his exit.

As sincere admirers of Mr. Hume, in the Historian, the Philosopher, and the Man; we felt much regret in hearing announced to the public, "The Life of David Hume, Esq.; written by Himself." It is an undertaking which we hesitate not to pronounce impossible to be executed with propriety: egotism is disgusting; vanity intolerable; and a just estimation of one's self, the most difficult thing in life.

Upon reading this performance, however, which has been dished out into a pamphlet, we find that it only incurs a general charge of insipidity, perhaps in some articles of injustice. Mr. Hume's natural temper disposed him to feel, with exquisite sensibility, every thing which affected his literary fame; and, notwithstanding his boasted equanimity, philosophy did not shield him from the excessive chagrin which he felt from those arrows, which Envy and Prejudice darted at his reputation. Anxiety about his difference with the whimsical Rouffeau extracted from him a personal, but complete justification. The illiberal criticisms which Mr. Gray[1]

---

[1] Perhaps the mercenary Mason is more deserving of this censure than Mr. Gray. In order to swell his volume, and to fill his pockets, the former has published a loose and desultory Correspondence, which the latter never dreamt would see the light, and would have reprobated could he ever have conceived the idea of his worst papers being put to this ungenerous and ungrateful use. – Nevertheless, in return to a benefactor, who conferred essential favours upon him, Mr. Mason has, as far as he was able, sacrificed his patron's reputation at the sordid altar of Plutus. The posthumous Poetical Pieces of Mr. Gray, though infinitely valuable, are few in number, and were not likely to answer the interested purposes of the hungry Editor by much emolument. This gentleman, therefore, resolving to establish

threw out against him, in his Epistolary Correspondence, gave him much concern. He saw, with mortification, the laurel wreath which Oxford weaved to cover the bald reputation of Beattie, *his antagonist, not his rival.* And such was the antipathy that subsisted between him and Mr. Tytler, the author of the Vindication of Mary Queen of Scots; that not satisfied with a most acrimonious note[2], which has published in the last edition of his History, he would not even fit in company with him, and the appearance of the one effected the instantaneous withdrawing of the other.

Mr. Hume, in the History of his Life, has not informed us of his having stood candidate for the Professorship of Moral Philosophy, in the University of Edinburgh; of the opposition which the Scots clergy excited to his pretensions; nor of the enquiry which was moved for in the venerable assembly of the Church of Scotland, respecting the principles inculcated in his Writings; and of the censures proposed to be inflicted on him as the author of Heretical Doctrines.

He has observed in the nineteenth page of his Life, that

---

a literary property or estate, by the name and writings of another, which he honestly acquaints us he was unable to perform by his own, has given to the world, with little labour, a large but meagre Quarto, containing some puerile letters, superior, however, to the Editor's notes, with which they are garnished. And by entitling these "The Poems of Mr. Gray," led the public to buy up a large impression before the deception was discovered. Thus has the ingenuous Mason bartered the high poetical and literary reputation of a worthy man who confided in him, for *money*.

Quid non mortalia pectora coges, Auri facra fames?

[2] This note deserves a place, as it will show that even Mr. Hume himself could occasionally be guilty of, *"the illiberal arrogance, petulance and scurrility which distinguish the Warburtonian School."*

"But there is a person, that has writ an 'Enquiry historical and critical into the evidence against Mary Queen of Scots;' and has attempted to refute the foregoing narrative. He quotes a single passage of the narrative in which Mary is said simply to refuse answering; and then a single passage from Goodall, in which she boasts simply that she will answer; and he very civilly and almost directly calls the author a liar, on account of this pretended contradiction. That whole Enquiry, from beginning to end, is composed of such *scandalous artifices*. And from this instance, the reader may judge of the *candour, fair dealing, veracity*, and *good manners* of the Enquirer. There are, indeed, three events in our history, which may be regarded as touchstones of partymen. An English Whig, who asserts the reality of the popish Plot, an Irish Catholic, who denies the massacre in 1641, and a Scotch Jacobite, who maintains the innocence of Queen Mary, must be considered as men beyond the reach of argument or reason, and must be left to their prejudices."

his History of Great Britain met at first with an indifferent reception. But with respect to this, Mr. Hume himself was mistaken. The first edition of the History of Great Britain, for the reigns of James the First and Charles the First, was printed at Edinburgh, A.D. 1754, for *Hamilton, Balfour and Neil*. Hamilton, upon his expectations from this book, took a shop, and settled in London. He applied to the London booksellers to take copies of the History from him, but none of them would deal with an *interloper*. Hamilton, sadly distressed, has recourse to *his friend*, Mr. Millar; Millar *obliges him* by taking fifty copies: but when gentlemen, in his well-frequented shop, asked for the book, "Pho (says Millar generously) it is incomplete, another volume is coming out soon. You are welcome to the use of this in the mean time." Thus did Millar circulate the fifty copies among some hundred readers, without selling one, And by this ingenious device attained his favourite purpose, of getting Hamilton to sell him his right in the copy for a trifle, as being an insignificant performance.

Mr. Hume, and the late Reverend Dr. Jardine, one of the ministers of Edinburgh, lived in habits of much intimacy. Religion, *natural* and *revealed*, was frequently the subject of their conversation. It happened one night, after they had entertained themselves with theological controversy, that Mr. Hume's politeness, when bidding adieu, would not permit Dr. Jardine (whose œconomy was not incumbered with many domestics) to light him down stairs. Mr. Hume stumbled in the dark, and the Doctor hearing it, ran to his assistance with a candle, and when he had recovered his guest said to him "David, I have often told you not to rely too much upon yourself, and that *natural light* is not *sufficient*." This pleasantry Mr. Hume never relished.

As a proof of the steadiness of Mr. Hume's sceptical tenets it may be observed, that when he published the first volume of his History of Great Britain, he was advised, that the opinions he had delivered concerning matters of religion, would hurt the sale of his work; and that some apology would be proper. He accordingly in his second volume, p. 449, when speaking of the religious parties, subjoins the following note, which when his fame was established beyond the reach of party, he cancelled as unworthy of admission.

"This sophism, of arguing from the abuse of any thing against the use of it, is one of the grossest, and at the same time, the most common, to which men are subject. The history of all ages, and none more than that of the period, which is our subject, offers us examples of the abuse of religion; and we have not been sparing, in this volume more than in the former, to remark them: But whoever would thence draw an inference to the disadvantage of religion in general, would argue very rashly and erroneously. The proper office of religion is to reform men's lives, to purify their hearts, to inforce all moral duties, and to secure obedience to the laws and civil magistrate. While it pursues these salutary purposes, its operations, tho' infinitely valuable, are secret and silent, and seldom come under the cognizance of history. That adulterate species of it alone, which inflames faction, animates sedition, and prompts rebellion, distinguishes itself on the open theatre of the world, and is the great source of revolutions and public convulsions. The historian, therefore, has scarce occasion to mention any other kind of religion; and he may retain the highest regard for true piety, even while he exposes all the abuses of the false. He may even think, that he cannot better show his attachment to the former than by detecting the latter, and laying open its absurdities and pernicious tendency.

It is no proof of irreligion in an historian, that he remarks some fault or imperfection in each sect of religion, which he has occasion to mention. Every institution, however divine, which is adopted by men, must partake of the weakness and infirmities of our nature; and will be apt, unless carefully guarded, to degenerate into one extreme or the other. What species of devotion so pure, noble, and worthy the Supreme Being, as that which is most spiritual, simple, unadorned, and which partakes nothing either of the senses or imagination? Yet is it found by experience, that this mode of worship does very naturally, among the vulgar, mount up into extravagance and fanaticism. Even many of the first reformers are exposed to this reproach; and their zeal, though in the event, it proved extremely useful, partook strongly of the enthusiastic genius: Two of the judges in the reign of Charles the Second, scrupled not to advance this opinion even from the bench. Some mixture of ceremony, pomp, and ornament may seem to correct the abuse; yet will it be found very difficult to prevent such a form of religion from sinking sometimes into superstition. The church of England itself, which is perhaps the best medium among these extremes, will be allowed, at least during the age of archbishop Laud, to have been somewhat infected with a superstition, resembling the Popish; and to have payed a higher regard to some positive institutions, than the nature of the things, strictly speaking, would permit. It is the business of an historian to remark these abuses of all kinds; but it belongs also to a prudent reader to confine the representations, which he meets with, to that age alone of which the author treats. What absurdity, for instance, to suppose, that the Presbyterians, Independants, Anabaptists, and other sectaries of the present age partake of all the extravagancies, which we remark in those, who bore these appellations in the last century? The inference indeed seems juster; where sects have been noted for fanaticism during one period, to conclude, that they will be very moderate and reasonable in the subsequent. For as it is the nature of fanaticism to abolish all slavish submission to priestly power, it follows, that as soon as the first ferment is abated, men are naturally in such sects left to the free use of their reason, and shake off the fetters of custom and authority."

To say barely, that Mr. Hume in his moral character was unexceptionable, would be doing him injustice; he was truly amiable, gentle, hospitable, humane. His temper was cast in the happiest mold, if we may not except to his anxious and extreme sensibility, in every thing which affected his literary reputation. It is told, that an elderly woman in the suburbs of Edinburgh, whose excess of zeal was proportionable to her want of sense and discretion, called on Mr. Hume; declaimed violently against his sceptical principles, as she had learned them by report; represented, that he was nodding on the brink of everlasting destruction; and delivered an earnest prayer, that it would please divine grace to give him to *see* the error of his ways. Mr. Hume listened to her with attention and good humour, thanked the lady for her concern about his future welfare, and expressed a desire to know what was her line in life. She informed him, that she was a married woman, and that her husband was a tallow-chandler in the neighbourhood; upon which Mr. Hume replied,

> "Good woman, since you have expressed so earnest a desire that I should be inspired with *inward light*, I beg you will supply me with *outward light* also."

The matron retired, not a little satisfied with the commission which he gave her, and her husband thenceforwards supplied Mr. Hume's family with candles.

Notwithstanding the ideas which zealots may have formed of Mr. Hume's principles, as latitudanarian, as atheistical, as damnable: his brother's notions of them were very different. For, speaking of the Historian one day, he expressed himself in this manner, "My brother Davie is a good enough sort of a man, *but rather narrow minded*."

As to Mr. Hume's abilities as a Philosopher, and an Historian, his Works are the basis on which posterity will rear his everlasting fame.

A few months before his death, Mr. Hume was persuaded by his friends to try the effects of a long journey, and the Bath waters: but finding his malady to increase, he resigned all hopes of life. He maintained, however, his usual chearfulness; and being resolved to make the most of the short remainder of his lease, he wrote to his friends in Edinburgh, informing them of his resolution to be in that city by a certain day, which he named; and separately requested their company to dinner on the day following. Accordingly, Lord Elibank, Professor Ferguson, Mr. Home the Dramatic Poet, Dr. Smith, Dr. Blair, Dr. Black, and others of his literary friends, obeyed the summons, and took a sort of farewel dinner with their dying friend. His *flowery* rival in historic fame was also invited. But, alas! the Lord Advocate of Scotland invites this *Reverend Doctor* on that very day to a turtle feast. What was to be done? both invitations could not be embraced; – the contest was short: For as it would seem, this Historian's taste is almost as elegant in eating, as in writing, he judiciously preferred the *turtle* of my Lord Advocate to the *mutton* of David Hume.

Never did death make more regular and visible approaches than to Mr. Hume. He met these with a chearfulness and resignation, which could only be the result of a vigorous understanding, and a well-spent life. He still went abroad, called upon his friends, but as the fatigue of a chaise was now become intolerable, he went in a sedan chair, and his ghastly looks bore the most striking appearances of speedy death. His situation was the more uncomfortable, that in his weak emaciated state, the physicians prescribed to him instead of a down bed, to lie on a rugged pallet[3].

He had already settled his affairs, and his facetiousness still suggested to him to make some verbal legacies, which would not have been so suitable to the gravity of a solemn deed. His friend Mr. Home the Poet, affected a delicacy which abhorred even the taste of Port wine; this whimsical nicety had often been the subject of Mr. Hume's raillery, and he left verbally to his friend the poet, *one bottle* of Port, and ten dozen of Claret, but on this condition, that the poet should drink the Port at two sittings, before he tasted the Claret.

Such was the estimation in which Mr. Hume was held, from his amiable qualities as a citizen, as well as from his literary fame, that for some weeks before his death, his situation became the universal topick of conversation and enquiry; each individual expressing an anxious solicitude about his health, as if he had been his intimate and particular friend.

On the twenty-fifth of August, Mr. Hume's character was put beyond the reach of being sullied by human frailty[4]. As soon as he conceived himself to be in a dying way, he purchased a spot for the depositing of his ashes; the south-west corner of the Calton burying ground at Edinburgh, *a rock wherein never man had been laid.* And from the particular charge he gave about his corpse, it would seem he was not altogether devoid of apprehensions of its being treated with insult.

The anxious attention with which the public viewed every circumstance respecting Mr. Hume's illness was not terminated even by his death. From the busy curiosity of the mob, one would have presumed them to entertain notions that the

[3] His disease was a diarrhœa; the physicians were divided about the seat of the malady. There is a reason however to conjecture, that his disorder originated from a course of eating rather fully, without drinking in proportion.

[4] Mr. Hume, after his circumstances became affluent, lived very hospitably and genteely. Yet he left to his relations upwards of 10,000l. of his own acquiring. He had a pension from the government of 500l. per annum.

ashes of Mr. Hume were to have been the cause or the object of miraculous exertion. As the physicians of London and Edinburgh were divided about the seat of his disorder, those of the city where he died, proposed that his body should be opened: but this, his brother who was also his executor, agreeably to the orders of the deceased, would not permit.

It is hardly to be credited, that the grave-diggers, digging with pick-axes Mr. Hume's grave, should have attracted the gaping curiosity of the multitude. That, notwithstanding a heavy rain, which fell during the interment, multitudes of all ranks gazed at the funeral procession[5], as if they had expected the hearse to have been consumed in livid flames, or encircled with a ray of glory; that people in a sphere much above the rabble would have sent to the sexton for the keys of the burying-ground, and paid him to have access to visit the grave. And that on a Sunday evening (the gates of the burying-ground being opened for another funeral) the company, from a public walk in the neighbourhood, flocked in such crouds to Mr. Hume's grave, that his brother actually became apprehensive upon the unusual concourse, and ordered the grave to be railed in with all expedition.

After his interment, two trusty persons, watched the grave for about eight nights. The watch was set by eight at night; at which time a pistol was fired, and so continued to be every hour till day-light. Candles in a lanthorn were placed upon the grave, where they burned all night; and the grease which dropped in renewing or snuffing the candles was to be seen upon the grave afterwards.

We cannot conclude this Supplement to the Life of Mr. Hume more properly than by applying to him and to his Works, those nervous lines, which Ovid has applied to himself.

"Quod nec Jovis ira, nec ignis,
Nec poterit serrum, nec edax abolere vetustas.
Cum volet illa dies, quæ nil nisi corporis hujus
Jus habet, incerti spatium mihi finiat ævi:
Parte tamen meliore mei super alta perennis

---

[5] When the mob were assembled round Mr. Hume's door to see the corpse taken out to interment, the following short dialogue passed between two of the refuse of the rabble: "Ah, (says one) he was an Atheist." "No matter, (says another) he was an *honest man.*

Astra ferar: NOMENQUE ERIT INDELEBELE NOSTRUM.
Quaque patet domitis; Romana potentia terris;
Ore lega populi: PERQUE OMNIA SECULA FAMA
(SI QUID HABENT VERI VATUM PRAESAGIA) VIVAM."

OVID

AN ACCOUNT OF THE LIFE AND WRITINGS OF DAVID HUME, ESQ. BY THOMAS EDWARD RITCHIE

Anonymous

Source: The Monthly Review, vol. 62, 1810

THIS volume contains most if not all of the papers and documents which are worthy of notice, relative to the life and writings of the philosopher to whom it is devoted. Of original composition, the portion is small; and had it been still less, the writer's fame and the value of the work would not have suffered. To collect together, from the various sources in which they lie, the materials which form this piece of history, is an useful if a humble service: but it gives the compiler no right to announce himself as the author of "An Account of the Life and Writings of Mr. Hume," to which distinction he has scarcely a better claim than the printer or the publisher. The insertion of a few puerile cavils, and of a few shreds of narrative, does not change the nature of the production.

Hume himself would induce us to suppose that he allotted scarcely any of his time to the ponderous writers on civil law: but were we to form our notions on the subject from his writings, we should not depart from the opinion which the present editor endeavours to convey, when he remarks; "it is probable, that the mere circumstance of directing his attention, although in a superficial degree, to the Roman code and the municipal laws of his own country, gave a slight bias to his studies, which, being seconded by favourable events, suggested at a future period the project of compiling his History: a task which he undertook, not from a wish to detail battles, and exhibit a tedious succession of political broils, but for the more dignified purpose of tracing the progress of legislation and civility." [*civilization.*]

If we except the last ill expressed and scarcely intelligible sentence, the observations in the following passage are just and applicable:

"So many discouragements as Hume had encountered by the untoward fortune of his literary productions, would doubtless have had their full influence on a more timid mind. But our author's temporal circumstances were now easy; and being totally independent of the sale of his works, he did not look to his pen for support: he sought only the reputation of a man of letters. No sense of the necessity of labour, no privations, no clamorous wants, obtunded his powers. In so favourable a situation, he could give full reins to his inclination: there was no call to haste, no urgency to toil; and he was not constrained to sit down, *invita Minerva*, to his cheerless task. Every new performance, therefore, matured in the bosom of tranquillity, may be regarded as a fair criterion of his talents at the time; and from his unremitting perseverance, he seems to have imbibed the true *cacoethes scribendi*."

We are induced to insert a paragraph from a letter left by Mr. Hume with his bookseller for an anonymous antagonist, who afterward proved to be Mr. James Balfour, a Scotish barrister, because it is penned in a spirit which is truly philosophical, and at the same time completely exhibits the man.

"SIR,

When I write to you, I know not to whom I am addressing myself; I only know he is one who has done me a great deal of honour, and to whose civilities I am obliged. If we be strangers, I beg we may be acquainted, as soon as you think proper to discover yourself: if we be acquainted already, I beg we may be friends: if friends, I beg we may be more so. Our connection with each other as men of letters is greater than our difference as adhering to different sects or systems. Let us revive the happy times, when Atticus and Cassius the Epicureans, Cicero the academic, and Brutus the Stoic, could all of them live in unreserved friendship together, and were insensible to all those distinctions, except so far as they furnished agreeable matter to discourse and conversation. Perhaps you are a young man, and being full of those sublime ideas, which you have so well expressed, think there can be no virtue upon a more confined system. I am not an old one; but, being of a cool temperament, have always found, that more simple views were sufficient to make me act in a reasonable manner;

νηθε, και μεμνησο απιττειν; in this faith have I lived, and hope to die."

The reception which most of Mr. Hume's productions experienced, on their first appearance, strongly corroborates the notion, that very superior merit is slow in establishing its claims. Of the first volume of the History of the House of Stuart, Mr. Ritchie says;

"The sale of the work was extremely dull, insomuch that Mr. Hume felt it necessary to hold a consultation with his bookseller, the late Mr. John Balfour of Edinburgh, as to what should be done to lessen the load of expence he had incurred. The indefatigable Andrew Millar was then taking the lead as a bookseller in London, and his name and extensive correspondence with the country dealers were sufficient to buoy up, in some degree, the character of a book, and facilitate its circulation. Mr. Balfour urged the necessity of obtaining the aid of Millar, in order to push the work into notice; and this advice was prudently followed.

Another incident had lately occurred, which not a little chagrined our author. The professorship of Moral Philosophy, in the university of Edinburgh, having become vacant by the death of Mr. William Cleghorn. Mr. Hume appeared as a candidate for the chair, which is in the gift of the town-council. But the interest of his friends proved unsuccessful: his philosophical opinions were misrepresented, his character was traduced, and so great an outcry raised by the religious zealots as to endanger his personal safety. The clergy were particularly active on this occasion, some of whom represented Mr. Hume's principles to be those of an atheist, while others charitably branded them as the dogmas of deism. Their remonstrances succeeded; but the event gave rise to a rooted antipathy on the part of Hume towards the Scotish clergy, although at this time he lived, and continued afterwards to live, in the strictest intimacy, and most cordial friendship, with Blair, Wallace, Drysdale, Wishart, Jardine, Home, Robertson, Carlysle, and a few others.

The election took place on the 28th of August, and the office was conferred on Mr. James Balfour of Pilrig, advocate and sheriff-depute of the county of Edinburgh."

This successful candidate was the same person with the anonymous opponent to whom Mr. Hume addressed the letter from which we have made an extract above.

We believe it to be little known in this part of the island, that an attempt was made by fanatical zeal to stigmatize our philosopher by involving him in ecclesiastical censures: but, as it is here observed;

"It is in vain to conceal, that deism, or a religious creed approximating to it, had begun to spread among the literary circles at Edinburgh; and Lord Kames and Mr. Hume, being the only persons who had ventured to commit their philosophical tenets to writing, were considered as the grand apostles of infidelity. What rendered this more dangerous in the opinion of the puritanical party was, that both these authors were men of great amenity of manners; and not only was their acquaintance valued and sought by most of the eminent characters in their neighbourhood, but they lived in habits of the strictest intimacy with the more respectable clergymen of the city.

The rigid notions of Calvin and John Knox were not yet in disrepute, and the prevalence of science had not altogether effaced the ancient intolerant spirit of the clerical profession. In the General Assembly, which is the supreme ecclesiastical judicature of the Scotish church, two great parties had long subsisted, the one professing more liberal and moderate principles than the other. The zealots, in the warmth of opposition, affected to take great offence at many of their opponents for cultivating the friendship of Kames and Hume, in whose writings they now began to discover the most noxious doctrines; and finally resolved, by attacking these, to expose their enemies to popular obloquy, if not to defeat.

In taking this step they were encouraged by an event, which had lately happened in England. Towards the end of the year 1754, the learned world beheld with astonishment, indignation, and dismay, the presentment of Lord Bolingbroke's philosophical works, and of David Mallet, their editor, by the Grand Jury of Middlesex."

The charge was first brought forwards in the General Assembly which met in 1755, but the matter was postponed by the assembly to their next meeting. From what is here

stated, it would seem as if these reverend fathers deemed it
more important to regulate the mode of psalm-singing, than
to check the progress of infidelity; for we learn that

> "The usual shortness of the session prevented the assembly
> from taking any farther notice of the matter, which was
> accordingly postponed to their next meeting. An affair of
> superior magnitude had engrosed the deliberations of that
> venerable body; for at this time the Scotish church was
> thrown into a general ferment by an attempt to introduce
> the reformed music. In accomplishing this the most inde-
> cent scenes were exhibited. It was not uncommon for a
> congregation to divide themselves into two parties, one of
> which, in chaunting the psalms, followed the old, and the
> other the new mode of musical execution; while the infidel,
> who was not in the habit of frequenting the temple, now
> resorted to it, not for the laudable purpose of repentance
> and edification, but from the ungodly motive of being a
> spectator of the contest."

This contest seems to have borne some resemblance to a late
dramatic struggle, except that it appears that the latter was
carried on with more decency; since we are informed that,
while the psalm-singing-squabble continued,

> "It was customary for the partizans of the different kinds
> of music to convene a-part, in numerous bodies, for the
> purpose of practising, and to muster their whole strength
> on the sabbath. The moment the psalm was read from
> the pulpit, each side, in general chorus, commenced their
> operations; and as the pastor and clerk, or precentor, often
> differed in their sentiments, the church was immediately in
> an uproar. Blows and bruises were interchanged by the
> impassioned songsters, and in many parts of the country,
> the most serious disturbances took place. In Edinburgh the
> magistracy declared in favour of the modern improvement,
> and appointed a committee of ministers, among whom was
> the Rev. Mr. Hugh Blair, to concert the proper means for
> introducing it. As the author of this work is not a gifted
> son of Apollo, he is unable to decide on the merits of so
> momentous a question: and feeling no inclination to be
> inquisitive as to the issue of the controversy, he is uncertain

which of the parties obtained the ascendancy, but inclines
to believe that the ancients were discomfited and silenced."

At the next Meeting of the Assembly in 1756, the matter was
regularly brought on before the Committee of Overtures;

"It was moved, that the Assembly should be desired to take
notice of some of the infidel writings published of late in
this nation, and of their authors; and in case it should be
found difficult or improper to make this notice too general,
it was proposed to confine the inquiry at present to one,
viz. David Hume, Esq. because he had publicly avowed his
writings, at least, some of the most offensive of them, by
prefixing his name. This motion was seconded, and some
paragraphs of the Confession of Faith and Form of Process
were read, asserting the propriety, and appointing the exercise of discipline in such cases, on which a long and warm
debate ensued.

The party who introduced the question, gave in a written
overture of the following purport – 'The General Assembly
judging it their duty to do all in their power to check the
growth and progress of infidelity; and considering that as
infidel writings have begun of late years to be published in
this nation, against which they have hitherto only testified
in general, so there is one person styling himself David
Hume, Esq. who hath arrived at such a degree of boldness
as publicly to avow himself the author of books containing
the most rude and open attacks upon the glorious gospel of
Christ, and principles evidently subversive even of natural
religion, and the foundations of morality, if not establishing
direct atheism: therefore the Assembly appoint the following persons as a committee to inquire into the writings of
this author, to call him before them, and prepare the matter
for the next General Assembly.'"

The opposers of the overture maintained,

"That the inquisition could serve no good purpose, and
that it was not to be supposed, that prosecution or censure
would convince Mr. Hume, or make him change his
opinions, in which he seemed to be so firmly rivetted.

That it would be a tedious and difficult enquiry, and
would lead to the discussion of many philosophical
opinions. They reminded the committee of the many long

and fierce debates, which had formerly agitated the Christian church, about fate, free will, and the the like; so that the affair, if entered upon, might last for many years, and become, in a manner, the sole business of the Assembly."

"That however wrong Mr. Hume's opinions were, his writings were mostly of an abstract and metaphysical kind, unintelligible to the multitude; and, therefore, as little danger could arise from them, liberty of judgment ought to be allowed. In fine, they were not proper objects of censure, which ought rather to be applied to practical errors, and cases more immediately criminal.

"The opponents of the motion likewise objected, that it would highly gratify Mr. Hume himself, and promote the sale of the book. They related several anecdotes to shew, how booksellers had artfully solicited the authoritative condemnation of books, in order to get them off their hands. It was represented by some as very dangerous to spread such writings in this manner, and bring them into the hands of common or country people, who would not otherwise have looked into them; and the consequences of this were pointed out very strongly.

"Some of the members insisted, that Mr. Hume could, in no respect, be deemed a Christian; that he had openly and publicly thrown off the profession of it, and was therefore one of those who, in the language of scripture, *are without*, and consequently not proper objects of Christian discipline.

"This was the objection chiefly insisted upon; and with a discussion of it, by mutual interrogations, the debate was closed. The friends of the overture allowed, that one who was not in any sense a member of the visible church was no subject of discipline. But they observed, that whatever gross crimes Mr. Hume had committed, he had neither been formally excluded by a sentence, nor had excluded himself by any formal declaration; that he had not renounced his baptism; that he frequently, in his writings, ranked himself among professing Christians, saying *our holy religion*, & c., words which, however plainly they were in the way of contempt and derision, shewed more forcibly the necessity of a visible separation. Professing Christians held voluntary and unnecessary communication with him; and even ministers were seen freely conversing with him, which it was presumed they would not do, if he were formally excluded."

The overture was happily thrown out, the votes for it being only 17 and against it 50.

The persecuting party, though thus discomfited, were not inclined to sit down without making a farther attempt to signalize their zeal; and having failed in their attacks against the authors, they piously assailed the publishers of Lord Kames's book. Our limits will not permit us to state the particulars of this interesting affair: suffice it to say that the process was dismissed, and that the Edinburgh "No Popery" party of that day were disappointed in their intolerant designs.

Determined as Mr. Hume was in his scepticism, he appears to have lived on terms of the greatest intimacy with the divines who at this time reflected so much honor on the northern capital by their literary productions; and it would seem that he subjected himself to no restraint in his intercourse with them. Writing to Dr. Blair respecting Dr. Campbell's answer to his Essay on Miracles, he says;

"I wonder the author does not perceive the reason why Mr. John Knox and Mr. Alexander Henderson did not work as many miracles as their brethren in other churches. Miracle-working was a popish trick, and discarded with the other parts of that religion. Men must have new and opposite ways of establishing new and opposite follies. The same reason extends to Mahomet. The Greek priests, who were in the neighbourhood of Arabia, and many of them in it, were as great miracle-workers as the Romish; and Mahomet would have been laughed at for so stale and simple a device. To cast out devils and cure the blind, where every one almost can do as much, is not the way to get any extraordinary ascendant over men. I never read of a miracle in my life, that was not meant to establish some new point of religion. There are no miracles wrought in Spain to prove the Gospel; but St. Francis Xavier wrought a thousand well-attested ones for that purpose in the Indies. The miracles in Spain, which are all so fully and completely attested, are wrought to prove the efficacy of a particular crucifix or relic, which is always a new point, or at least not universally received."

He then thus expostulates with the Dr. himself;

> "Having said so much to your friend, who is certainly a very ingenious man though a little too zealous for a philosopher, permit me also the freedom of saying a word to yourself. Whenever I have had the pleasure to be in your company, if the discourse turned apon any common subject of literature or reasoning, I always parted from you both entertained and instructed. But when the conversation was diverted by you from this channel towards the subject of your profession; though I doubt not but your intentions were very friendly towards me, I own I never received the same satisfaction: I was apt to be tired, and you to be angry. I would therefore wish for the future, wherever my good fortune throws me in your way, that these topics should be forborn between us. I have long since done with all inquiries on such subjects, and am become incapable of instruction; though I own no one is more capable of conveying it than yourself."

Between Robertson and Hume, a most confidential friendship seems to have subsisted. Robertson's work no sooner appeared than the hemisphere of letters was in a blaze, and all eyes were fixed on the new meteor. Hume's breast seems not once to have admitted a particle of jealousy. Is this ascribable to his philosophy, or to an indifference arising from his temperament, or to the consciousness of his superiority? The History of Scotland claims a high place for its author, but vast is the distance between him and Hume. How tranquil and playful does the philosopher appear, jostled as he is by the indefatigable and expert bookmaker, and the consummate historiographer, when he thus writes to the latter:

> "Next week I am published; and then I expect a constant comparison will be made between Dr. Robertson and Mr. Hume. I shall tell you in a few weeks, which of these heroes is likely to prevail. Meanwhile, I can inform both of them for their comforts, that their combat is not likely to make half so much noise as that between Broughton and the one-eyed coachman. *Vanitas vanitatum, atque omnia vanitas.* I shall still except, however, the friendship and good opinion of worthy men."

He begins the letter with the following pleasant story:

"I forgot to tell you, that two days ago I was in the House of Commons, where an English gentleman came to me, and told me that he had lately sent to a grocer's shop for a pound of raisins, which he received wrapt up in a paper that he shewed me. How would you have turned pale at the sight! It was a leaf of your History, and the very character of Queen Elizabeth, which you had laboured so finely, little thinking it would so soon come to so disgraceful an end. I happened a little after to see Millar, and told him the story; consulting him, to be sure, on the fate of his new boasted historian, of whom he was so fond. But the story proves more serious than I apprehended. For he told Strahan, who thence suspects villany among his 'prentices and journey-men; and has sent me very earnestly to know the gentle-man's name, that he may find out the grocer, and so trace the matter to the bottom. In vain did I remonstrate, that this was sooner or later the fate of all authors, *serius, ocyus, sors exitura.* He will not be satisfied; and begs me to keep my jokes for another occasion. But that I am resolved not to do; and, therefore, being repulsed by his passion and seriousness, I direct them against you."

Shortly afterward, he writes to the same person again in the same strain:

"But though I have given a high character of your work to Monsieur Helvetius, I warn you that this is the last time, that either to Frenchman or Englishman I shall ever speak the least good of it. A plague take you! Here I sat near the historical summit of Parnassus, immediately under Dr. Smollet; and you have the impudence to squeeze yourself directly under his feet. Do you imagine, that this can be agreeable to me? and must not I be guilty of great simplicity to contribute by my endeavours to your thrusting me out of my place in Paris as well as at London? But I give you warning, that you will find the matter somewhat difficult, at least in the former city. A friend of mine, who is there, writes home to his father the strangest accounts on that head, which my modesty will not permit me to repeat, but which it allowed me very deliciously to swallow."

All the papers which relate to the intercourse of Hume with Rousseau are here inserted, and, we think, properly. The

letter of explanation, which Mr. Hume's spirited remon-
strance exorted from the morbid philosopher, affords a deeper
insight into his temperament, and more completely exhibits
him as the artificer of his own misfortunes, than any thing else
that has been written by him or respecting him.

If the satisfaction which we have received from seeing the
materials before us collected together, and the pleasure which
we have derived from casting our eye over them, were not
sufficient to induce us to suppress our objections to an
improper and too ostentatious title-page, much less will they
avail to lessen the disgust which the cavils of the compiler
against the statements of his original, and the pitiful criticisms
on his works, have excited in our minds. More glaring proofs
of ignorance and presumption are no where to be found. Of
the criticism, we submit to our readers one specimen only:

> "It may, perhaps, appear to be a homely remark, but it is not
> the less just, that, in perusing any work of a disquisitionary
> nature, the first thing to which a reader ought to direct his
> attention is the table of contents. It is not a mere enumer-
> ation of the different topics treated of in the text, which this
> table presents to an intelligent inquirer. If he finds in it a
> *lucidus ordo* in the arrangement of the plan; if he finds that
> natural succession, or connected series of discussion, which
> gives perspicuity and precision to a literary performance, he
> is inclined to form a favourable opinion of the abilities of
> the writer. A very slight inspection of the tables of contents
> prefixed to the writings of Adam Smith or Dr. Reid, who
> were contemporaries of Mr. Hume, will enable a man of
> ordinary capacity to observe the intimate dependence which
> each successive chapter has on that preceding it, and to
> comprehend at one view the general scope and object of the
> author: but we look for this in vain in Mr. Hume's Treatise;
> and the consequence of his failure or neglect in correctness
> of arrangement and division of the subject, is a tiresome
> repetition of arguments and opinions, which tends to
> involve the whole in confusion and obscurity."

The censure which we thus pass on incompetence, in a
pretended critic, will not be ascribed to any predilection for
the erroneous principles and theories which have been maintained or countenanced by a great genius.

II. Dialogues Concerning Natural Religion

DIALOGUES CONCERNING NATURAL RELIGION BY DAVID HUME
Anonymous

Source: The Gentlemen's magazine, vol. 49, 1779

In these dialogues the disputants are Cleanthes, Philo, and Demea. The first, as the author himself remarks, is distinguished by an accurate and philosophical turn; the second, by a careless scepticism; the third, by a rigid and inflexible orthodoxy. We need not say on which side this sceptical metaphysician inclines the balance, but must observe, that the weapons with which Philo attracts the moral attributes of the Deity are the same with those which were employed by Lord Bolingbroke, and were most ably parried by Bishop Warburton. And, not to mention later writers, who, that has read Cicero *de Natura Deorum*, can think that the Divine Goodness required any other advocate?

DIALOGUES CONCERNING NATURAL RELIGION BY DAVID HUME, ESQ.

Anonymous

Source: The Monthly Review, vol. 61, 1780

WE have here a very elaborate performance. It treats on the most important and interesting subject that can possibly employ the thoughts of a reasonable being. It is written with great elegance; in the true spirit of ancient dialogue; and, in point of composition, is equal, if not superior, to any of Mr. Hume's other writings. Nothing new, however, is advanced on the subject. The Author, indeed, has attempted little more than to throw the most exceptionable parts of his philosophical works into a new form, and to present them in a different dress.

The conversation is supported by CLEANTHES, DEMEA, and PHILO. – Cleanthes, to use Mr. Hume's own words, is a person of an accurate philosophical turn; Philo, a careless sceptic; and Demea, a rigid, inflexible, orthodox divine. Cleanthes, however, defends a good cause very feebly, and is by no means entitled to the character of an accurate philosopher. Demea supports the character of a sour, croaking divine, very tolerably; but PHILO is the hero of the piece; and it must be acknowledged, that he urges his objections with no inconsiderable degree of acuteness and subtlety.

We shall endeavour to give our Readers a concise, but clear view, of what is advanced by each of the speakers; and, not to weaken the force of their arguments, we shall give their own words.

"No man; no man, at least," says Demea, "of common sense, I am persuaded, ever entertained a serious doubt of the being of a God. The question is not concerning the BEING, but the NATURE of GOD. This I affirm, from the infirmities of human understanding, to be altogether incomprehensible and unknown to us. The essence of that supreme mind, his attributes, the manner of his existence, the very nature of his duration; these, and every particular, which regards so divine a Being, are mysterious to men. Finite, weak, and blind creatures, we ought to humble ourselves in his august presence, and, conscious of our frailties, adore in silence his infinite perfections, which eye hath not seen, ear hath not heard, neither hath it entered into the heart of man to conceive. They are covered in a deep cloud from human curiosity: it is profaneness to attempt penetrating through these sacred obscurities; and next to the impiety of denying his existence, is the temerity of prying into his nature and essence, decrees and attributes.–

The ancient Platonists were the most religious and devout of all the Pagan philosophers: yet many of them, particularly Plotinus, expressly declare, that intellect or understanding is not to be ascribed to the Deity, and that our most perfect worship of him consists, not in acts of veneration, reverence, gratitude, or love; but in a certain mysterious self-annihilation, or total extinction of all our faculties. These ideas are, perhaps, too far stretched; but still it must be acknowledged, that, by representing the Deity as comprehensible, and similar to a human mind, we are guilty of the grossest and most narrow partiality, and make ourselves the model of the whole universe.–

It is my opinion, that each man feels, in a manner, the truth of religion within his own breast; and from a consciousness of his imbecility and misery, rather than from any reasoning, is led to seek protection from that Being, on whom he and all nature is dependent. So anxious, or so tedious, are even the best scenes of life, that futurity is still the object of all our hopes and fears. We incessantly look forward, and endeavour, by prayers, adoration, and sacrifice, to appease those unknown powers, whom we find, by experience, so able to afflict and oppress us. Wretched creatures that we are! what resource for us amidst the innumerable ills of life, did not religion suggest some methods of atonement, and appease those terrors, with which we are incessantly agitated and tormented? – The miseries of life, the unhappiness of man, the general corruptions of our nature, the unsatisfactory enjoyment of pleasures, riches, honours; these phrases have become almost proverbial in all languages. And who can doubt of what all men declare from their own immediate feeling and experience? – Look round this library of Cleanthes. I *shall* venture to affirm that, except Authors of particular sciences, such as chymistry or botany, who have no occasion to treat of human life, there is scarce one of those innumerable writers, from whom the sense of human misery has not, in some passage or other, extorted a complaint and confession of it. At least, the chance is entirely on that side; and no one Author has ever, so far as I can recollect, been so extravagant as to deny it. – The whole earth, believe me, Philo, is cursed and polluted. A perpetual war is kindled among all living creatures. Necessity, hunger, want, stimulate the strong and courageous; fear, anxiety, terror, agitate the weak and infirm. The first entrance into life gives anguish to the new born infant and to its wretched parent: weakness, impotence, distress, attend each stage of that life: and 'tis at last finished in agony and horror. – Though the external insults from animals, from men, from all the elements, which assault us, form a frightful catalogue of woes, they are nothing in comparison of those, which arise within ourselves, from the distempered condition of our mind and body. How many lie under the lingering torment of diseases? And the disorders of the mind, though more secret, are not perhaps less dismal and vexacious. Remorse, shame, anguish, rage, disappointment, anxiety, fear, dejection, despair; who has ever passed through life without cruel inroads from these tormentors? How many have scarcely ever felt any better sensations? Labour and poverty, so abhorred by every one, are the certain lot of the far greater number: and those few privileged persons, who enjoy ease and opulence, never reach contentment or true felicity. All the goods of life united would not make a very happy man: but all the ills united would make a wretch indeed; and any one of them almost (and who can be free from every one?) nay often the absence of one good (and who can possess all?) is sufficient to render life ineligible. –

Nothing can be more surprising than to find a topic like this, concerning the wickedness and misery of man, charged with no less than atheism and profaneness. Have not all pious divines and preachers, who have indulged their rhetoric on so fertile a subject; have they not easily, I say, given a solution of any difficulties which may attend it? This world is but a point in comparison of the universe: this life but a moment in comparison of eternity. The present evil phenomena, therefore, are rectified in other regions, and in some future period of existence. And the eyes of men, being then opened to larger views of things, see the whole connection of general laws, and trace, with adoration, the benevolence and rectitude of the Deity, through all the mazes and intricacies of his providence."

Such are the sentiments of the rigid, inflexible, orthodox DEMEA; such are the arguments which he employs to prove the mysterious, incomprehensible nature of the Deity, and by which he endeavours to shew, that the infirmities of our nature do not permit us to attain any ideas, which in the least correspond to the ineffable sublimity of the divine attributes. Let us now hear what the "accurate" philosopher CLEANTHES says.

Demea asserts, as we have already mentioned, that the present evil phenomena are rectified in some future period of existence. – "No! replied Cleanthes, No! These arbitrary suppositions can never be admitted, contrary to matter of fact, visible and uncontroverted. Whence can any cause be known but from its known effects? Whence can any hypothesis be proved but from the apparent phenomena? To establish one hypothesis upon another is building entirely in the air; and the utmost we ever attain, by these conjectures and fictions, is to ascertain the bare possibility of our opinion; but never can we, upon such terms, establish its reality."

"The only method of supporting divine benevolence (and it is what I willingly embrace), is to deny absolutely the misery and wickedness of man. Your representations are exaggerated: your melancholy views mostly fictitious: your inferences contrary to fact and experience. Health is more common than sickness; pleasure than pain; happiness than misery. And for one vexation, which we meet with, we attain, upon computation, a hundred enjoyments."

"I have been apt to suspect," says this *accurate philosopher*, "the frequent repetition of the word *infinite*, which we meet with in all theological writers, to favour more of panegyric than of philosophy, and that any purposes of reasoning, and even of religion, would be better served, were we to rest contented with more accurate and more moderate expressions.   The terms, *admirable, excellent, superlatively great, wise, and holy*; these sufficiently fill the imaginations of men; and any thing beyond, besides that it leads into absurdities, has no influence on the affections or sentiments.   Thus, in the present subject, if we abandon all human analogy, as seems your intention, Demea, I am afraid we abandon all religion, and retain no conception of the great object of our adoration.   If we preserve human analogy, we must for ever find it impossible to reconcile any mixture of evil in the universe with infinite attributes; much less, can we ever prove the latter from the former. But supposing the Author of Nature to be finitely perfect," (a strange supposition, surely!) "though far exceeding mankind; a satisfactory account may then be given of natural and moral evil, and every untoward phenomenon be explained and adjusted.   A less evil may then be chosen, in order to avoid a greater; inconveniences be submitted to, in order to reach a desirable end; and, in a word, benevolence, regulated by wisdom, and limited by necessity may produce just such a world as the present."

The principal points which Cleanthes endeavours to establish are, – that the works of nature are similar to those of art; that the Deity is similar to a human mind and understanding, and that our ideas of his attributes, as far as they go, are just and adequate, and correspondent to his real nature.

"Look round the world, says he, contemplate the whole and every part of it; you will find it to be nothing but one great machine, subdivided into an infinite number of lesser machines, which again admit of subdivisions, to a degree beyond what human senses and faculties can trace and explain.   All these various machines, and even their most minute parts are adjusted to each other with an accuracy, which ravishes into admiration all men, who have ever contemplated them.   The curious adapting of means to ends, throughout all nature, resembles exactly, though it much exceeds, the productions of human contrivance, of human design, thought, wisdom, and intelligence.   Since therefore the effects resemble each other, we are led to infer, by all the rules of analogy, that the causes also resemble; and that the Author of Nature is somewhat similar to the mind of man; though possessed of much larger faculties, proportioned to the grandeur of the work, which he has executed. By this argument *a posteriori*, and by this argument alone, do we prove at once the existence of a Deity, and his similarity to human mind and intelligence."

In regard to the argument *a priori*, as it is called, Cleanthes endeavours to shew its fallacy, and that it is of very little consequence to the cause of true piety or religion.

"I shall begin, says he, with observing, that there is an evident absurdity in pretending to demonstrate a matter of fact, or to prove it by any argument *a priori*. Nothing is demonstrable, unless the contrary implies a contradiction. Nothing, that is distinctly conceivable, implies a contradiction. Whatever we conceive as existent, we can also conceive as non-existent. There is no being, therefore, whose non existence implies a contradiction. Consequently there is no being, whose existence is demonstrable. I propose this argument as entirely decisive, and am willing to rest the whole controversy upon it."

Cleanthes, our Readers have already seen, is of opinion that the ascribing of *infinite* perfections to the Deity leads into absurdities, and has no influence on the affections or sentiments; and that, if we suppose the Author of Nature to be *finitely* perfect, we may give a satisfactory account of natural and moral evil, explain and adjust every untoward phenomenon.

Now, if the Author of Nature be *finitely* perfect, his perfections are limited, or, in other words, he is an imperfect Being; and yet Cleanthes, in another passage, says that he is a Being perfectly good, wise, and powerful.

"The most agreeable reflection, says he, which it is possible for human imagination to suggest, is that of genuine Theism, which represents us as the workmanship of a Being perfectly good, wise, and powerful; who created us for happiness, and who, having implanted in us immeasurable desires of good, will prolong our existence to all eternity, and will transfer us into an infinite variety of scenes in order to satisfy those desires, and render our felicity complete and durable. Next to such a Being himself (if the comparison be allowed) the happiest lot which we can imagine, is that of being under his guardianship and protection." – O SI SIC OMNIA!

It is not our business to answer Mr. Hume, but it is obvious to remark, that a Being *finitely* perfect, cannot be *perfectly* wise and good. The character of Cleanthes, therefore, is not consistent; nor is it properly supported; for an accurate philosopher should have shewn, clearly and distinctly, upon philosophical principles, by what steps he rose to the idea of a perfectly wise and good Being, and what reasons he had for concluding that this Being would prolong our existence to all eternity, and make us completely happy.

But we now proceed to lay before our Readers Mr. Hume's own sentiments in the character of the "careless sceptic," PHILO. – He acknowledges that a purpose, an intention, a design, strikes every where the most stupid thinker, the most careless observer of nature, that no man can be so hardened in absurd systems, as at all times to reject it; that in many views of the universe, and of its parts, particularly the latter, the beauty and fitness of final causes strike us with such irresistible force, that all objections appear (what he believes they really are) mere cavils and sophisms; and that we cannot then imagine how it was ever possible for us to lay any stress on them. But there is no view of human life, he tells us, from which, without the greatest violence, we can infer the moral attributes, or learn infinite benevolence, conjoined with infinite power and infinite wisdom, which we must discover by the eyes of faith alone. He thinks it extremely unreasonable to form our ideas of the Author of Nature from our experience of the narrow productions of human design and invention, and says that it is impossible for us to tell, from our limited views, whether the present system of things deserves any considerable praise, if compared to other possible, and even real systems.

"Could a peasant, says he, if the ÆNEID were read to him, pronounce that poem to be absolutely faultless, or even assign to it its proper rank among the productions of human wit, he, who had never seen any other production?

But were this world ever so perfect a production, it must still remain uncertain, whether all the excellencies of the work can justly be ascribed to the workman. If we survey a ship, what an exalted idea must we form of the ingenuity of the carpenter, who framed so complicated, useful, and beautiful a machine! And what surprize must we feel, when we find him a stupid mechanic, who imitated others, and copied an art, which, through a long succession of ages, after multiplied trials, mistakes, corrections, deliberations, and controversies, had been gradually improving! Many worlds might have been botched and bungled, throughout an eternity, ere this system was struck out: much labour lost: many fruitless trials made: and a slow, but continued improvement carried on during infinite ages in the art of world making. In such subjects, who can determine, where the truth, nay, who can conjecture where the probability, lies, amidst a great number of hypotheses which may be proposed, and a still greater number, which may be imagined?–

In a word, CLEANTHES, a man, who follows your hypothesis, is able, perhaps, to assert, or conjecture, that the universe, sometime, arose from something like design: but beyond that position he cannot ascertain one single circumstance, and is left afterwards to fix every point of his theology, by the utmost licence of fancy and hypothesis. This world, for aught he knows, is very faulty and imperfect, compared to a superior standard; and was only the first rude essay of some infant Deity, who afterwards abandoned it, ashamed of his lame performance: it is the work only of some dependent, inferior Deity; and is the object of derision to his superiors: it is the production of old age and dotage in some superannuated Deity; and ever since his death, has run on at adventure, from the first impulse and active force, which it received from him. You justly give signs of horror, DEMEA, at these strange suppositions: but these, and a thousand more of the same kind, are CLEANTHES's suppositions, not mine. –

There occurs to me another hypothesis, which must acquire an air of probability from the method of reasoning so much insisted on by CLEANTHES. That like effects arise from like causes: this principle he supposes the foundation of all religion. But there is another principle of the same kind, no less certain, and derived from the same source of experience; that where several known circumstances are observed to be similar, the unknown will also be found similar. Thus, if we see the limbs of a human body, we conclude, that it is also attended with a human head, though hid from us. Thus, if we see through a chink in a wall, a small part of the sun, we conclude, that were the wall removed, we should see the whole body. In short, this method of reasoning is so obvious and familiar, that no scruple can ever be made with regard to its solidity.

Now if we survey the universe, so far as it falls under our knowledge, it bears a great resemblance to an animal or organized body, and seems actuated with a like principle of life and motion. A continual circulation of matter in it produces no disorder; a continual waste in every part is incessantly repaired: the closest sympathy is perceived throughout the entire system; and each part or member, in performing its proper offices, operates both to its own preservation and to that of the whole. The world then, I infer, is an animal, and the Deity is the SOUL of the world, actuating it, and actuated by it.–

Were I obliged to defend any particular system (which I never willingly should do), I esteem none more plausible, than that which ascribes an eternal, inherent principle of order to the world; though attended with great and continual revolutions and alterations. This at once solves all difficulties; and if the solution, by being so general, is not entirely complete and satisfactory, it is, at least, a theory, that we must, sooner or later, have recourse to, whatever system we embrace.–

Our friend CLEANTHES asserts, that since no question of fact can be proved otherwise than by experience, the existence of a Deity admits not of proof from any other medium. The world, says he, resembles the works of human contrivance: therefore its cause must also resemble that of the other. Here we may remark, that the operation of one very small part of nature, to wit man, upon another very small part, to wit, that inanimate matter lying within his reach, is the rule, by which CLEANTHES judges of the origin of the whole; and he measures objects, so widely disproportioned, by the same individual standard. But to wave all objections drawn from this topic; I affirm that there are other parts of the universe (besides the machines of human invention) which bear still a greater resemblance to the fabric of the world, and which therefore afford a better conjecture concerning the universal origin of this system. These parts are

animals and vegetables. The world plainly resembles more
an animal or a vegetable, than it does a watch or a knitting
loom. Its cause, therefore, it is more probable, resembles
the cause of the former. The cause of the former is generation or vegetation. The cause, therefore, of the world, we
may infer to be something similar or analogous to generation or vegetation.

But how is it conceivable, said DEMEA, that the world
can arise from any thing similar to vegetation or generation? Very easily, replied PHILO. In like manner as a tree
sheds its seed into the neighbouring fields, and produces
other trees; so the great vegetable, the world, or this planetary system, produces within itself certain seeds, which,
being scattered into the surrounding chaos, vegetate into
new worlds. A comet, for instance, is the seed of a world;
and after it has been fully ripened, by passing from sun to
sun, and star to star, it is at last tost into the unformed
elements, which every where surround this universe, and
immediately sprouts up into a new system.–

I have all along asserted, and still assert, that we have no
data to establish any system of cosmogony. Our experience,
so imperfect in itself, and so limited both in extent and
duration, can afford no probable conjecture concerning the
whole of things. But if we must needs fix on some hypothesis; by what rule, pray, ought we to determine our
choice? Is there any other rule than the greater similarity
of the objects compared? And does not a plant or an animal,
which springs from vegetation or generation, bear a
stronger resemblance to the world, than does any artificial
machine, which arises from reason and design? –

In this little corner of the world alone, there are four
principles, *Reason, Instinct, Generation, Vegetation*, which
are similar to each other, and are the causes of similar
effects. What a number of other principles may we naturally suppose in the immense extent and variety of the
universe, could we travel from planet to planet, and from
system to system, in order to examine each part of this
mighty fabric? Any one of these four principles above mentioned (and a hundred others which lie open to our
conjecture) may afford us a theory, by which to judge of
the order of the world; and it is a palpable and egregious
partiality, to confine our view entirely to that principle, by

which our own minds operate. Were this principle more intelligible on that account, such a partiality might be somewhat excusable; but reason, in its internal fabric and structure, is really as little known to us as instinct or vegetation; and perhaps even that vague, undeterminate word, *Nature*, to which the vulgar refer every thing, is not at the bottom more inexplicable. The effects of these principles are all known to us from experience: but the principles themselves, and their manner of operation are totally unknown: nor is it less intelligible, or less conformable to experience to say, that the world arose by vegetation from a seed shed by another world, than to say that it arose from a divine reason or contrivance, according to the sense in which CLEANTHES understands it.–

That vegetation and generation, as well as reason, are experienced to be principles of order in nature, is undeniable. If I rest my system of cosmogony on the former, preferably to the latter, 'tis at my choice. The matter seems entirely arbitrary. And when CLEANTHES asks me what is the cause of my great vegetative or generative faculty, I am equally intitled to ask him the cause of his great reasoning principle. These questions we have agreed to forbear on both sides; and it is chiefly his interest on the present occasion to stick to this agreement. Judging by our limited and imperfect experience, generation has some privileges above reason: for we see every day the latter arise from the former, never the former from the latter."–

PHILO proceeds to inform us that he could, in an instant, propose various other systems of cosmogony, which would have some faint appearance of truth; though it is a thousand, a million to one, he says, if any one of them were the true system. – Motion, we are told, in many instances, from gravity, from elasticity, from electricity, begins in matter, without any known voluntary agent, and to suppose always, in these cases, an unknown voluntary agent, is mere hypothesis; and hypothesis attended with no advantage; the beginning of motion in matter itself being as conceivable *a priori* as its communication from mind and intelligence.

"All religious systems, it is confessed, says he, are subject to great and insuperable difficulties. Each disputant triumphs in his turn; while he carries on an offensive war, and exposes the absurdities, barbarities, and pernicious tenets of his antagonist. But all of them, on the whole, prepare a complete triumph for the *Sceptic*; who tells them, that no system ought ever to be embraced with regard to such subjects: for this plain reason, that no absurdity ought ever to be assented to with regard to any subject. A total suspense of judgment is here our only reasonable resource. And if every attack, as is commonly observed, and no defence, among theologians, is successful; how complete must be *his* victory, who remains always, with all mankind, on the offensive, and has himself no fixed station or abiding city, which he is ever, on any occasion, obliged to defend?"

PHILO, in a word, is of opinion, that as no system of cosmogony ought ever to be received from a slight analogy, so neither ought any to be rejected on account of a small incongruity; since that is an inconvenience, from which we can justly pronounce no one to be exempted.

The object of that curious artifice and machinery, which nature has displayed in all animals, PHILO tells us, is the preservation alone of individuals and propagation of the species. It seems enough for her purpose, he says, if such a rank be barely upheld in the universe, without any care or concern for the happiness of the members that compose it. No resource for this purpose: no machinery, in order merely to give pleasure or ease; no fund of pure joy and contentment: no indulgence without some want or necessity, accompanying it. At least, the few phenomena of this nature, we are told, are over-balanced by opposite phenomena of still greater importance.

"Allowing, says he, what never will be believed, at least, what can never possibly be proved, that animal, or at least, human happiness in this life exceeds its misery; we have yet done nothing; for this is not, by any means, what we expect from infinite power, infinite wisdom, and infinite goodness. Why is there any misery at all in the world? Not by chance surely. From some cause then. Is it from the intention of the Deity? But he is perfectly benevolent. Is it contrary to his intention? But he is almighty. Nothing can shake the solidity of this reasoning, so short, so clear, so decisive; except we assert, that these subjects exceed all human capacity, and that our common measures of truth and falsehood are not applicable to them; a topic, which I have all along insisted on, but which you have, from the beginning, rejected with scorn and indignation.

But I will be contented to retire still from this intrenchment: for I deny, CLEANTHES, that you can ever force me in it: I will allow, that pain or misery in man is *compatible* with infinite power and goodness in the Deity, even in your sense of these attributes: what are you advanced by all these concessions? A mere possible compatibility is not sufficient. You must *prove* these pure, unmixt, uncontrollable attributes from the present mixt and confused phenomena, and from these alone.   A hopeful undertaking! Were the phenomena ever so pure and unmixt, yet being finite, they would be insufficient for that purpose. How much more, where they are also so jarring and discordant?"

There seem to be *four* circumstances, PHILO says, on which depend all, or the greatest part of the ills, that molest sensible creatures, none of which appear to human reason, in the least degree, necessary or unavoidable; nor can we suppose them such, without the utmost licence of imagination.

The *first* circumstance which introduces evil, we are told, is that contrivance of œconomy or the animal creation, by which pains as well as pleasures are employed to excite all creatures to action, and make them vigilant in the great work of self-preservation.   Now pleasure alone, in its various degrees, seems to human understanding sufficient to this purpose. – The *second* circumstance is, the conducting of the world by general laws; and this seems no way necessary to a very perfect being. – The *third* circumstance is, the great frugality, with which all powers and faculties are distributed to every particular being. Nature, 'tis said, seems to have formed an exact calculation of the necessities of her creatures; and like a *rigid master*, has afforded them little more powers or endowments, than what are strictly sufficient to supply those necessities. An *indulgent parent* would have bestowed a large stock, in order to guard against accidents, and secure the happiness and welfare of the creature, in the most unfortunate concurrence of circumstances. Every course of life would not have been so surrounded with precipices, that the least departure from the true path, by mistake or necessity, must involve us in misery and ruin. Some reserve, some fund would have been provided to ensure happiness; nor would the powers and the necessities have been adjusted with so rigid an œconomy.

The *fourth* circumstance, whence arises the evil and misery of the universe, is the inaccurate workmanship of all the springs and principles of the great machine of nature. One would imagine, PHILO says, that this grand production had not received the last hand of the maker; so little finished is every part, and so coarse are the strokes with which it is executed.

"On the concurrence, then, continues he, of these *four* circumstances does all, or the greatest part of natural evil depend. Were all living creatures incapable of pain, or were the world administered by particular volitions, evil never could have found access into the universe; and were animals endowed with a large stock of powers and faculties, beyond what strict necessity requires; or were the several springs and principles of the universe so accurately framed, as to preserve always the just temperament and medium; there must have been very little ill in comparison of what we feel at present. What then shall we pronounce on this occasion? Shall we say, that these circumstances are not necessary, and that they might easily have been altered in the contrivance of the universe? This decision seems too presumptuous for creatures, so blind and ignorant. Let us be more modest in our conclusions. Let us allow, that, if the goodness of the Deity (I mean a goodness like the human) could be established on any tolerable reasons *a priori*, these phenomena, however untoward, would not be sufficient to subvert that principle; but might easily, in some unknown manner, be reconcilable to it. But let us still assert, that as this goodness is not antecedently established, but must be inferred from the phenomena, there can be no grounds for such an inference, while there are so many ills in the universe, and while these ills might so easily have been remedied, as far as human understanding can be allowed to judge on such a subject. I am sceptic enough to allow, that the bad appearances, notwithstanding all my reasonings, may be compatible with such attributes as you suppose: but surely they can never prove these attributes. Such a conclusion cannot result from scepticism; but must arise from the phenomena, and from our confidence in the reasonings, which we deduce from these phenomena."

In regard to the influence of religious principles on the conduct of mankind, PHILO says, it is certain from experience, that the smallest grain of natural honesty and benevolence has more effect on men's conduct, than the most pompous views, suggested by theological theories and systems. And when we have to do with a man who makes a great profession of religion and devotion; this, we are told, has no other effect upon several, who pass for prudent, than to put them on their guard, lest they be cheated and deceived by him. He further says, that the steady attention alone to so important an interest as that of eternal salvation, is apt to extinguish the benevolent affections, and beget a narrow, contracted selfishness; and that when such a temper is encouraged, it easily eludes all the general precepts of charity and benevolence. In regard to the worship of the Deity, hear what he says:

"*To know God*, says SENECA, *is to worship him*. All other worship is indeed absurd, superstitious, and even impious. It degrades him to the low condition of mankind, who are delighted with intreaty, solicitation, presents, and flattery. Yet is this impiety the smallest of which superstition is guilty. Commonly, it depresses the Deity far below the condition of mankind; and represents him as a capricious demon, who exercises his power without reason, and without humanity. And were that divine Being disposed to be offended at the vices and follies of silly mortals, who are his own workmanship; ill would it surely fare with the votaries of most popular superstitions. Nor would any of the human race merit his *favour*, but a very few, the philosophical theifts, who entertain, or rather indeed endeavour to entertain, suitable notions of his divine perfections: as the only persons, intitled to his *compassion* and *indulgence*, would be the philosophical sceptics, a fact almost equally rare, who, from a natural diffidence of their own capacity, suspend, or endeavour to suspend, all judgment with regard to such sublime and such extraordinary subjects."

Such are the sentiments, such the doctrines contained in the

Dialogues before us; and it is natural now, surely, to ask, what gratitude is due to Mr. Hume for this legacy to the public? If the principles which he has laboured with so much zeal and earnestness to establish be true, the wicked are set free from every restraint but that of the laws; the virtuous are robbed of their most substantial comforts; every generous ardor of the human mind is damped; the world we live in is a fatherless world; we are chained down to a life full of wretchedness and misery; and we have no hope beyond the grave.

Mr. Hume had been long floating on the boundless and pathless ocean of scepticism; it is natural, therefore, to imagine that, in the evening of his day, he would have been desirous of getting into some peaceful harbour; of breathing a pure air; of viewing a clear and unclouded sky, free from those unwholesome mists that hang over the gloomy regions of darkness and uncertainty; and of passing through the closing scenes of life with tranquillity and pleasing hopes. But his love of paradox, his inordinate pursuit of literary fame, continued, whilst life continued; it is scarce possible, indeed, with the utmost stretch of candour and charity, to assign any other motives for publishing what must shock the sense and virtue of his fellow-mortals, or to reconcile it with the character of a good citizen, and a friend to mankind.

We know it will be said, that Mr. Hume, notwithstanding his principles, was a very benevolent and a very amiable man; we *know* he was, and are as ready to allow him all the praise he is intitled to, on account of his good qualities, as the warmest of his admirers. But, surely, it cannot be inferred from this, that principles have little or no effect on human conduct. A man, who is naturally of a cool dispassionate turn of mind; of a studious disposition; whose education, fortune, and other accidental circumstances, connect him with the upper ranks of life, may not only have fashionable manners, be an agreeable companion, but may, by the mere force of natural temper, be a benevolent, good-humoured man, and act his part in life with great decency. But suppose that Mr. Hume's principles are let loose among mankind, and generally adopted, what will then be the consequence? Will those who think they are to die like brutes, ever act like men? Their language will be, *let us eat and drink, for to-morrow we die.* When men are once led to believe that death puts a final period to their existence, and are set free from the idea of their being accountable creatures, what is left to restrain them from the gratification of their passions but the authority of the laws? But the best system of laws that can be formed by human wisdom, is far from being sufficient to prevent many of those evils which break in upon the peace, order, and welfare of society. A man may be a cruel husband, a cruel father, a domestic tyrant; he may seduce his neighbour's wife or his daughter, without having any thing to fear from the law; and if he takes pleasure in the gratification of his irregular appetites, is it to be supposed that he will not gratify them? What, indeed, is to restrain him?

But we leave it to our Readers to pursue these reflexions, – into which we were naturally led, and for which, we hope, we need make no apology. – Mr. Hume's Dialogues cannot possibly hurt any man of a philosophical turn, or, indeed, any man of common sense; and it is only the high reputation which the Author of them has so justly acquired by his other writings, and the influence of this reputation, that give them any claim to notice. They may serve, indeed, to confirm the giddy, the profligate, and the unprincipled in their prejudices against religion and virtue, but must be despised by every man who has the smallest grain of seriousness and reflection. No virtuous father will ever recommend them to the perusal of his son, except in point of composition; and every impartial judge must pronounce them unworthy of a writer of such distinguished abilities as Mr. HUME.

PAMPHILUS, a young man, who relates to HERMIPPUS the conversation which passed between Cleanthes, Philo, and Demea, concludes the Dialogues in the following manner.–

"Upon a serious review of the whole, says he, I cannot but think, that Philo's principles are more probable than Demea's; but that those of Cleanthes approach still nearer to the truth." –

Our Readers will make their own comment upon this, and with them we leave it.

REMARKS ON MR. HUME'S DIALOGUES CONCERNING NATURAL RELIGION
Thomas Hayter

MR. HUME, in the Introduction to his Dialogues (p. 10.) exhibits the following sketch of the personages between whom the Dialogues are supposed to be maintained.

> "The remarkable contrast in their characters still farther raised your expectations; while you opposed the accurate philosophical turn of CLEANTHES to the careless scepticism of PHILO, or compared either of their dispositions with the rigid inflexible orthodoxy of DEMEA."

From this representation one might at first be led to look for Mr. HUME himself under the mask of CLEANTHES, and to expect from the mouth of CLEANTHES the celebrated Metaphysician's own sentiments. Let us consider however that Mr. HUME, after the great nominal superiority attributed to CLEANTHES, could not possibly, without appearance of vanity, have appointed CLEANTHES his representative. The fact indeed indisputably is, that PHILO, not CLEANTHES, personates Mr. HUME. CLEANTHES assumes at times (p. 242 and 244) the tone of DEMEA: while PHILO possesses in general the sole exclusive priviledge of retailing the purport of Mr. HUME's former Philosophical productions. – Every remarkable trait and feature of those productions may be traced in the parts of the Dialogue assigned to PHILO.

Part I

THE first part of Mr. HUME's Dialogues is employed in proposing and canvassing different systems of cosmogony – The system of CLEANTHES deducing (p. 47) the universe from an intelligent cause (after being confronted by various intermediate theorys) is allowed (at p. 196) to prevail over its rivals, and to convert their advocate, PHILO – Neither the system of CLEANTHES, in its original state, nor any of its rivals are proposed as the objects of the present disquisition. The sole aim of these remarks is to contravert PHILO's own additions to the system of CLEANTHES, viz. PHILO's disavowal of God's moral attributes, and his proscription of popular religion.

PHILO's objection to the existence of benevolence in the divine nature is grounded principally on the circumstance of human misery. Of this melancholy object he[1] exhibits (from p. 173 to p. 192.) a most uncomfortable, forlorn, and, I trust, overcharged description – Some of the darkest shades in the frightful picture are borrowed from the Pencils of writers in general, particularly of Poets. Their testimony PHILO appeals to (p. 173 and 174) as decisive,

> "The Poets (p. 173.) who speak from sentiment, without a system, and whose testimony has therefore more authority, abound in images of this nature."

Again, (p. 174.)

> "Look round the library of CLEANTHES. I shall venture to affirm that, except authors of particular sciences such as chemistry and botany, who have no occasion to treat of human life, there is scarce one of those innumerable writers, from whom the sense of human misery has not in some passage or other, extorted a complaint and confession of it."

Let us here, by PHILO's leave, recall to recollection an old remark "Omnes ingeniosos esse melancholicos." Suppose now any individual of the pensive tribe to labour under a real misfortune or under the spleen, and to have, at that critical moment, a pen in his hand: He instantly, in all human probability upon the slightest provocation in his subject, gives a dash at the condition of mortal affairs: vents his particular emotions in general terms: expands a partial posture of private concerns into an universal representation: and etches a copy of human life from the present complexion of his own

---

[1] I am aware that the topic of human wretchedness is (from p. 174 to p. 185.) frequently handled by DEMEA. But as the assertions of DEMEA on this point (from p. 174 to p. 181.) are (at p. 181.) most cordially assented to by PHILO; and as the remainder of DEMEA's tragic declamation (down to p. 185.) meets in that page with a similar warm acquiescence from his friend; we may surely venture to set down PHILO a complete proselyte to the dismal creed.

situation – With respect to Poets, we need not conceive them in any actual distress in order to justify a suspicion of some misrepresentation in the affair of human calamity. What pathetic incident ever passed through the hands of a genuine bard without receiving many touches of amplification? And is the interesting argument of mortal misery likely to be dismissed naked, and unadorned, totally destitute of its poetical finishing? Without calling in the supposition of absolute fiction, how greatly does the warm animated language alone of poetry vary the aspect, without altering the circumstances, of a fact; and magnify, without seeming to depart from, truth? In what doth oratory consist? not professedly, nor yet visibly in falsification. Yet, hear the same identical narrative at one time from an eloquent, at another time from a plain man; you will perceive the one to have heated, you know not why, your passions and imagination, while the other best satisfies your judgement. In a word, the testimony of authors, especially of "the inspired train", as PHILO calls the poets, does not seem worthy of the great stress laid upon it by PHILO.

RENOUNCING then the illusions of fancy, let us listen to PHILO's own representation of the horrid scene.

"You ascribe (p. 186) CLEANTHES, (and, I believe, justly) a purpose and intention to nature. But what, I beseech you, is the object of that curious artifice and machinery, which she has displayed in all animals? The preservation alone of individuals and propagation of the species. It seems enough for her purpose, if such a rank be barely upheld in the universe, without any care or concern for the happiness of the members that compose it. No resource for this purpose: no machinery in order merely to give pleasure or ease: no fund of pure joy and contentment: no indulgence, without some want or necessity accompanying it. At least the phenomena of this nature are overbalanced by opposite phenomena of still greater importance. Our sense of music harmony and indeed beauty of all kinds gives satisfaction, without being absolutely necessary to the preservation and propagation of the species. But what racking pains, on the other hand, arise from gouts, gravels, megrims, tooth-achs, rheumatisms; where the injury to the animal-machinery is either small or incurable? Mirth, laughter, play, frolic seem gratuitous satisfactions, which have no farther tendency: Spleen, melancholy, discontent, superstition are pains of the same nature". Again, (at p. 191.) "You must at the same time allow, that if pain be less frequent (which is extremely doubtful) than pleasure, it is infinitely more violent and durable. One hour of it is often able to out-weigh a day, a week, a month of our common insipid enjoyments; And how many days, weeks, and months are passed by many in the most acute torments? Pleasure scarcely in one instance is ever able to reach ecstasy and rapture: And in no one instance can it continue for any time at its highest pitch and altitude. The spirits evaporate; the nerves relax; the fabric is disordered; and the enjoyment quickly degenerates into fatigue and uneasiness. But pain, often, good God, how often! rises to torture and agony; and the longer it continues, it becomes still more genuine agony and torture. Patience is exhausted; courage languishes; melancholy seizes us; and nothing terminates our misery but the removal of its cause, or another event, which is the sole cure of all evil, but which, from our natural folly, we regard with still greater horror and consternation."

Let us analyse this tale of woe. It positively asserts, at setting out "that the sole object (pray mark the expression 'sole') of nature's curious machinery is the preservation of individuals and the propagation of the species". At the distance of a few sentences, however, the tale enumerates several sources of delight "not absolutely necessary to the preservation and propagation of the species". Is this reasoning, PHILO, or prating? would not a single instance (you recite several) of "gratuitous satisfaction" completely exclude the supposition of a total insensibility and unfeelingness, if we may so speak, in the determinations of nature? She does not, you say, grant as much as I could reasonably wish – But, if she had been perfectly and entirely inattentive to your accommodation, would she have granted any thing at all? "The phenomena of her graciousness, you reply, are overbalanced by opposite phenomena of still greater importance". How does this subterfuge demonstrate your first doctrine of a total uniform obduracy? If nature had been so unequivocally void of goodness as you pretend, she would have exposed you to the evils you describe without any, the slightest mixture of alleviation:

she would never have imparted any solace, that could possibly have been dispensed with: and you would have drunk from her cup nothing but dregs. You must surely retract your first accusation.

DISLODGED from this post you next retreat to the position, that evil does, upon the whole, predominate in the canvass of nature: the picture is cast in shades. Before we adopt your representation, let us survey the facts on which it is grounded. Your own catalogue of evils is nearly equal in point of number, with your list of blessings. Thus far your argument looks almost equally both ways: it will quickly, I hope, set its face against you. If, for instance, your evils, though rather more numerous than your blessings, be found to center in a comparatively small number of individuals, while your blessings are pretty generally diffused through the human race, there will evidently result, in regard to the whole creation, a far greater measure of happiness, than of misery. This conclusion cannot be denied, if the two first branches of the sentence are established. To establish them is my task – In regard to the first branch, namely, the comparatively narrow operation of PHILO's evils; are most of those evils, let us ask, any thing else than various species of ill health? And is health or sickness, let us next ask, the most usual visitant to the sons of men? A great proportion of mankind in every civilized country live in a state of idleness: if a great part of the remainder was sick, how could the business of the world go on? Let every one, in a word, from his own experience strike an estimate of the actual balance between sickness and health, and then answer my question. PHILO has, it must be confessed, two evils, discontent and superstition, not strictly reducible to the head of sickness. Are not both these evils, however, of a very precarious, fluctuating nature? Chearful company, a fine day, the flightest amusement, the most trivial employment suspend, sometimes cure, their influence. May they not therefore fairly be considered as a sort of neutral powers; hanging at equal distances between the attractions of pleasure and pain, and not decisively gravitating towards either? PHILO's evils, upon the whole, appear evidently to have a much more contracted range in human life than PHILO was willing to ascribe to them – Let us next see, if PHILO's blessings (which is the second branch of the sentence I am to demonstrate) do not move in a pretty large circle? Is any man so unfortunate, as not frequently to have tasted some of these blessings? Is any man so forlorn, as to despair of all future access to the rich feast? – The reader does, I flatter myself, by this time think me entitled to the conclusion, which I drew from the two branches of my sentence now discussed, viz. That good, not evil, is the leading feature in the state of mortal affairs.

BUT though PHILO should allow pleasure to have the ascendancy, in point of frequency, over pain; PHILO still laments (p. 191 and 192) that the former sensation is inferior to the latter both in duration and degree. "Pleasure, he cryes, scarcely in any instance is ever able to reach ecstasy and "rapture". What a complaint from a Philosopher! who tells us (at p. 259) of these very dialogues "That there is no state of mind so happy as the calm and equable." Without however pressing the Philosopher either with his character or declarations, let us look abroad into the world, and see whether the want of "ecstasy and rapture" be very generally and seriously deplored. That part of mankind, which is engaged in constant employment, and which possesses at the same time either a competence or at worst a bare sufficiency of necessarys, comprehends probably near two thirds, at all events half of the human race. Now amongst this very large body it is much to be doubted if the scarcity of "ecstasy and rapture" has, ever since the creation, been the transient occasion of a single sigh. These contented mortals dream not of raptures, but enjoy satisfaction: they have not the word ecstacy in their mouths, but solid tranquility in their hearts: they wish not to be angels, and are happy men: they have not yet schooled themselves into discontent: nor learnt the sublime science of becoming metaphysically miserable – PHILO's estimate of pain now claims our attention. "Pain, often, good God, how often! rises to torture and agony". That pain is sometimes excessive, it is more our business to lament, than to deny. Let us remark however, for the consolation of mankind, that this melancholy grievance appears often of greater magnitude and in far larger dimensions to the spectator, than to the sufferer. Persons, condemned by sickness to lasting confinement and quick returns of pain, wear, not uncommonly very strong marks of serenity and acquiescence. The goodness of God's providence infuses, no doubt, some drops of comfort into the bitter draught of agony, to attemper its malignity and restrain its excessive operation. – At the worst, an event, not far distant from any of us, is, according even to PHILO's account (p. 192), "A cure of all evil." PHILO indeed adds, "But which, from our natural folly, we regard with horror and consternation." But pray, if death be really a cure of all evil, are we not, when it comes, cured by it, whether we wished to be so, or not? does death, when it actually takes place, lose its efficacy, as a remedy, through our previous misconceptions of its nature? – Let us here remark, that when men of sense shudder at death, their emotion, it is to be feared, arises more from depravity, than folly. The profligate and irreligious may naturally recoil from the approach of that futurity whose reality they have questioned; and may justly dread the frowns of that being whose authority they have defied. But thousands of virtuous men in all ages have received, and will doubtless, to the end of time continue to receive the final summons of their Creator with calm undisturbed composure.

PHILO from (p. 199 to p. 102) repeatedly echoes to us, that the whole sublunary scene (human life of course included) wears no stamp or signature of a benevolent author. This idea (at p. 201) sprouts up into the following allusion.

"Did I show you a house or palace, where there was not one apartment convenient or agreeable; where the windows, doors, fires, passages, stairs and the whole œconomy of the building were the source of noise, confusion, fatigue, darkness and the extremes of heat and cold, you would certainly blame the contrivance without any farther examination."

Instead of examining his imaginary building, let us ask PHILO a simple question, namely, whether he has already entirely forgot "the sense of music harmony and beauty?" of p. 187. "The mirth, laughter, play, frolic" of p. 188? Has, in a word, the whole fair train of "gratuitous satisfactions," enumerated by himself, totally escaped from his recollection? If a single trace of them had survived in his memory, he would surely not have represented his miserable allegorical lodging so shockingly ill-furnished, so completely deficient in every, the smallest, article of accommodation.

FROM p. 205 to p. 217 PHILO employs himself in displaying four circumstances, on which, to use his own words (p. 203),

"All or the greatest part of the ills that molest sensible creatures depend" and by the removal of which the creation would, in his conception (p. 217.) be prodigiously improved. – Notwithstanding however PHILO's present apparent acquiescence in his new mundane arrangements, we find him, no farther off than p. 218, staggering into the following reflexion,

> "Shall we say that these circumstances are not necessary, and that they might easily have been altered in the contrivance of the universe? This decision seems too presumptuous for creatures so blind and ignorant."

What a pity, PHILO, is it, that this very natural obvious sentiment did not occur to you, a few pages back, at your first entrance into the intricacys of cosmogonic criticism! How endless is it to object to what we do not understand! How idle is the proposal of altering what we do not know if we can improve! To erect card-constructed houses indeed with the infant, to weave straw-crowns with the maniac seem far more rational employments of time and intellect than for blind mortals to revise creation, and ignorant theorists to new-model the universe.

DESCENDING then from these illusive, air-built speculations, let us hasten to the final result of all the foregoing theories, namely, to PHILO's representation, inferred from the said theories, of the divine attributes.

PHILO's first position on this head (p. 221.) runs thus,

> "There may four hypotheses be framed concerning the first causes of the universe: that they are endowed with perfect goodness: that they have perfect malice: that they are opposite and have both goodness and malice: that they have neither goodness nor malice: mixt phenomena can never prove the two former principles: and the uniformity and steadiness of general laws seems to oppose the third; the fourth therefore, seems by far the most probable."

In opposition however to the fourth supposal, let it be asked, whether one single solitary instance (Philo has recounted several) of "gratuitous satisfaction," would not forbid us to consider the Deity as absolutely regardless of our welfare? Let it next be remarked, that to those, who adopt my estimate of human happiness and misery, the belief of God's benevolence acquires instant confirmation, and stands erected upon a fair ample, immoveable foundation.

PHILO's next feature in the divine nature is thus sketched (p. 222.)

"What I have said concerning natural evil will apply to moral, with little or no variation; we have no more reason to infer, that the rectitude of the supreme being resembles human rectitude than that his benevolence resembles the human."

In subversion of this doctrine I will beg leave to cite a passage from "Mr. HUME's 11th essay on the practical consequences of natural religion," where EPICURUS, in a speech ascribed to him (p. 217.) thus expresses himself,

"I acknowledge that in the present order of things virtue is attended with much more peace of mind than vice, and meets with a more favourable reception in the world. I am sensible, that according to the past experience of mankind, friendship is the chief joy of human life, moderation the only source of tranquility and happiness. I never balance between the virtuous and vicious course of life; but am sensible, that to a well disposed mind every advantage is on the side of the former."

The supreme being then, has (by the confession of a person not to be suspected of bigotry) interwoven in the very frame and constitution of things, a testimony to the superiority of virtue above vice: in other words, the Almighty hath provided, that the preference due to the former quality beyond the latter, should be suggested to us, at every step of our existence, by the striking evidence of familiar facts. With this glaring document of the deity's love for moral uprightness in us, let us couple PHILO's assertion, (p. 236.) that the nature of the supreme being does, in point of intelligence, "bear a considerable resemblance to ours." And will this nature, in the direction of its intelligence, totally renounce the rules recommended by itself for the government of our analogous intelligence? shall the declared lover of righteousness not do right? shall the determined patron of justice be himself unjust?

Part II

PHILO opens his charge (p.243) against religion with the following invective.

> "How happens it then, if vulgar superstition[2] be so salutary to society, that all history abounds so much with accounts of its pernicious consequences on public affairs? factions, civil wars, persecutions, subversions of government, oppression, slavery; these are the dismal consequences which always attend its prevalency over the minds of men. If the religious spirit be ever mentioned in any historical narration, we are sure to meet afterwards with a detail of the miseries which attend it."

We shall be extremely mistaken, if we consider all the mischiefs in which the word religion has been held out, or in which religionists had concern, as the genuine fruit of mere religious influence.   The name of religion has often hung upon the tongue, where no particle of her holy energy reached the heart.   PHILO himself will inform us (p. 244.) that "religion is (only) a cover to faction and ambition," which are the real prompters of those turbulent scenes where religion alone appears upon the stage.   Now ambition and faction are durable permanent principles; and, if religion had

---

[2] What PHILO means by vulgar superstition may be learnt from p. 244. CLEANTHES there remarks, "That when religion distinguishes itself and acts as a separate principle over men, it has departed from its proper sphere, and has become only a cover to faction and ambition." To this PHILO replies "And so will all religion, except the philosophical and rational." All religion then, according to PHILO, except the philosophical and rational will become the cover to faction and ambition.   To be the cover of faction and ambition is, in the ordinary acceptation of the words, to be the source of all the mischiefs ascribed to vulgar superstition in the present page. All religion therefore, except the philosophical and rational, is evidently, in PHILO's view of things, vulgar superstition.

The professors of philosophical religion are said (p. 261) to be extremely few.   The faith of these professors is represented (at p. 262) as centering entirely in one solitary speculative tenet, which (to use the very words there employed in characterizing it) affords no inference that can affect human life, or can "be the source of any action or forbearance," so simple a code of divinity can evidently not incumber its proselytes with temples, modes of worship, or fear of heavenly power.   The professors of this pure theology are of course easy to be distinguished.   These pure theologists, once distinguished, negatively ascertain to us the vulgarly superstitious part of mankind, namely, all other persons, except atheists, and these contemplative single-teneted religionists.

never existed, would undoubtedly, on some pretence or other, have found vent. Passions, in a word, that use religion simply as a veil, will, though stripped of the veil, present an undaunted front: though detected, they will not be dismayed. Ambition and faction are no bigots. Divested of their religious disguise, they instantly assume some other; immediately new-dress their indefatigable characters, nor remain a single moment absent from the stage. They substitute perhaps popularity for prayers; Agrarian laws for alms; and largesses to the mob instead of donations to saints. – They have, it is true, often borrowed the vizor of religion; must religion therefore be made their voucher? must that chaste and holy principle be loaded with the infamy of actions, which she had not the smallest concern in giving birth to? must she be rendered responsible for measures, which she was not allowed to direct; and be represented as the adviser of those, by whom she was never consulted? – What? – Some men have basely prostituted the name of religion, all men therefore ought to renounce her precepts! some persons, not really under her guidance, have acted wrong, she must therefore no longer teach us to act right! We must strip ourselves of the substance, because others have put on the semblance. Religion, in fine, having been accommodated to bad ends, must on that account, not be permitted to promote good ones[3]. By this mode of reasoning the worthy man, whose signature is counterfeited for the purposes of forgery, ought to suffer capital punishment: and honesty, because personated now and then by hypocrisy, should be proscribed as a species of villany.

PHILO (p. 243.) declares positively that "no periods of time can be happier or more prosperous than those in which it (religion) is never heard of nor regarded." Before we assent to this proposition, let us recollect, that at no period probably of time whatever was religion so little heard of or regarded, as in the æra immediately preceding the dissolution of the Roman republick. – In this immaculate æra (let us briefly trace its happiness and prosperity) one man concerted and had nearly executed a general massacre of the supreme magistrates, with a total subversion of a free government. – Gover-

---

[3] The inestimable benefits resulting from religion will be displayed in a subsequent paragraph.

nors of extensive provinces constantly ravaged the unhappy objects of their jurisdiction, with merciless, and more than hostile licentiousness. – Fortunes of an almost imperial amplitude, vanished daily at the touch of dissipation: while, to repair the mighty ruins, crimes of every complexion and enormity were, without fear or compunction, had recourse to – one general alone, in pursuit of wealth and power, desolated Gaul, threw his own country into convulsions, nor finished his career till near two millions of his fellow-creatures had fallen victims to his ambition. – Can one meditate without horror on almost any of the principal transactions in PHILO's golden age! religion had indubitably no concern in those dreadful scenes: and may securely exclaim in the language of our Poet; "Thou canst not say, I did it" – Let us now suppose for a moment, that religion had actually happened to have interested, in PHILO's favorite age, the passions of mankind. What would have been the consequence? she would, in all human probability, have been appointed the nominal president, the ostensible high-priestess at the dreadful rites. CæSAR would have been a CROMWELL: would have waved a dagger in one hand, his manual in the other: would have pretended, while he sought only his own aggrandisement, "to seek the Lord[4]". If this imaginary state of things indeed had really taken place; religion, we may be assured, would have been marked by PHILO, as principal instigatress of CæSAR's worst actions, as the sole mover of his way-ward ambition!

PHILO proceeds (p. 244.) to depreciate the efficacy of future rewards and punishments.

> "The inference is not just, because finite rewards and pun-
> ishments have so great influence, that therefore such as are
> infinite and eternal must have so much greater. Consider,
> I beseech you, the attachment we have to present things,
> and the little concern we discover for objects so remote and
> uncertain. When divines are declaiming against the
> common behaviour and practice of the world, they always
> represent this principle as the strongest imaginable (which
> indeed it is) and describe almost all human kind as lying
> under the influence of it, and sunk into the deepest lethargy
> and unconcern about their religious interests. Yet these

---

[4] A favorite expression of CROMWELL.

same divines, when they refute their speculative antagonists, suppose the motives of religion to be so powerful, that, without them, it were impossible for civil society to subsist; nor are they ashamed of so palpable a contradiction."

They need not PHILO, be ashamed of it, for it is not, (if my conjectures are right) a contradiction. The meaning of the divines (if I could be referred to their works) would prove, I really believe, consistent. It probably runs thus, sensible objects, take strong and lasting hold of the human mind; and powerfully detach it from the doctrines of eternity: the doctrines of eternity however, by means of exhortation and meditation, do in many instances find entrance into the heart, once admitted they operate potently; mightily convert the inclinations; and prevent numberless enormities. Without their salutary influence, society would be deluged with insufferable profligacy; and be rendered incapable of subsisting. – In opposition to these very rational suggestions of the divines, PHILO remarks (p. 245.)

"It is certain from experience, that the smallest grain of natural honesty and benevolence, has more effect on men's conduct, than the most pompous views suggested by theological theories and systems."

Supposing, though not admitting, the truth of this position, how PHILO does it answer your present purpose? in what shape does it constitute a plea for the entire renunciation of religion? in recommending the exterminating system, 'tis your business to prove – not, that religion has little influence: but, that she has none at all. This latter position however, you will scarce venture absolutely to maintain, after having declared (p. 246.) that religion "operates by starts and bounds," that is, that religion has some influence: – calculate PHILO, the amount of this influence at your discretion: does it direct one half, one third, or one fourth of human agency? deliver your estimate. Morality will accept it at your hands; and rejoice in the friendly tender. SAUL slew his thousands, DAVID his ten thousands; yet, both surely merited the applause of their countrymen. Is the general, who wins five battles, to be disgraced, because another general wins ten? no judicious person, in a word, will, in the great task of curbing human wickedness, reject any, the very slightest, cooperation. – Aware perhaps of some reasoning of this kind PHILO employs, (p. 246.) in still farther disparaging the energy of the religious principle: representing it as an inert, lifeless spring of action; a monitor, easy to be silenced; a lawgiver, without difficulty eluded; an adviser whom no one pays more attention to, than passion and inclination permit. – Fully to convince us indeed, that the caput mortuum of religion may be easily dispensed with in society, PHILO peremptorily asserts (p. 247.) that

> "none but fools ever repose less trust in a man, because they hear, that from study and philosophy, he has entertained some speculative doubts on theological subjects."

Notwithstanding this testimonial to the innocency and uprightness of irreligion; which person, in the name of common sense, is most worthy of confidence and dependance; the man, who is restrained solely by a regard to character and interest: or the man, who in addition to the above motives, has the controul likewise of divine vengeance, hanging incessantly, like DAMOCLES's sword, over his every procedure?

PHILO, not content with detracting from the influence of religion in the article of enforcing virtue, proceeds to accuse her of encouraging vice – The first species of proof, employed by PHILO in the support of his bold charge, is the exhibition of certain odious, unworthy religious characters.

> "When we have to do (p. 247) with a man, who makes a great profession of religion and devotion; has this any other effect upon several, who pass for prudent, than to put them on their guard, lest they be cheated and deceived by him?" Again (p. 248) "Amongst ourselves some have been guilty of that atrociousness, unknown to the Grecian and Egyptian superstitions, of declaiming, in express terms, against morality."

The figure of "pars pro toto," though tolerated in composition, is intolerable in argument. PHILO, in the passages before us, points out certain reprehensible characters, by no means predominant in the religious Drama, and represents them as the principal actors. He would, no doubt, wish us to imagine, that the Pharisaical Hypocrite in the first extract, and the unprincipled enthusiast in the second are faithful samples of the generality of religionists: that they have the true family-face; and may serve as models of their brethren.

p. 248. PHILO launches at religion the following invective,

"Even though superstition or enthusiasm should not put itself in direct opposition to morality; the very diverting of the attention, the raising up a new and frivolous species of merit, the preposterous distribution which it makes of praise and blame, must have the most pernicious consequences, and weaken extremely men's attachment to the natural motives of justice and humanity."

Let us here pause; and bestow a thorough examination upon that "new frivolous species of merit" practical religion: let us ascertain its intrinsic value: let us enquire, if the pretended mass of dross wear not an imperial superscription; be not stamped with a divine image.

FOR the origin of religion I shall appeal solely to the authority[5] of Mr. HUME; who (in his dissertation on the natural history of religion, sect. 4. p. 24,) remarks

"That the only point of theology, in which we shall find a consent of mankind almost universal, is, that there is invisible, intelligent power in the world."

Again, (sect. 15. p. 114.)

"The universal propensity to believe in invisible, intelligent power, if not an original instinct, being at least a general attendant of human nature, it may be considered as a kind of mark or stamp, which the divine workman has set upon his work – Before we proceed to decypher this heaven-imprinted character, this hand-writing, as it were, of nature; let us step back for a moment, to the dialogues, and listen to PHILO, haranguing (at p. 228) in the following strain,"
"*That nature does nothing in vain*, is a maxim established in all the schools, merely from the contemplation of the works of nature, without any religious purpose; and, from a firm conviction of its truth, an anatomist who had observed a new organ or canal, would never be satisfied till he had also discovered its use and intention."

---

[5] Better authority might, doubtless, be produced: but none, probably, so satisfactory to PHILO.

The all-sagacious architect has therefore, surely, not *in vain* implanted in our nature the religious propensity: nor swerved in this single important instance from her usual maxims of providence. Let us now then endeavour to unfold her counsels in this particular: and develop, as far as we are able, the "use and intention" or final cause, as it is often called, of religion[6] – The human body, it has been repeatedly observed, is incapable of perpetual exertion. Certain pauses are occasionally requisite to relieve the strained machine, and readjust its disordered springs. All nations accordingly, without exception, have invariably indulged themselves in periodical seasons of relaxation – A state of inactivity, let it next be remarked, is to men in general, particularly to the lower orders of our species a state of danger. The human mind no sooner stagnates, than it putrefies – How fortunate then would it be, if mankind could be engaged, during part of their day of rest in some innocent employment; which might fill up some intervals of a very perilous season unexceptionably; and render leisure, the source of mischief, in some degree innoxious! But how would our satisfaction redouble, if the much-wished for employment should prove not simply inoffensive; but should consist in calling mankind together[7] to the performance of offices of a composed, solemn, awful cast; replete with stilness and sobriety; and calculated to settle the heart into a salutary calm. The effect of such a soul-steadying exercise would surely not be entirely momentary; but would follow the mind probably beyond the walls of the temple; and fortify it for some time, against the suggestions of idle levity. To an avocation of the kind here described can every religion under heaven perhaps boast itself to amount – But if paganism be all this, what is not Christianity? In the religious assemblies of those regions, where the celestial ray of revelation shines with free lustre, we shall hear a heaven-descended performance constantly recited, pregnant with the purest maxims of morality, and rich in interesting displays of future existence – The very prayers too, in the well-con-

---

[6] Though my conjectures on this momentous subject should not be deemed satisfactory, still let it be remembered, that the religious propensity, according to the well-founded maxim of the schools quoted by PHILO, indisputably has a final cause.

[7] Mere association, if regulated by decorum, has a most efficacious tendency, in the opinion of intelligent judges, to civilize and polish the human race.

structed religious assemblies of those regions, will not merely implore divine protection; but will, in doing so, briefly recall to view, the most effectual recommendation to divine protection, moral excellency – The persuasions of a holy orator will, at the close, reinforce the general impression. From such a fertile field of instruction, from such a matchless school of morality, what barbarian can depart totally unmeliorated? There is no one, I firmly believe, scarcely the most hardened, but what carries away from the religious meetings of true protestantism some degree of improvement, some sense of duty. Suppose, with PHILO, this improvement, this sense of duty "to operate by starts and bounds," to prevent bad actions only occasionally, at particular seasons: still will the benefit resulting from them be great, superlative, and inestimable!

BUT PHILO entertains quite different conceptions; and maintains religion to be the parent of evil, rather than of good: more a friend to vice, than virtue – The instance of the bad tendency of religion, produced by PHILO at p. 249, carries a very striking peculiar air.

"Many religious exercises are entered into with seeming fervour, where the heart at the time, feels cold and languid: a habit of dissimulation is by degrees contracted: and fraud and falshood become the predominant principle."

Concise piece of demonstration! A man performs certain religious offices negligently – is rendered by that means a hypocrite – quickly after a complete rogue! when such unbounded licentiousness of inference is freely and unblushingly practised, there seems to be no reason, why one man, as well as another, may not presume to draw conclusions. I will try therefore, if from the same premises, which have afforded PHILO so much scandalous deduction against religion, I cannot derive a position of a dissimilar and perfectly opposite nature. From PHILO's premise then at the beginning of the above extract I reason, as follows: A consciousness of the described infirmity throws the religionist into a state of humiliation, prostration of soul, and abasement – which penitential emotions soon terminate in their congenial habitudes to lowliness, and Christian meekness – PHILO, in the concluding sentence of p. 249. carries on his lately-fabricated religious hypocrite through the fiery regions "of the highest zeal in religion and the deepest hypocrisy" till, in the first paragraph of p. 250. the wretch is calcined into "an enthusiastic zealot whom no morality can be forcible enough to bind." That such miscreants, as are here exhibited, have existed, no candid person will deny: but mark: PHILO can reap not the least benefit from the concession, till he prove the generality of religionists to be of a similar diabolical stamp – PHILO here, as upon a former occasion, lets loose upon us the figure of "Pars pro toto": a most paltry, surely, exceptionable, and inadequate engine of persuasion.

In the second paragraph of p. 250. PHILO brings forward a most unheard of accusation against religion, complaining

"That the steady attention alone to so important an interest as that of eternal salvation, is apt to extinguish the benevolent affections, and beget a narrow, contracted selfishness."

Rather, will not the contemplation of so truly interesting an object as immortal bliss absorp, as it were, the soul; swallow up all its lower attachments; and completely disengage it from the attraction of those sublunary concerns in which selfishness and narrow-mindedness principally center?

I SHALL entirely pass over PHILO's reflections (p. 251 and 252.) upon the degree of ascendancy and influence, proper to be allowed the priesthood. A discussion of these topics would not materially affect, so far as I can judge, the subject in debate; which is the native excellence and general good tendency of religion. These attributes of religion, if proved, must eternally remain unsullied, unaltered, unimpaired; neither sympathizing with political arrangements; nor susceptible of tarnish from the misconduct of particular priests.

IT has often been urged in favour of religion, that it gives efficacy to oaths. To invalidate this plea, PHILO first (p. 253) represents several circumstances (perfectly independant of religion) as forming "the chief restraint" upon a swearer's tongue. That the circumstances, enumerated by PHILO, have a tendency to enforce truth in depositions, we allow. But has not religion a similar tendency, in an infinitely greater degree? PHILO insinuates, that she has little or none! – In farther support of his hypothesis, PHILO apprizes us (p. 253) "That custom-house oaths and political oaths are but little regarded even by some who pretend to principles of honesty and religion." From this fact PHILO wishes us, probably, to reason in the following manner: An appeal is equally made to heaven, in custom-house oaths and political oaths, as in other oaths of a more valid nature: the more valid oaths therefore do evidently not derive their validity from that appeal to heaven, which belongs, in an equal degree, to them, and to the invalid custom-house or political oath. To this suggestion let us thus reply; The contempt in which many persons hold the rights of the public,[8] in comparison with the rights of individuals, may easily lead such wrong-headed casuists to conceive, that an appeal to heaven, in regard to the former, is less noticed by the most High, than when it relates to the latter branch of rights. These motley moralists, therefore, while they lay no stress upon the inspection of omniscience in public, may possibly be greatly influenced by a sense of it in private depositions: may, in a word, partially elude, while they by no means totally abjure the belief of celestial cognizance in the transaction of swearing – Let us farther remark, that the generality of religionists would, it is to be hoped, recoil from the crime of perjury in one scene, no less than in another: at the custom-house, equally as in a court of judicature – PHILO's next surmise, (p. 253) in derogation to the utility of religion in attestations, is founded upon the validity of a Quaker's asseveration. PHILO means, no doubt, by this instance, to intimate, that veracity is attainable in depositions, without the help of religious enforcements. An examination however of the fact adduced will decisively forbid any such inference. From what, may we ask, does a Quaker's obstinate adherence to the scheme of simple asseveration proceed, but from an extreme veneration for the authority of scripture? Now the same scripture, which teaches the Quaker, through the medium of erroneous construction, never to exceed the line of simple affirmation, does more clearly and more explicitly teach him never, in his affirmation, to exceed the line of truth. A Quaker's asseveration, is therefore, we may well conclude, often purified by a recollection of scriptural precepts: its veracity, in a word, results, in no

---

[8] The interests of the community are certainly, though one scarce knows upon what ground, deemed far less sacred by the generality of mankind, than the rights of individuals. Many persons, for instance, of unquestionable honesty in private concerns, will, without shame or scruple, engage in the purchase or disposal of contraband commodities, though such practices are palpable, indisputable frauds upon the interests of the community.

small degree, from the influence of religious impression. – PHILO next endeavours to gainsay that opinion of POLYBIUS, which ascribes the infamy of Greek faith to the prevalency of the EPICUREAN philosophy.

> "But I know also (replies PHILO p. 254) that PUNIC faith had as bad a reputation in ancient times, as IRISH evidence has in modern; though we cannot account for these vulgar observations by the same reason."

But what? Because a commercial spirit of avarice, or any other cause unknown to us, has accidentally engendered habits of perjury; do irreligious tenets, on that account, cease to produce a similar effect? Avarice frequently instigates men to dishonesty, *therefore* ambition does not. An ordinary fire yields heat, *therefore* the sun affords none. – PHILO makes one struggle more (p. 254) to enervate POLYBIUS's conjecture; attempting to convince us, from a passage in EURIPIDES, "That Greek faith was infamous before the rise of the EPICUREAN philosophy." Without entering into a discussion of the passage in EURIPIDES, let us peremptorily and determinately object to touches of poetry, as competent evidence of national manners. A single well known instance of any crime, existing in a person whom a poet wishes, but is afraid directly to attack, will easily give birth to a poetical effusion of general sarcasm, no way expressive of general truth: The sole purpose of such sarcasm being to glance upon, without seeming to aim at some particular individual; and to insinuate, not avowedly point, a private imputation.

PHILO (p. 256.) vents the following murmur;

> "The terrors of religion commonly prevail above its comforts. – It is allowed, that men never have recourse to devotion, so readily as when dejected with grief, or depressed with sickness. Is not this a proof that the religious spirit is not so nearly allied to joy, as to sorrow?"

Let us apply the argumentative process of this sentiment, to another strictly similar set of ideas. – It is allowed that men never have recourse to the offices of friendship, so readily as when dejected with grief, or oppressed with sickness. Is not this a full proof that the spirit of friendship is not so nearly allied to joy, as to sorrow? – How many things, or, rather how easily may any thing be proved by the admission of such lax reasoning?

In p. 257, 258, 259. PHILO laments that the prospects of a future state, exhibited by popular religions, wear universally a dismal, inauspicious appearance. – Before we object to this representation, let us briefly remark, that the representation, though admitted, affords no pretence for the renunciation of religion. For if religion as was formerly attempted to be shown, result from a divine impulse, and produce the most extensive benefits, her authoritative practical supremacy will for ever remain unshaken, whatever be the complexion of her future remuneratory system. Though our attention, in a word, should be unwilling to follow religion, into the other world, it will still be our duty and our interest to adhere to her in this. – This being premised, let us now, upon very familiar grounds of exception, express unwillingness to hear a single syllable from PHILO, on the subject of a future state. That awful scene, like all other scenes of a mixed chequered nature, is, doubtless, viewed in different lights by different imaginations: chearfulness, supposing criminality out of the question, fixes on the bright, despondency on the cloudy part of the horizon. To the gaiety of PHILO's temper his picture of human life, examined at the opening of this performance, bears ample testimony. A passage too (in Mr. HUME's dissertation on the natural history of religion) may serve to throw farther light upon the complexion of PHILO's posthumous meditations. Mr. HUME (in the passage alluded to, Sect. 15. p. 115.) remarks, "that the most open impiety is attended with a secret dread and compunction." PHILO upon the whole, does not seem a person, to whom any cool dispassionate man, ought to apply for a description of futurity.

PHILO concludes his elaborate declamation against religion, with informing us (p. 259.)

"That though this opinion (about future happiness and misery) be seldom so steady in its operation, as to influence all the actions; yet it is apt to make a considerable breach in the temper, and to produce that gloom and melancholy, so remarkable in all devout people."

PHILO seems in this passage, to forget a former piece of information of his, (at p. 246.)

> "That religious motives where they act at all, operate only by starts and bounds; and it is scarcely possible for them to become altogether habitual to the mind."

Religious motives, we see (at p. 246.) work only temporary effects: while (at p. 249.) they produce lasting operations. Religious motives indeed, seem in PHILO's hands to be susceptible, like Milton's angels, of occasional contraction and dilatation, just as circumstances require. When we talk of their salutary influence, "They act only (PHILO tells us) by starts and bounds." On a sudden however as soon as PHILO himself handles the pensive tendency of these narrowly-operating principles, they swell on the imagination; acquire formidable magnitude; and "make a considerable breach in the temper." – Without availing ourselves of PHILO's inconsistency, without endeavouring to render the philosopher an evidence against himself, let us dispassionately enquire into the reality of that gloom and melancholy, ascribed by PHILO to all devout people. – A short appeal on this topic may first, with propriety, be made to the actual experience of man-kind. Are religion and chearfulness, in general incompatible? let every man's personal observation answer the question. – Let us next remark, that (when the gloom of a religionist arises, as in innumerable instances it certainly does, from natural temper) the religionist, though gloomy with, would indisputably have been so without religion. The unfortunate man carries that within him, which spreads an unvarying shade round his steps: and which, if not exerted upon religious truth, would undoubtedly fasten on and discolour some other object. – Let us in the last place, ask PHILO this simple, but material question: whatever be the nature of the religionist's sorrow, does PHILO tender him a cure? Has sceptical philosophy any balm to comfort the devout heart; any medicine to refresh the religiously-afflicted spirit? let us, in imagination, consign the religionist to PHILO's direction, and watch the result. – PHILO, it will here be proper to recollect, launches (at p. 244.) into the following exclamation,

> "consider, I beseech you, the attachment which we have to present things, and the little concern we discover for objects so remote and uncertain, viz. eternal rewards and punishments."

Apply this doctrine to the case of PHILO's patient.   The unhappy man was melancholy from the contemplation of objects *remote and uncertain*; turned over to PHILO he instantly hears[9] such a horrid representation of things *present*, as will harrow up his soul, and hurry him into the excesses of phrensy and desperation.   He was anxious while directed by devotion: touched by the wand of infidelity he feels his anxiety redouble, his horrors infinitely accumulate.   Under the influence of religion he moped: under the guidance of PHILO he will perhaps destroy himself.

Pol me occidistis, amici,
Non fervastis. Hor.

The picture, or rather caricature, of religion, exhibited by PHILO in the dialogues, may perhaps not unhappily be contrasted with a short etching of irreligion, which appears in Mr. HUME's dissertation on the natural history of religion. Sect. 16. p. 116.

"Look out (cries the great philosopher) for a people entirely devoid of religion: If you find them at all, be assured, that they are but few degrees removed from brutes."

To what worse state, great and good God, can the strictest profession of thy holy religion reduce us!

---

[9] See PHILO's lamentations over the miseries of life, discussed at the beginning of this performance.

LETTER IX. AN EXAMINATION OF MR. HUME'S DIALOGUES ON NATURAL RELIGION
Joseph Priestley

Dear Sir,

I AM glad to find that you think there is at least some appearance of weight in what, at your request, I have urged, in answer to the objections against the belief of a God and a providence; and I am confident the more attention you give to the subject, the stronger will those arguments appear, and the more trifling and undeserving of regard you will think the cavils of atheists, ancient or modern. You wish, however, to know distinctly what I think of *Mr. Hume's posthumous Dialogues on Natural Religion*; because, coming from a writer of some note, that work is frequently a topic of conversation in the societies you frequent.

With respect to *Mr. Hume's metaphysical writings* in general, my opinion is, that, on the whole, the world is very little the wiser for them. For though, when the merits of any question were on his side, few men ever wrote with more perspicuity, the arrangement of his thoughts being natural, and his illustrations peculiarly happy; yet I can hardly think that we are indebted to him for the least real advance in the knowledge of the human mind. Indeed, according to his own very frank confession, his object was mere *literary reputation*[1]. It was not the *pursuit of truth*, or the advancement of virtue and happiness; and it was much more easy to make a figure by disturbing the systems of others than by erecting any of his own. All schemes have their respective weak sides which a man who has nothing of his own to risk may more easily find, and expose.

In many of his *Essays* (which, in general, are excessively wire-drawn) Mr. Hume seems to have had nothing in view

---

[1] See his Life, written by himself, p. 32, 33.

but to *amuse* his readers, which he generally does agreeably enough; proposing doubts to received hypotheses, leaving them without any solution, and altogether unconcerned about it. In short, he is to be considered in these *Essays* as a mere *writer* or *declaimer*, even more than Cicero in his book of Tusculan Questions.

He seems not to have given himself the trouble so much as to read *Dr. Hartley's Observations on Man*, a work which he could not but have heard of, and which it certainly behoved him to study. The doctrine of *association of ideas*, as explained and extended by Dr. Hartley, supplies materials for the most satisfactory solution, of almost all the difficulties he has started [*sic*], as I could easily shew if I thought it of any consequence; so that to a person acquainted with this theory of the human mind, *Hume's Essays* appear the merest trifling. Compared with Dr. Hartley, I consider Mr. Hume as not even a child.

Now, I will frankly tell you, that this last performance of Mr. Hume has by no means changed for the better the idea I had before formed of him as a metaphysical writer. The dialogue is ingeniously and artfully conducted. Philo, who evidently speaks the sentiments of the writer, is not made to say all the good things that are advanced, his opponents are not made to say any thing that is very palpably absurd, and every thing is made to pass with great decency and decorum.

But though Philo, in the most interesting part of the debate, advances nothing but common-place objections against the belief of a God, and hackneyed declamation against the plan of providence, his antagonists are seldom represented as making any satisfactory reply. And when, at the last, evidently to save appearances, he relinquishes the argument, on which he had expatiated with so much triumph, it is without alledging any sufficient reason; so that his arguments are left, as no doubt the writer intended, to have their full effect on the mind of the reader. And though the debate seemingly closes in favour of the theist, the victory is clearly on the side of the atheist. I therefore shall not be surprised if this work should have a considerable effect in promoting the cause of atheism, with those whose *general turn of thinking*, and *habits of life*, make them no ill-wishers to that scheme.

To satisfy your wishes, I shall recite what I think has most of the appearance of strength, or plausibility, in what Mr.

Hume has advanced on the atheistical side of the question, though it will necessarily lead me to repeat some things that I have observed already; but I shall endeavour to do it in such a manner, that you will not deem it quite idle and useless repetition.

With respect to the general argument for the being of God, from the marks of design in the universe, he says, p. 65,

> "Will any man tell me, with a serious countenance, that an orderly universe must arise from some thought and art, like the human, because we have experience of it. To ascertain this reasoning, it were requisite that we had experience of the origin of worlds, and it is not sufficient, surely, that we have seen ships and cities arise from human art and contrivance."

Now, if it be admitted that there are marks of design in the universe, as numberless fitnesses of things to things prove beyond all dispute, is it not a necessary consequence, that if it had a cause at all, it must be one that is capable of design? Will any person say that an eye could have been constructed by a being who had no knowledge of optics, who did not know the nature of light, or the laws of refraction? And must not the universe have had a cause, as well as any thing else, that is finite and incapable of comprehending itself?

We might just as reasonably say, that any particular ship, or city, any particular horse, or man, had nothing existing superior to it, as that the visible universe had nothing superior to it, if the universe be no more capable of comprehending itself than a ship, or a city, a horse, or a man. There can be no charm in the words *world* or *universe*, so that they should require no cause when they stand in precisely the same predicament with other things that evidently *do* require a superior cause, and could not have existed without one.

All that Mr. Hume says on the difficulty of stopping at the idea of an uncaused being, is on the supposition that this uncaused being is a *finite one*, incapable of comprehending itself, and, therefore, in the same predicament with a ship or a house, a horse or a man, which it is impossible to conceive to have existed without a superior cause. "How shall we satisfy ourselves," says he, p. 93, &c.

> "concerning the cause of that being whom you suppose the

author of nature. – If we stop and go no farther, why go so far, why not stop at the material world. How can we satisfy ourselves without going on in infinitum. – By supposing it to contain the principle of order within itself, we really assert it to be God, and the sooner we arrive at that Divine Being, so much the better. When you go one step beyond the mundane system, you only excite an inquisitive humour, which it is impossible ever to satisfy."

It is very true, that no person can satisfy himself with going backwards *in infinitum* from one thing that requires a superior cause, to another that equally requires a superior cause. But any person may be sufficiently satisfied with going back through finite causes as far as he has evidence of the existence of intermediate finite causes; and then, seeing that it is absurd to go on *in infinitum* in this manner, to conclude that, whether he can comprehend it or not, there *must* be some *uncaused intelligent being*, the original and designing cause of all other beings. For otherwise, what we *see* and *experience* could not have existed. It is true that we cannot conceive *how* this should be, but we are able to acquiesce in this ignorance, because there is no *contradiction* in it.

He says, p. 15,

"Motion, in many instances from gravity, from elasticity, from electricity, begins in matter without any known voluntary agent; and to suppose always in these cases an unknown voluntary agent, is mere hypothesis, and hypothesis attended with no advantage."

He also says, p. 118, "Why may not motion have been propagated by impulse through all eternity?"

I will admit that the powers of gravity, elasticity, and electricity, might have been in bodies from all eternity, without any superior cause, if the bodies in which we find them were capable of knowing that they had such powers, of that *design* which has proportioned them to one another, and of combining them in the wonderful and useful manner in which they are actually proportioned and combined in nature. But when I see that they are as evidently incapable of this as I am of properly producing a plant or an animal, I am under a necessity of looking for a higher cause; and I cannot rest till I come to a being *essentially different* from all visible beings whatever, so as not to be in the predicament that they are in, of requiring a superior cause. Also, if motion could have been in the universe without any cause, it must have been in consequence of bodies being possessed of the power of *gravity*, &c. from eternity, without a cause. But as they could not have had those powers without communication from a superior and intelligent being, capable of proportioning them, in the exact and useful manner in which they are possessed, the thing is manifestly *impossible*.

What Mr. Hume says with respect to the *origin of the world* in the following paragraph, which I think unworthy of a philosopher, and miserably trifling on so serious a subject, goes intirely upon the idea of the supreme cause resembling such beings as do themselves require a superior cause, and not (which, however, *must* be the case) a being that can have no superior in wisdom or power. I, therefore, think it requires no particular animadversion.

"Many worlds," he says, p. 106, "might have been botched and bungled throughout an eternity ere this system was struck out, much labour lost, many fruitless trials made, and a slow, but continued improvement, carried on during infinite ages in the art of world making."

"A man who follows your hypothesis," p. 111, "is able perhaps to assert, or conjecture, that the universe some time arose from something like design; but beyond that position he cannot ascertain one single circumstance, and is left afterwards to fix every point of his theology by the utmost licence of fancy and hypothesis. This world, for ought we know, is very faulty and imperfect, compared to a superior standard, and was only the first rude essay of some infant deity, who afterwards abandoned it, ashamed of his own performance. It is the work only of some dependent inferior deity, and is the object of derision to his superiors. It is the production of old age and dotage, in some superannuated deity, and ever since his death has run on at adventures, from the first impulse and active force, which it received from him."

In reading *Mr. Hume's life*, written by himself, one might be surprised to find no mention of a *God*, or of a *providence*, which conducted him through it; but this cannot be any longer wonderful, when we find that, for any thing he certainly believed to the contrary, he himself might be the most considerable being in the universe. His maker, if he had any, was either a careless playful infant, a trifling forgetful dotard, or was, perhaps, dead and buried, without leaving any other to take care of his affairs. All that he believed of his maker was, that he was capable of *something like design*, but of his own comprehensive intellectual powers he could have no doubt.

Neither can we think it at all extraordinary that Mr. Hume should have recourse to *amusing books* in the last period of his life, when he considered the author of nature himself as never having had any serious object in view, and when he neither left any thing behind him, nor had any thing before him, that was deserving of his care. How can it be supposed that the man, who scrupled not to ridicule his maker, should consider the human race, or the world, in any other light than as objects of ridicule, or pity. And well satisfied might he be to have been so fortunate in his passage through the world, and his easy escape out of it, when it was deserted by its maker, and was continually exposed to some unforeseen and dreadful catastrophe. How poor a consolation, however, must have been his *literary fame*, with such gloomy prospects as these!

What Mr. Hume says with respect to the deficiency in the proof of the *proper infinity* of the divine attributes, and of a probable *multiplicity of deities*, all goes on the same idea, viz. that the ultimate cause of the universe is such a being as must himself require a superior cause; whereas, nothing can be more evident, how incomprehensible soever it may be, than that the being which has existed from eternity, and is the cause of all that does exist, must be one that *cannot* have a superior, and, therefore, must be infinite in knowledge and power, and consequently, as I have endeavoured to shew before, can be but *one*.

"As the cause," he says, p. 104, "ought only to be proportioned to the effect, and the effect, so far as it falls under our cognizance, is not infinite, what pretensions have we to ascribe that attribute to the Divine Being? – By sharing the work among several we may so much farther limit the attributes of each, and get rid of that extensive power and knowledge which must be supposed in one deity."

– This I think unworthy of a philosopher on so grave and interesting a subject.

It is owing to the same inattention to this one consideration, that, in order to get rid of the idea of a supreme intelligent cause of all things, Mr. Hume urges the superior probability of the universe resembling a *plant*, or an *animal*.

"If the universe," says he, p. 129, "bears a greater likeness to animal bodies, and to vegetables, than to the works of human art, it is more probable that its cause resembles the cause of the former than that of the latter; and its origin ought rather to be ascribed to generation, or vegetation, than to reason or design."

On this, Demea, the orthodox speaker, very properly observes, p. 137,

"Whence could arise so wonderful a faculty but from design, or how can order spring from any thing which perceives not that order which it bestows."

In reply to which Philo contents himself with saying, ib.

"A tree bestows order, and organization, on that tree which springs from it, without knowing the order; an animal, in the same manner, on its offspring," and p. 140, "Judging by our limited and imperfect experience, generation has some privileges above reason; for we see every day the latter to arise from the former, never the former from the latter."

Manifestly unsatisfactory as this reply is, nothing is advanced in answer to it by either of the other disputants. But it is obvious to remark, that, if an animal has marks of design in its construction, a design which itself cannot comprehend, it is hardly possible for any person to imagine that it was originally produced without a power superior to itself, and capable of comprehending its structure, though he was not himself present at the original formation of it, and, therefore, could not see it. Can we possibly believe that any particular *horse* that we know, originated without a superior cause?

Equally impossible is it to believe, that the *species of horses* should have existed without a superior cause.

How little then does it avail Mr. Hume to say, p. 135, that "reason, instinct, generation, vegetation, are similar to each other, and the causes of similar effects;" as if *instinct, generation*, and *vegetation*, did not necessarily imply *design*, or reason, as the cause of them. He might with equal reason have placed other powers in nature, as *gravity, elasticity*, &c. in the same rank with these; whereas all these must equally have proceeded from reason, or design, and could not have had any existence independent of it. For design is conspicuous in all those powers, and especially in the proportion and distribution of them.

Pursuing the analogy of plants and animals, he says, p. 152,

"In like manner as a tree sheds its seeds into the neighbouring fields, and produces other trees; so the great vegetable the world, or this planetary system, produces within itself certain seeds, which being scattered into the surrounding chaos, vegetate into new worlds. A comet, for instance, is the seed of a world, and after it has been fully ripened by passing from sun to sun, and star to star, it is at last tossed into the unformed elements, which every where surround this universe, and immediately sprouts up into a new system."

"Or, if we should suppose this world to be an *animal*, a comet is the *egg* of this animal; and in like manner as an ostrich lays its egg in the sand, which, without any farther care, hatches the egg, and produces a new animal; so – Does not a plant or an animal," p. 134, "which springs from vegetation or generation, bear a stronger resemblance to the world, than does any artificial machine, which arises from reason and design?"

Had any friend of religion advanced an idea so completely absurd as this, what would not Mr. Hume have said to turn it into ridicule. With just as much probability might he have said that Glasgow grew from a seed yielded by Edinburgh, or that London and Edinburgh, marrying, by natural generation, produced York, which lies between them. With much more probability might he have said that *pamphlets* are the productions of large *books*, that *boats* are young *ships*, and that *pistols* will grow into great *guns*; and that either there never were any first towns, books, ships, or guns, or that, if there were, they had no makers.

How it could come into any man's head to imagine that a thing so complex as this world, consisting of land and water, earths and metals, plants and animals, &c. &c. &c. should produce a seed, or egg, containing within it the elements of all its innumerable parts, is beyond my power of conception.

What must have been that man's knowledge of philosophy and nature, who could suppose for a moment, that a comet could possibly be the seed of a world? Do comets spring from worlds, carrying with them the seeds of all the plants, &c. that they contain? Do comets travel from sun to sun, or from star to star? By what force are they tossed into the *unformed elements*, which Mr. Hume supposes every where to surround the universe? What are those elements? and what evidence has he of their existence? or, supposing the comet to arrive among them, whence could arise its power of vegetating into a new system?

What Mr. Hume objects to the arguments for the *benevolence* of the deity is such mere cavilling, and admits of such easy answers, that I am surprised that a man whose sole object was even *literary reputation* should have advanced it.

"The cause of nature," p. 186, "tends not to human or animal felicity, therefore it is not established for that purpose." He might as well have said that *health* is not agreeable to the [cause] of nature, as that enjoyment and *happiness* are not, since the one is the necessary consequence of the other.

> "It is contrary," he says, in fact, p. 193, "to every one's feeling and experience to maintain a continued existence in this world to be eligible and desirable. It is contrary to an authority so established as nothing can subvert."

And yet almost all animals and all men *do* desire life, and, according to his own account, his own life was a singularly happy and enviable one.

> "You must prove," p. 195, "these pure unmixed and uncontrollable attributes from the present mixed and confused phenomena, and from these alone: a hopeful undertaking."

If *evil* was not, in a thousand ways, necessarily connected with, and subservient to *good*, the undertaking would be hopeless, but not otherwise.

"It seems plainly possible," p. 205, "to carry on the business of life without any pain. Why then is any animal ever rendered susceptible of such a sensation?"

But pain, *as such*, we have seen to be excellently useful, as a guard against more pain, and greater evils; and no man can pretend to say that the same end *could* have been attained by any other means.

"The conduct of the world by general laws," p. 206, "seems no wise necessary to a very perfect being." But without general laws there could have been little or no room for *wisdom*, in God or man; and what kind of happiness could we have had without the exercise of our rational powers. To have had any *intellectual enjoyments* in those circumstances (and the sensual are of little value in comparison with them) we must have been quite other kind of beings than we are at present, probably much inferior to what we are now.

"Almost all the moral as well as natural evils of human life," p. 213, "arise from *idleness*; and were our species, by the original constitution of their frame, exempt from this vice, or infirmity, the perfect cultivation of the land, the improvements of arts and manufactures, the exact execution of every office and duty, immediately follows, and men at once may fully reach that state of society which is so imperfectly attained by the best regulated government. But as industry is a power, and the most valuable of any, nature seems determined, suitable to her usual maxims, to bestow it on men with a very sparing hand."

And yet this writer can say, p. 259, that "no state of mind is so happy as the calm and equable." But would not more industry, and *activity*, necessarily disturb this calm and happy temperament, and be apt to produce quarrels, and, consequently, more unhappiness?

"I am sceptic enough," he says, p. 219, "to allow that the bad appearances, notwithstanding all my reasonings, may be compatible with such attributes as you suppose; but surely they can never prove such attributes."

But if present appearances prove *real benevolence*, I think they will go very near to prove *unbounded* benevolence, for reasons that I have alledged before, and which I shall not repeat here.

It is pretty clear to me, that Mr. Hume was not sufficiently acquainted with what has been already advanced by those who have written on the subject of the being and attributes of God. Otherwise he either would not have put such weak arguments into the mouth of his favourite Philo, or would have put better answers into those of his opponents. It was, I imagine, his dislike of the subject that made him overlook such writers, or give but little attention to them; and I think this conjecture concerning his aversion to the subject the better founded, from his saying, p. 259, that "there is a gloom and melancholy remarkable in all devout people."

No person really acquainted with true devotion, or those who were possessed with it, could have entertained such an opinion. What Mr. Hume had seen must have been some miserably low superstition, or wild enthusiasm, things very remote from the calm and sedate, but chearful spirit of rational devotion.

Had he considered the nature of true devotion, he must have been sensible that the charge of gloom and melancholy can least of all apply to it. Gloom and melancholy certainly belong to the system of atheism, which intirely precludes the pleasing ideas of a benevolent author of nature, and of a wise plan of providence, bringing good out of all the evil we experience; which cuts off the consoling intercourse with an invisible, but omnipresent and almighty protector and friend; which admits of no settled provision for our happiness, even in this life, and closes the melancholy scene, such as Mr. Hume himself describes it, with a total annihilation.

Is it possible to draw a more gloomy and dispiriting picture of the system of the universe than Mr. Hume himself has drawn, in his tenth dialogue? No melancholy religionist ever drew so dark a one. Nothing in the whole system pleases him. He finds neither *wisdom*, nor *benevolence*. Speaking on the supposition of God being omnipotent and omnificient, he says, p. 185,

"His power we allow infinite; whatever he wills is executed; but neither man nor any other animal is happy; therefore he does not will their happiness. His wisdom is infinite; he is never mistaken in choosing the means to any end; but the course of nature tends not to human or animal felicity; therefore it is not established for that purpose."

"Look round the universe," says he, p. 219, "what an immense profusion of beings, animated and organized, sensible and active. You admire this prodigious variety and fecundity. But inspect a little more narrowly these living existences, the only beings worth regarding. How hostile and destructive to each other. How insufficient all of them for their own happiness. How contemptible, or odious, to the spectator. The whole presents nothing but the idea of a blind nature, impregnated by a great vivifying principle, and pouring forth from her lap, without discernment, or parental care, her maimed and abortive children."

Compare this with the language of the pious writers of the scriptures.

"Thou art good and doest good. The Lord is good to all, and his tender mercies are over all his works. The earth is full of the goodness of the Lord. The eyes of all wait upon thee, and thou givest them their meat in due season. Thou openest thine hand, and satisfiest the desires of every living thing. The Lord reigneth: let the earth rejoice, let the inhabitants of the isles be glad thereof. Clouds and darkness are round about him, righteousness and judgment are the habitation of his throne."

In the scriptures the Divine Being is represented as "encouraging us to cast all our care upon him who careth for us." The true christian is exhorted to *rejoice evermore*, and especially to *rejoice in tribulation*, and persecution for righteousness sake. Death is so far from being a frightful and disgusting thing, that he triumphs in it, and over it. *O death, where is thy sting? O grave, where is thy victory?*

Would any person hesitate about chusing to *feel* as these writers felt, or as Mr. Hume must have done. With his views of things, the calmness and composure with which, he says, he faced death, though infinitely short of the *joyful expectation* of the christian, could not have been any thing but affectation. If, however, with his prospects he really was as calm, placid, and chearful, as he pretends, with little reason can he charge any set of *speculative principles* with a tendency to produce gloom and melancholy. If *his* system did not produce this disposition, it never can be in the power of *system* to do it.

Notwithstanding I have differed so much from Mr. Hume with respect to the principles of his treatise, we shall, in words, at least, agree in our conclusion. For though I think the being of a God, and his general benevolence and providence, to be sufficiently demonstrable, yet so many cavils may be started on the subject, and so much still remains, that a rational creature must wish to be informed of concerning his maker, his duty here, and his expectations hereafter, that what Mr. Hume said by way of cover and irony, I can say with great seriousness, and I do not wish to say it much otherwise, or better.

"The most natural sentiment," he says, p. 363, "which a well-disposed mind will feel on this occasion, is a longing desire and expectation, that heaven would be pleased to dissipate, at least alleviate, this profound ignorance, by affording some more particular revelation to mankind, and making discoveries of the nature, attributes, and operation of the divine object of our faith. A person seasoned with a just sense of the imperfection of natural reason will fly to *revealed truth* with the greatest avidity. To be a philosophical sceptic is, in a man of letters, the first and most essential step towards being a sound believing christian."

I am, &c.

REMARKS ON MR. HUME'S DIALOGUES CONCERNING NATURAL RELIGION BY T. HAYTER
Anonymous

Source: The Monthly Review, vol. 64, 1781

These Remarks are such as must naturally and obviously occur to those readers who are conversant with moral and theological subjects, and acquainted with Mr. Hume's writings. They chiefly relate to the moral attributes of the Deity, and the influence of religious principles upon human conduct. The Author writes in a lively and animated manner; and his style, after a little more practice and attention to the rules of composition, will, we doubt not, become more chaste, correct, and uniformly elegant.

DAVID HUME
John Hunt

Source: The Contemporary Review, vol. 11, 1869

MRS. MALLET, the wife of David Mallet, "the beggarly Scotchman" on whose head Samuel Johnson poured out the concentrated essence of his hatred of Scotland, once said to Hume, "Allow me, Mr. Hume, to introduce myself to you. It is right that we Deists should know each other." "*Madam,*" replied Hume, "*I am not a Deist, and do not wish to be known under that name.*" If Hume had been asked what he was, and by what name he wished to be known, he would probably have declined to answer. If he had been willing to answer, he would probably have found it difficult. No mind would have rebelled more than his against being classed and labelled.

Hume's first publication was the "Treatise of Human Nature." As this work was afterwards disowned by its author, we need not do more than mention it. Its place was supplied by the "Essays," in which the chief questions were treated with more accuracy and clearness, while many of the more intricate and ingenious but less important reasonings were omitted.

We shall best begin by viewing Hume in his relation to Locke. He was avowedly an experimentalist, holding the senses to be the only channels of knowledge. Through them the mind has what Hume calls *impressions*. The *memory* of these impressions constitutes ideas. Upon these the mind works. It arranges them, transposes them, and reasons upon them. There is here an unusual meaning attached to the word *ideas*, but that meaning is definite, and the peculiarity itself clearly marks Hume as on the side of the sensuous philosophy. He cannot find in the mind any innate ideas or any infinite ideas, such as those of infinite time or infinite space.

The title generally applied to Hume is that of Sceptic, and this both in philosophy and religion. He follows experience till he finds there is something beyond experience. Then he either acknowledges that we must fall back upon natural instincts, and trust to reason, such as it is, or he gives way to despair, and with an easy indifference flings the problem aside as insoluble, bidding us be content with our ignorance, for all is an enigma, a riddle, and a mystery. These two states of mind are clearly distinguishable in Hume. They are both called Scepticism, yet they are so different that the one leads to inquiry, the other to indolence.[1] The one was a quality of his own keen intellect, the other was learned in France. It is only the first which we care to notice further.

Locke imagined that he found in experience the grand remedy for the reveries of schoolmen and metaphysicians. It was a method which suited the practical character of the English mind. Hume, who was not disposed to be a meta-physician, but a man of the world, accepted it readily; but being by nature a metaphysician, he could not escape a pre-vious question, What is the foundation of all conclusions from experience? nor a subsequent inquiry as to how we were to solve questions not soluble by experience. Every subject in philosophy which he touches plays round this word. The first inquiry always is, How far do we know it by Locke's method? This knowledge in Hume's searching analysis invariably turns out to be small. It was objected to Locke by Stillingfleet that he discarded substance out of the world. Bishop Berkeley, for an object in no way sceptical, showed the impossibility of our ever being able to demon-strate the existence of a material world. Hume accepted Berkeley's arguments and Berkeley's conclusions. We are conscious of mind. There is an intellect which perceives, – but what does it perceive? Impressions and ideas that belong to it? or impressions and ideas that belong to an external world? Without the mind to perceive, where would be that

---

[1] This has been well expressed by Professor Maurice in his admirable remarks on Hume. "It is not when he is pushing his investigations as far as they will go that we ever complain of him; *then* he is doing a service to truth and to mankind. It is when, as often happens in this treatise, he declines investigation, laughs at the effort to make it as useless and ridicu-lous, flings himself into his arm-chair, becomes as indolently and con-temptuously acquiescent as any priest ever wished his disciples to be; it is then that he exhibits the state of mind to which we are all tempted; and against which, whatever others do, the believer in a God of truth must wrestle to the death." – *Modern Philosophy.*

which we suppose to be perceived? The mind is conscious only of its own impressions and ideas, but it has no certainty of any existence beyond that of which it is conscious. So far Hume went with Berkeley. But experience not only fails to guide us to an external world, it does not even prove to us the existence of mind. When we say we are conscious of mind we assume as much as when we say we are conscious of matter. Our consciousness extends only to impressions and ideas, so that the existence of a mind perceiving is as much beyond demonstration as the existence of an external world perceived. Here is the first of the shortcomings of experience. The existence of matter and mind is demitted to the limbo of scepticism.

The common-sense philosophers have always reckoned themselves certain of matter and motion – that motion could not exist without a mover, nor any effect without a cause. But how did they come by this knowledge? Hume showed that it can never be reached by experience. We cannot discover that force or energy which produces an effect. We can never see what that is which makes an effect the infallible consequence of a cause. All we know is that one follows the other. The impulse of one billiard ball is attended with motion in the second. This is all that is manifest to the *outward* senses. From the first appearance of any object we never know what effect will result from it. By experience we know that certain effects follow certain causes – that heat, for instance, is the constant attendant on flame. But prior to experience we do not know that flame contains that force which we call heat. The idea is evidently not derived from the contemplation of bodies. Some philosophers say it is an inward impression, or an idea derived from reflection on the operation of our minds, or a conclusion reached by our reasonings guided by experience. These are suppositions. All that we can say is simply that such a thing follows another because we have seen before a similar conjunction. What the connection is we do not know. The first time a man saw the communication of motion by impulse or by the shock of two billiard balls, he could not pronounce that the one event was connected with the other, but only that they were conjoined. It is not till after he has felt these events to be connected, by having observed several instances of the same nature, that he can foretell the existence of the one from the appearance of the other.

When Hume writes of morals, experience is still playing its part. For a time it is a guide, then it fails, and Hume, after stumbling on other philosophies not experimental, falls finally into doubt and uncertainty. He proves by observations drawn from experience that virtue is the interest of man. He proves also, though this is not his object, that the distinctions of right and wrong exist anterior to all experience. For those who deny the reality of these distinctions he has no other name but "disingenuous disputants." Their reality must be admitted. The only questions are those which concern their extent and their foundation. The pleasure of a virtuous deed may be the motive which leads to it. This motive Hume founded on what he calls a *sentiment*. This is, in opposition to the philosophers who find the motives of virtue in reason. This *sentiment* he calls an internal sense, or fine feeling. It is, in fact, the "moral sense" of Lord Shaftesbury – an intuition of the mind not in any way derived from the impressions of the external world or from experience of human life. To separate this from reason could only be done by giving reason a limited meaning – a meaning which it may have had in Locke's philosophy, but to which it was never limited in any other philosophy. With Hume, reason means merely reasoning. It does not include what the Germans understand by *Vernunft*, nor what Plato and the ancient philosophers meant by that reason in which the world is constituted. Hume accordingly finds that these ancient philosophers, and such as Shaftesbury among the moderns, were confused between *reason* and *sentiment*. The former, he says, often affirmed that virtue is nothing but conformity to reason, and yet they considered morals as deriving their existence from taste or sentiment. The moderns talk much about the beauty of virtue and the deformity of vice, yet they commonly account for this distinction by metaphysical reasonings, and by deductions from the most abstract principles of the understanding. Having in this way placed "sentiment" in opposition to "reason," Hume admits that there are many specious arguments for both sides, and concludes with something of the confusion of which he complains in others. "In many orders of beauty," he says, "particularly those of the fine arts, it is requisite to employ much reasoning in order to feel the

proper sentiment, and a false relish may be frequently corrected by argument and reflection. There are just grounds to
conclude that moral beauty partakes much of the latter species, and demands the assistance of our intellectual faculties
in order to give it a suitable influence on the human mind."
After saying this he announces that he will confine himself
to the experimental method; fact and observation being the
only ground for a system of ethics. From this ground he
comes to a conclusion partly sceptical; regarding virtue as
unquestionably the interest of man, yet adding an exception
perhaps in the case of justice. "*That honesty is the best policy*
may be a good general rule, but it is liable to many exceptions,
and he, it may perhaps be thought, conducts himself with
most wisdom who observes the general rule and takes advantage of all the exceptions." In the treatise on "Human Nature"
the question was discussed, if moral distinctions are to be
found in nature. The answer is, that if by natural we are to
understand the opposite of miraculous, they are in nature,
and also if by natural is to be understood the opposite of
unusual; but in the sense of natural as opposed to artificial,
some virtues are said to be natural and others artificial.

Experience always landed Hume in scepticism, but in his
really philosophical moods he was never willing to stay there.
He believed in an external world as much as the most
ordinary individual who puts his foot on this firm earth. He
no more doubted the existence of his mind than he doubted
of his doubts. Nature provides a remedy for scepticism.
Hume could not discover the connection between cause and
effect, but he never denied its existence nor the validity of
our reasonings concerning it. "Allow me to tell you," he says
in one place, "that I never asserted so absurd a proposition
as that anything might arise without a cause. I only maintained that our certainty of the falsehood of that proposition
proceeded neither from intuition nor from demonstration,
but from another source . . . . There are many different kinds
of certainty, but some are satisfactory to the mind, though
perhaps not so regular as the demonstrative kind."

Hume refused the name of Deist, but it is probable that he
would not have refused to be called by the Greek equivalent,
Theist. There is a story that once dining with a large company
at the Baron D'Holbach's, the discourse turning on natural
religion, Hume said that as for Atheists he did not believe

there ever was one. "You have been a little unfortunate," said the baron; "you are now at table with seventeen for the first time." It is not generally admitted that Hume was a Theist. He came with his experience to find out if it could lead him to a demonstration of the being of God. As in other cases, it came short. He had never seen God, he was not with Him before the mountains were brought forth. He saw effects in the world, but no agent producing them. He saw workmanship, but no hand at work. His experience did not reach a handbreadth into the deep that is infinite. Hume, however, brings forward his objections avowedly as "sceptical paradoxes" with a distinct affirmation that he does not approve of them. In the essay, "Of a Providence and Future State," a philospher of the sect of the Epicureans is supposed to address the common people of Athens. He urges them to abide by the ancient religious traditions of their forefathers, and not to attempt to establish religion upon reason. The religious philosophers indulged a rash curiosity. They excite doubts which they never satisfy – they paint in the most magnificent colours the order, beauty, and wise arrangement of the universe, and then ask if such a glorious display of intelligence could proceed from the fortuitous concourse of atoms, or if chance could produce what the greatest genius can never sufficiently admire. This is an argument from effects to causes. It is inferred from the order of the work that there must have been design and forethought in the worker. The Epicurean philosopher answers that he allows the argument to be solid so far as it goes, but its advocates must not pretend to establish the conclusion in a greater latitude than the phenomena of nature will justify. When we infer any particular cause from an effect, we must proportion the one to the other, and can never be allowed to ascribe to the cause any qualities but what are exactly sufficient to produce the effect. We cannot return back upon the cause and infer other effects from it besides those by which it is known to us. No one merely from the sight of Zeuxis' pictures could know that he was also a statuary or architect. We may fairly conclude the workman to be possessed of the talents and taste displayed in his works, but we have no right to infer that he has any talents beyond what he manifests. Supposing the Deity to be the Author of the existence and order of the universe, we can ascribe to Him that precise degree of power, intelligence, and benevolence which appear in His workmanship, but nothing more. The supposition of further attributes is mere hypothesis, and so too is the supposition that in distant regions of space or periods of time there will be a more magnificent display of these attributes. We can never be allowed to mount up from the effect to the cause, and then descend downwards to infer any new effect from that cause. It is objected that as we reason from a half-finished building that it is a work of design and contrivance, and justly return to the cause to infer that the building will soon be finished, so may we infer the completion of what is wanting to the perfection of this world. If we find on the seashore the print of a human foot, we conclude that a man had passed that way, though the sand may have effaced the print of the other foot. Why then may we not reason that the Author of nature is capable of producing something greater than nature at present manifests? The answer is, human art and divine are not the same; man is a being whom we know by experience, and from our knowledge of him and his works we can draw a hundred inferences of what may be expected from him. The print of *a* foot in the sand can only prove that there was some figure adapted to it by which it was produced, but the print of a *human* foot proves likewise from our other experience that there was probably another foot which also left its impression.

> "The case is not the same with our reasonings from the works of nature. The Deity is known to us only by His productions, and is a single Being in the universe, not comprehended under any species or genus, from whose experienced attributes or qualities we can by analogy infer other attributes or qualities in Him. As the universe shows wisdom and goodness we infer wisdom and goodness. As it shows a particular degree of these perfections we infer a particular degree of them precisely adapted to the effect which we examine."

The source of our mistake is said by the Epicurean philosopher to be that we tacitly consider ourselves as in the place of the Supreme Being, and conclude that –

> "He will act on every occasion according to our ideas of what is reasonable. But the ordinary course of nature might

convince us of the contrary. It is regulated by principles and maxims very different from ours. We cannot reason from ourselves to a Being so remote and incomprehensible, who bears much less analogy to any other being in the universe than the sun to a waxen taper."

Bolingbroke had already reasoned in this way with reference to the divine attributes of power and justice, but by a singular inconsistency he did not hold his reasoning applicable to the attributes of wisdom and goodness. Hume proposes to introduce these objections as "sceptical paradoxes," nothing more than curious; but in a note to the essay, where he speaks in his own person, he says it may be established as a maxim that, when any cause is known only by its particular effects, it must be impossible to infer any new effects from that "cause."

It is still, however, not evident how far Hume agreed with the philosophy of his Epicurean philosopher. The subject was resumed in a tract, which was published after his death. This was called "Dialogues on Natural Religion." The principal disputants are Philo and Cleanthes. The one is a Sceptic, the other a Theist. The author of Hume's Life, John Hill Burton, says that Hume showed most sympathy with Cleanthes, and, indeed, very nearly professed the theistical doctrine for his own. Philo says that the inquiry can never be concerning the *being*, but only concerning the nature of the Deity. The being of God is not to be questioned. It is a truth self-evident. Nothing exists without a cause, and the original cause of the universe we call God, and piously ascribe to Him every perfection. But as all perfection is purely relative, we ought never to imagine that we can comprehend the attributes of the Divine Being, or suppose that His perfections have any analogy or likeness to the perfections of a human creature. We justly ascribe to Him wisdom, thought, design, knowledge, because these words are honourable among men, and we have no other language nor other conception by which we can express our admiration of Him. But we must not think that His attributes have any resemblance to these qualities among men. He is infinitely superior to our limited view and comprehension, and is "more the object of worship in the temple than of disputation in the schools." Cleanthes saw in the world but one great machine, subdivided into an infinite number of lesser machines, which again admit of subdivision to a degree beyond what human senses and faculties can trace or explain. All these various machines, and even the most minute parts, are adjusted to each other with an accuracy which ravishes into admiration all men who have ever contemplated them. The curious adapting of means to ends throughout all nature resembles exactly, though it much exceeds, the productions of human contrivance, or human design. And since the effects resemble each other, we are led to infer, by all the rules of analogy, that the causes also resemble each other, and that the Author of nature is in some way similar to man, though possessed of much greater faculties, proportioned to the grandeur of His work. By this argument, *a posteriori*, and by this argument alone, do we prove at once the existence of Deity and the likeness of the divine mind to the human.

Philo answers that if we see a house we conclude with the greatest certainty that it had an architect or builder, because this is precisely the species of effect which we have experienced to proceed from that species of cause. But we cannot affirm that the universe bears such resemblance to a house that we with the same certainty infer a similar cause, or that the analogy is here entire and perfect.

Cleanthes dwells on the resemblance, which he maintains is not slight, on the economy of final causes – the order, proportion, and arrangement of every part. And Philo points out to Demea, another of the speakers, that Cleanthes tacitly allows that order, arrangement, or the adjustment of final causes, is not of itself any proof of design, but only so far as we have experienced it to proceed from design. For anything we know, *a priori*, matter may contain the spring or source of order originally within itself as well as mind, and there is no more difficulty in conceiving that the several elements, from an internal unknown cause, may fall into the most exquisite arrangement, than in conceiving that these ideas in the great universal mind, from a like internal unknown cause, fall into the same arrangement.

Cleanthes allows the equal possibility of both suppositions, but finds from experience that there is an original principle of order in mind, not in matter, and as from similar effects we can infer similar causes, so he concludes that the adjustment of means to an end is the same in the universe as in a machine of human contrivance, and, therefore, the causes of both must resemble each other.

Philo is scandalized with this comparison made between the mind of God and the created mind. Thought, design, or intelligence, he says, such as we discover in men and animals, is no more than one of the springs and principles of the universe, as well as heat and cold, attraction or repulsion, and a hundred others, which fall under daily observation. Why should thought be the model of the whole universe? It is true that in this minute globe of earth, stone, wood, brick, iron, brass, have not an order or arrangement without human art or contrivance, but it does not follow that the universe has not its order without something similar to human art. Is a part of nature a rule for the whole? Is a very small part a rule for the universe? This is not to be allowed. The inhabitants of other planets, have they thought, intelligence, and reason, or anything similar to these faculties in man? When nature has so extremely diversified her manner of operation in this small globe *can we imagine that she incessantly copies herself throughout the universe,*[2] and if thought is confined to this narrow corner, with what propriety can we assign it as the original cause of all things?

Cleanthes answers that if even in common life we assign a cause for an event, it is no objection that we cannot assign a cause for that cause, and answer every new question that may be started. What philosophy could submit to so rigid a rule? Philosophers, who confess ultimate causes to be unknown, are sensible that the most refined principles into which they trace the phenomena are still as inexplicable as the phenomena themselves are to the vulgar. The order and arrangement of nature, the curious adjustment of final causes, the place, use, and intention of every part and organ, all these bespeak, in the clearest language, an intelligent Cause, an Author. The heavens and the earth give in the same testimony. The whole chorus of nature raises a hymn to the praise of the Creator. "You alone," says Cleanthes to Philo, "or almost alone, disturb the general harmony. You start abstruse doubts, cavils, and objections. You ask me, What is the cause of the cause? I know not; I care not; that concerns not me.

---

[2] Had the discoveries now known as morphology and typology been known in Hume's day he would scarcely have made Philo reason after this fashion.

I have found a Deity, and here I stop my inquiry. Let them go further who are wiser or more enterprising."

Philo admits that the grandeur and magnificence of nature are arguments for Deity, but shows that on Cleanthes' *a posteriori* principles they become objections by removing the Deity further off from likeness to man. He also points out to Cleanthes that by confining himself to this method of reasoning he renounces all claim to infinity in any of the attributes of Deity. For as the cause ought to be proportioned to the effect, and the effect, so far as it falls under our cognizance, is not infinite, we cannot ascribe this attribute to the Divine Being. Nor can we, on Cleanthes' principles, ascribe perfection to God, for there are many inexplicable difficulties in the works of nature which, if we allow a perfect Author to be proved *a priori*, are easily solved, and become only seeming difficulties, from the narrow capacity of man, who cannot trace infinite relations. But on the rigid final cause supposition these difficulties become real; and, further, were the world ever so perfect a production, it must still remain uncertain whether all the excellencies of the work can justly be ascribed to the Workman. He may have botched and bungled many worlds throughout an eternity. Ere this system was struck out much labour may have been lost, many fruitless trials made, and a slow but continual improvement in the art of world-making carried on during infinite ages. Nor by this reasoning solely can we prove the unity of God as in a piece of human workmanship – a house, a ship, or a city; though unity be in the work, a great number of men may be employed in working.

In the essay on the "Natural History of Religion," Hume, speaking in his own person, declares himself decidedly on the side of Theism. The whole frame of nature, he says, bespeaks an intelligent Author; and no rational inquirer can, after serious reflection, suspend his belief a moment with regard to the primary principles of genuine Theism and religion. This belief Hume thinks is not an original instinct or primary impression. It is the result of reasoning. There are nations, he says, without any sentiment of religion, and there are no two nations, perhaps no two men, that ever precisely agreed in their religious ideas. By studying the works of nature we come inevitably to the conclusion that there is an Author of nature; but if we leave the works of nature and trace the footsteps of invisible power in the various and contrary events of life, we are necessarily led to Polytheism. From this Hume argues that Polytheism preceded Monotheism. The apparently capricious powers of nature would be the first divinities – beings corresponding to the elves and fairies of our ancestors. As men advanced in the knowledge of nature they would see that the work of nature could not be ascribed to these deities. The idea of the unity of God being once reached, the human mind could never again lose sight of it. The intelligent Pagans never ascribed the origin and fabric of the universe to these imperfect beings. Hesiod and Homer suppose gods and men to have sprung equally from the unknown powers of nature. Ovid speaks of the creating Deity in the doubtful terms, "*Quisquis fuit ille Deorum;*" and Diodorus Siculus, beginning his work with the enumeration of the most reasonable opinions concerning the origin of the world, makes no mention of a Deity, or intelligent mind. Hume denies the universality of the religious sentiment in order that he may deny the existence of a primary instinct, which, as a mere experimental philosopher, he was bound to do; yet here, as in other places, he is forced to go beyond his own philosophy to find a rational explanation of the phenomena of religion. A people, he says, destitute of religion are but a few degrees removed from the brute. And again, he says, that if the propensity to believe in invisible intelligent power be not an original instinct, it is, at least, a general attendant on human nature, and may be considered as a mark or stamp which the divine Workman has set upon His work, and "nothing, surely," Hume adds, "could more dignify mankind than to be thus selected from all other parts of the creation to bear the image or impression of the universal Creator. What a noble privilege is it of human reason to attain the knowledge of the Supreme Being, and from the visible works of nature be enabled to infer so sublime a principle as its Supreme Creator!" After saying all this, Hume's natural dislike to religion comes upon him. He finds ignorance the mother of devotion, revolts at the corruptions of theological systems and the evils to which they have given rise, and finally sinks into his wonted scepticism, finding that all is an "inexplicable mystery;" that the result of inquiry is, "doubt and uncertainty, from which our only escape is into the calm though obscure regions of philosophy."

Hume was in Paris about two years after the great excitement that had been raised by the miracles supposed to have been performed at the tomb of the Abbé Paris. He had many conversations with the priests about the reality of these and other miracles. A Jesuit of La Flèche once answered Hume that the same objections which he urged against Catholic miracles were valid against those of the Gospel. Hume says he admitted this as a sufficient answer. If there are no real miracles but those recorded in the Bible, they become so exceptionable that there is a very strong probability against their being genuine. The order of nature is visible to us; a Gospel miracle comes to us only on the authority of testimony; which, then, is the stronger evidence, our senses or testimony? Archbishop Tillotson had already weighed the question in arguing against the doctrine of the *real presence*. This doctrine might have the authority of Scripture or tradition, but these cannot overbalance the testimony of our senses. The Apostles saw the miracles of Jesus. To them the evidence was equal to the evidence of the senses; but to us, who have only their testimony, it is not equal. When we believe anything on human testimony the principle of our belief is founded on an observation of the veracity of human testimony, and of the usual conformity of facts to the reports of witnesses. Here all the experiments and observations give a probability in favour of the truth of that to which testimony is made. But when the fact attested is such a one as has seldom fallen under our observation, there is a contest of two opposite experiences. The Indian prince who refused to believe the first relations concerning the effects of frost reasoned justly. It required very strong testimony to engage his assent to facts which bore so little analogy to the events of which he had constant and uniform experience. The action of frost was not *contrary* to his experience, but it was not conformable to it. It was *extraordinary*, not miraculous. In a wider knowledge of nature it was found to be within the operations of nature. A miracle Hume defines as a *violation* of the laws of nature; and as a firm and unalterable experience has established these laws, the proof against a miracle is as entire as any argument from experience can possibly be. The Indian prince rightly required strong testimony to believe in ice, but no testimony is sufficient to evidence a miracle.

No writer on miracles omits to notice Hume. To refute

him has been the ambition of every Christian apologist for the last hundred years; but what could really be said in reply was said in his lifetime. It is recorded of a professor in the University of Edinburgh that he annually refuted the great sceptic, and with as much complacency as regularity. A portion of his lectures was always introduced with the words – "Having considered these different systems, I will now, gentlemen, proceed to refute the ingenious theories of our late respected townsman, Mr. David Hume." As there really was but one answer, that answer has been repeated with variations and amplifications by all who have undertaken to meet his objections.

William Adams, who is described as chaplain to the Bishop of Llandaff, was one of the first who wrote on miracles with reference to Hume's argument. Adams at once objected to the definition of miracle as a "transgression of the law of nature." If the Author of nature performs any work different from what we see going on every day, He does not thereby violate or transgress any law. He does not even depart from the order of nature, but only from what we know of the order of nature. Our idea of a natural law is nothing more than our observation of what usually goes on in the world. It is not contrary to nature that the dead should be raised, or that the winds should be controlled by a word. It only supposes a power in nature greater than what is manifested in our daily experience. Our individual observation may testify to a uniformity of sequences in nature, but we have no right to make this the universal measure where so much evidently lies beyond our knowledge. Extraordinary occasions may require extraordinary manifestations of power. For the truth of these we must depend on testimony. If they became frequent they would cease to be extraordinary, and so cease to serve the end for which a miracle is wrought. The uniformity of nature must be acknowledged before we can acknowledge a miracle. This, says Adams, is a position which has been laid down by all who write in defence of miracles, and he expresses wonder to see it now pleaded as decisive against them. Adams sometimes speaks of God changing or subverting His laws, which are not much better words than "transgressing" or "violating." He confesses a necessity of speaking in this way, for a miracle is apparently a subversion of law, but in reality it is conformable to nature.

This was taking the force out of the distinction which Hume made between the extraordinary and the miraculous.

It appears from Dr. Campbell's "Dissertation on Miracles," that Hume in the first edition of his "Essay" maintained the impossibility of miracles. Some of the reasoning still looks in that direction, and many who replied to Hume argued against the thesis that miracles are impossible. In the early editions there was a passage which read thus – "Upon the whole, it appears that no testimony for any kind of miracle *can* ever possibly amount to a probability, much less to a proof." The passage now reads thus – "Upon the whole, it appears that no testimony for any kind of miracle *has* ever amounted to a probability, much less to a proof." This fairly changes the question from possibility to probability. While Hume maintained that miracles were improbable, Campbell held that they were not only probable, and might be proved from testimony, but that the miracles on which the belief in Christianity is founded *are* sufficiently attested.

Campbell refuses to admit that our belief in testimony has its foundation in experience. He regards it rather as an original instinct or intuition. It is not, therefore, to be put into the balance against experience. He makes this simple illustration of the case between him and Hume: – He lived near a ferry; he had seen the ferry-boat cross the river a thousand times and return safe. One day a stranger comes to his door and seriously tells him that the boat is lost; he stood on the bank, and saw it upset. Here is what Hume would call "a contest of opposite experiences;" but Campbell maintains that his having seen the boat cross and recross a thousand times in safety is no proof against the testimony of the stranger – that must be overthrown by contrary testimony. Another person testifies that he had seen the boat safe; that it has not been upset. Here the things balanced are homogeneal, here is testimony against testimony; but until the second testimony came there was no inconsistency in believing that, though the boat had crossed a thousand times in safety, it was now upset. A fallacy may be noticed in the application of this illustration. It might be said that we have experience that boats are upset, but we have none that dead men are raised to life. But in making this objection we should be carrying with the word experience an ambiguity which Campbell is careful to mark. Did Hume mean by experience his own, personally? If so, there is no fallacy in Campbell's illustration. He may never have seen a ferry-boat upset. Did Hume mean by experience that of men in general? If so, what did he know of other men's experience except by testimony? This boasted uniformity of nature, then, has only testimony for its foundation, the same as that on which miracles depend; so that testimony really forms the greater part of that experience which was to overthrow the validity of testimony. To make Hume's case valid, evidence is required from experience that ferry-boats have never been upset. This is a considerable change from Dr. Tillotson's argument about transubstantiation, with which Hume began his "Essay." That argument rested on the superiority of sense over testimony. The apostles saw the miracles of Jesus; they had the evidence of their senses. But if our senses cannot be trusted, – if what appears bread and wine is not bread and wine, but flesh and blood, – we overthrow not only testimony, but the evidence on which testimony rests, which is the veracity of sense. Here the things opposed are the evidence of our senses and an external authority. In Hume's argument the opposition is between his own personal experience, added to what he knows traditionally of the general experience of mankind, and an external testimony of certain facts which, though out of the range both of general experience and his own experience personally, are yet not incompatible with either. This seems to be the force of Campbell's argument, but Hume had sheltered himself by a subtle distinction which it was necessary to examine. The Indian prince who did not believe in ice because he had never seen it, and could not conceive the possibility of it, having no conception of the conditions on which its existence was possible, reasoned rightly on the whole. It required strong testimony to convince him. Both sides agree in this. Both sides also agree that the testimony might be such as it would be unreasonable for him to reject. Hume says that his unbelief might be overcome by testimony, because, though it is not *conformable to his experience* that water should be turned into ice, it is yet *not contrary to it*. This is just what Campbell says of miracles. They are not contrary to our experience, but they are outside of it or not conformable to it. Our acquaintance with the laws of nature is only partial. In the idea of a miracle as contrary to experience, Hume is still working upon his definition that it is "a transgression of law," which Campbell of course rejects. To illustrate his meaning, Hume says it is no miracle that a man in seeming good health should die suddenly, but it is a miracle that a dead man should rise to life. The main difference here is, according to Campbell, that the one is common – conformable to experience, – the other is not conformable to experience; so that the Indian prince would not have been more unreasonable in refusing on the strongest testimony to believe in ice, than we should be in refusing on the same testimony to believe that a man was raised from the dead.

But Hume comes even nearer to his opponents than this. He grants that there may possibly be "miracles, or violations of the usual course of nature, of such a kind as to admit of proof from human testimony." There may be; but he does not grant that there has been. Suppose, he says, there was a universal testimony that for the first eight days in January, 1600, there was a total darkness over the whole earth. Such a testimony ought to be received by philosophers, and the cause of the miracle investigated. By "miracle" Hume evidently means here something natural, for philosophers are to investigate the cause of it. But this is not surely the kind of "miracle" concerning which he wrote his "Essay;" yet into something of this kind Dr. Campbell resolves all the miracles which he defends, – miracles which are variations from the usual course of nature, but not violations of the *actual* system of nature. The conclusion is, that the kind of miracle against which Hume writes, is a kind of miracle whose existence Christians, as represented by Dr. Campbell, do not profess to believe.

John Douglas, Bishop of Salisbury, wrote "The Criterion; or, Rules by which the True Miracles in the New Testament are distinguished from the spurious Miracles of Pagans and Papists." Douglas connects Hume's argument against miracles with his doctrine of cause and effect. It is only when our experience connects a cause with a particular effect that we believe it. Testimony is not sufficient. The plain inference made by Douglas is that Hume's argument proves too much. It is equally valid against the Christian miracles, and everything wonderful in nature which has not yet come within the narrow limits of our experience. Douglas assumes the omnipotency of God, and from that reasons for miracles. He notices the contradiction pointed out by Campbell, that Hume in the plainest terms admits that human testimony may in some cases give credibility to a miracle. He also noticed a limitation which Hume expressly wished should be noticed, that only such miracles as are made the *foundation of a new system of religion* cannot be made credible by testimony. His previous reasoning had struck at all miracles; but "he is lost in a labyrinth, surely," says the author of "The Criterion," "when he now applies it only to miracles connected with religion." Bishop Douglas argues for the necessity of revelation. Socrates had seen this necessity when he told Alcibiades of a Great Teacher who was to teach men their duty towards God and man. The expediency of a revelation involves the expediency of miracles. The "rules" for testing miracles are that the accounts be not published too long after the time when the miracles were said to have been performed, nor distant from the place; and if published at the time and place, not allowed to pass without examination. The "Life of Apollonius Tyanæus," by Philostratus, was not published till a hundred years after the death of the hero. Moreover, the whole of that biography is made up of imitations of New Testament miracles. The "Life of Ignatius," by Ribadeneira, in the first two editions contained no miracles. These were first inserted in an abridgment printed at Ypres in 1612, fifty-five years after the death of Ignatius. Bishop Douglas examines at some length the miracles said to have been wrought by the influence of the Abbé Paris, and does not find that they were so wonderful as the cures of Valentine Greatrakes, which were attested not only by the Bishop of Dromore, but by such rational theologians as Dr. Cudworth, Henry More, Bishop Wilkins, and Bishop Patrick, with many eminent physicians, and yet they were not accounted miracles.

The introductory part of Dr. Paley's "Evidences of Christianity" is devoted to Hume's argument; but Paley only repeats, in a condensed form, the substance of Dr. Campbell's dissertation. The very first sentence of Paley's book assures us that the writer is a man who understands an argument and can reason calmly. The previous advocates of Christianity generally held it necessary to exalt the light of the Gospel, and to contrast with it the darkness and insufficiency of natural religion. This was done under the belief that the

Deists had exalted the light of natural religion so as to make Christianity unnecessary. Paley at once states the case as it appears to every dispassionate and unbiassed mind. It is unnecessary to prove that mankind stood in need of a revelation, because, he says, "I have met with no serious person who thinks that even under the Christian revelation we have too much light." On the supposition that there is a Creator and Governor of the world, and a future life for man, it is not unlikely that God would give a revelation. The probability that God would acquaint men with the fact of the future life, is not greater than the probability that He would do it by miracles. To say that these doctrines, or the facts connected with them, are violently improbable, is a prejudication which should be resisted. Hume's position is stated to be that it is contrary to experience that a miracle should be true, but not contrary to experience that testimony should be false. The narrative of a fact, Paley says, is only contrary to experience when the fact is related to have existed at such a time and place, at which time and place, we being present, did not perceive it to exist. This is properly contrary to experience. This was Tillotson's contrariety. There is no intelligible meaning that can be attached to the words contrary to experience, except that we ourselves have not experienced anything of the kind related, or that such a thing has not been generally experienced by others. We cannot say that *universal* experience is against it, for that would be to assume the whole question. Paley accepts it as a fair statement of the controversy, "whether it be more improbable that the miracle should be true, or the testimony false;" and he asks, in argumentative justice, that in considering the probability of the miracle we should be allowed to take in all that we know of the existence, power, and disposition of the Deity. A miracle will appear more incredible to one who does not believe in God than to one who does; and more improbable when no purpose can be assigned, than when it is done on an occasion which seems to require it. Paley concludes by defending the Christian miracles as well attested, and showing that some pretended miracles are not well attested.

When Dr. Chalmers wrote his "Evidences of Christianity," which were published in 1836, he reviewed the whole of the controversy which had been raised by Hume's "Essay." He remarked how differently it had been treated in the two countries – England and Scotland. The English mind, best represented by Paley, came directly to the argument with full confidence in the faculties with which nature has endowed us. The Scotch mind always started a previous question, and, with Hume, reasoned about our reasoning. He naturally sympathised with the metaphysical bent of his countrymen, yet he says the English apologists were not deceived in the result, just because nature has not deceived them. She has not given original principles to her children for the purpose of leading them astray. Chalmers would not agree to Dr. Campbell's position, that belief in testimony was an instinct anterior to experience. He returned to Hume's belief that it was resolvable into experience. The two things, then, experience and testimony, are homogeneal, and are fairly balanced against each other. Chalmers is willing to contend with Hume on this ground, and he undertakes to prove that the testimony for miracles may have a superiority of experimental evidence in its favour. Hume classed *all* testimony as one; and because some testimony had deceived, he concluded that all might deceive us. Chalmers claims that testimony should be separated into its kinds, and he affirms that a testimony is conceivable – nay, that a testimony has often been given having such marks and characteristics of unlikelihood or moral impossibility of its falsehood, that we can aver with the utmost confidence that it never has deceived us and never will.

Archbishop Whately's "Historic Doubts relative to Napoleon Buonaparte" illustrates the extend to which scepticism may be carried. All we know of the existence of Buonaparte is from testimony. We never saw him, and even the multitudes that did profess to have seen him may have been deceived as to the actual person. The whole story of his life is marvellous, incredible, extraordinary, miraculous, improbable, yet it is well authenticated. It reads like a romance, yet it is true. No one will justify the scepticism which doubts of the existence of Napoleon and his strange history. Hume would here make distinctions of extraordinary and miraculous, contrary to experience, and not conformable to it; but practically, and so far as the argument is concerned, the distinctions do not mark a difference. Hume himself, as Whately shows, uses the term *miraculous* as synonymous with *improbable*, and throughout Hume's "Essay" the difficulty of believing the miraculous is the same in kind as the difficulty of believing the marvellous.

Bishop Warburton wrote "Remarks on Hume's 'Natural History of Religion.'" They are not of much value; in fact, this is one of Warburton's poorest performances. His words were many and strong, his arguments few and feeble. Warburton defended Christianity by throwing mud at its opponents. He denied that Polytheism preceded Monotheism. His argument was "the authority of an old book." When Warburton reviewed Bolingbroke, he extolled Toland and Tindal as good reasoners. He described them as men who really had something to say, and could say it; "but as for Bolingbroke, he was the mere essence of emptiness and nonentity." Now that Hume is to be brow-beaten, Bolingbroke is extolled as a man who knew how to reason; but as for Hume, he "insults common sense," and defends "dogmatical nonsense with scepticism still more nonsensical."[3]

We have abstained in all the preceding papers from any remarks on Leland's "View of the Deistical Writers." Leland was industrious, he had good intentions, he was disposed to be candid, and yet he is one-sided. His book does not deserve the reliance which has generally been placed on it. Two of the writers especially were entirely beyond him. These were Hobbes and Hume. Of the former he does not say much; of the latter he says a great deal too much. He is most successful with Bolingbroke. He fails entirely with Hume. He says that the tendency of Hume's writings is to confound rather than to enlighten the understanding. But this depends on the character of the understanding. He marks a few things in Hume's writings that "strike at the foundations of natural religion." When Leland wrote this, the "Dialogues on Natural Religion" had not been published, so the reference was probably to the essay on "Providence and a Future State." Hume, as we have seen, distinctly avows that he did not approve the principles advocated by the Epicurean philosopher. The extent to which he did agree with him, as expressed in a note at the end, is only unfavourable to natural religion as different people may view it differently. The impossibility of tracing the connection between cause and effect Leland would have been willing to pass by as a display of metaphysical subtlety,

---

[3] The "Remarks" were published by Cadell, in 1777, as written by Bishop Hurd, in the form of a letter to Bishop Warburton, with the addition of a few lines at the beginning and a few at the end.

if Hume had not made it the foundation of conclusions relating to matters of great importance. Now this was just one of the things which Hume denied he had ever done. The inquiry was limited to the question of the source whence we have the idea of power in causation. The answer is that it is from experience, and not from intuition or demonstration, but the fact of its existence and the validity of our arguments depending on it remain the same. With his own interpretation of Hume's doctrine of causation, Leland finds Hume inconsistent, when treating of liberty and necessity he speaks of necessary connection.

It may be some excuse for Dr. Leland that he was not alone in supposing that Hume's principles were unfavourable to natural religion. The objection which Hume put into the mouth of Philo, that we had no ground for ascribing to the cause more than we found in the effect, did not invalidate the argument from design, but it showed that it had limitations. It might prove a Creator, but it did not prove an Infinite. It might prove that there was some analogy between the mind of God and the mind of man, but it could not annihilate the manifest interval between the Divine and the human. Yet the things suggested by Philo have been taken into account by all philosophical Theists. They are to be found in Plato and Plotinus, in John Scotus Erigena and Benedict Spinoza. The acknowledgment of them has caused all philosophy of religion to be charged with what is called Pantheism.

Hume's "Dialogues" were continued by Dr. Morehead, a clergyman of the Episcopal Church in Scotland. Philo becomes a Christian, defends the Berkeleyan philosophy, and "all for the best," while Cleanthes remains a simple Theist. In Dr. Morehead's "Dialogues" Philo admits that he never denied the validity of the design argument. His error, as he explains it, was in esteeming it merely analogical and founded on experience. Now he maintains that its foundation is deeper. Wherever he sees marks of order, disposition, plan, he must acknowledge a designing mind by a necessary decision of the understanding previous to all experience.[4] Were there no works of art in existence, we might still per-

---

[4] This was the argument of the Scotch metaphysicians, Stewart, Brown, and Reid, in reply to Hume.

ceive traces of intelligence in the universe of nature. The universe may be a machine, an animal, a vegetable, or the production of a concourse of atoms; in any case, the mind reads intelligence in it. Reason was employed in putting the machine together, generating the animal, sowing the seeds of vegetation, or reducing into form or order the irregular dance of atoms. What the supreme nature is we do not know, but we do know that the universe manifests an intelligent mind. The nature or reality of all things is hid from us. Inquiries into real essence invariably lead to scepticism; but there is another region accessible to us – that is, the natural sentiments which we cannot but form upon questions of this kind. The reality of existence may be very different from our conceptions of it, yet when we have reached the genuine and unbiassed apprehensions of the human mind, we have reached the only view on which it can be contemplated. Thus, to trust our faculties is to trust in God. Philo, in Dr. Morehead's "Dialogues," differs chiefly from the Philo of Hume in having added Christianity to his philosophy.

We should not omit altogether an ingenious argument against Hume's sceptic which is urged by Hugh Miller in his "Testimony of the Rocks." It is drawn from geology, and though not remarkable for metaphysical keenness, is yet, in its sphere, and, so far as it goes, such as Hume would have welcomed. Miller considers Hume as identical with Philo, and so supposes the argument against the perfections of Deity, from the singularity of the effect, as Hume's own. This misconception brings with it some confusion, for Miller has not seen that Hume, in his stern impartiality, was simply trying to mark out the precise boundaries of our knowledge as derived from the measure of the capacity of the human mind. Miller's reply to the sceptic is that we have in geology that experience in world-making which no longer makes the world a "singular effect." We have at least five distinct "footprints on the sand;" that is, five distinct creations, – the *Azoic*, the *Palaeozoic*, the *Secondary*, the *Tertiary*, and the *Human era*. In the first era it might have been said that it was unphilosophical to argue that the producing Cause was competent to form anything beyond gases and earths, metals and minerals; yet in the *Palaeozoic* we have tall araucarians and pines, reptiles of comparatively low standing, and highly organized fishes. It is evident now that in the first creation the producing Cause had put forth but a part of His power. In the *Secondary*, the manifestation of this power is still higher. In the *Tertiary*, we have noble forests of dicotyledonous trees with sagacious and gigantic mammals. In the *Human era*, the greatness of the Divine power is yet more fully revealed. Each creation has been higher than the one that preceded it. With this experience, Miller asks, is it still unphilosophical to reason that the producing Cause will yet put forth greater energy and realize the hopes of the deeply-seated instincts which lead us to look for new heavens and a new earth? There is certainly in this a probability that yet higher creations will succeed the present; but the point of Philo's argument is, that in strict reasoning we must always measure the producing Cause by precisely what is manifested in the effect.

The result of Hume's criticism of the design argument has been finally settled by Kant. In the *pure reason* which leads to scepticism, it loses its force, but it finds it again in what Kant calls the *practical reason*. It is valid as far as it goes. In concluding his Essay on Miracles, Hume said with a sneer that our religion is not founded on reason but on faith. Those who replied to him found at least that it was not against reason. The internal sense which men have of the truth of religion is properly called faith; not that it is opposed to reason, nor in the sense of implicit reliance on authority, but as designating a state of mind rather than an act of the mind. In this sense the most devout and rational Christians of the present day will not object to taking Hume's conclusion seriously, that the foundation of our belief in Christianity is not from a process of reasoning concerning miracles, or any other external evidence, but really has its foundation in something which is called *faith*. Why should Hume have sneered at this? He had proved that reason, as he understood it, had failed in everything, even in proving its own existence. He had shown, too, that our only escape from scepticism was to return to reason, such as it is, and to put faith in it. So that a rational faith really is practical reason.

Hume's biographer, Mr. Burton, claims that Hume's place should be not among the sceptics, but among the philosophers of the porch. There is some justice in this claim when the easy French philosophy is put off. Hume's character is that of the genuine Stoic – calm, patient, unbiassed, self-sacrificing. In the Essays on Epicurean, Stoic, Platonist, and Sceptic, each of the philosophers is made to speak as if Hume felt that each of them had some truth on his side. Though avowedly a disciple of the experimental philosophy, his eagerness to follow principles to their last results continually leads him to some region which that philosophy forbids its disciples to enter. He refused to engage in controversy. The agitation of mind which that kind of gladiatorship produces, he did not think conducive to the discovery of truth. When Dr. Campbell, through his friend Dr. Blair, submitted to him the manuscript of the "Dissertation on Miracles," Hume sent to Campbell one of the kindest letters ever written. If it had not the name of Christian, it had the reality without the name. To Dr. Blair he wrote that whenever they met it must be with the understanding, that no subjects relating to his profession were to be introduced in their conversation. He had made up his mind; and such subjects might destroy the good feeling which existed between them. The entire simplicity of Hume's character, as delineated by his friends, is in keeping with all that we know of him from his writings. It is traditionally recorded that his mother, speaking of her son David, once said, "Our Davie's a fine, good-natured cratur, but uncommon wake-minded." It is possible that David, destitute of the religious element, without prejudice or bias, may have appeared to his devout mother precisely in this light.

Hume lived in a dark age – dark, we mean, as regards religion. The eighteenth century had so many men remarkable for their virtues, their great human gifts, and their practical common sense, that we often wish it were possible to vindicate it from the usual charge of irreligion. But all the evidence is against us. Hume says that the clergy had lost their credit; their pretensions and doctrines were ridiculed; and even religion could scarcely support itself in the world. We have the same testimony from Bishop Butler, Archbishop Secker, and others. Hume was penetrated with the spirit of the age. There is no great man of whom we know anything who had by nature so little of the sentiment of religion. His mind was essentially pagan, without one Shemetic element. The whole spirit of the Bible was alien to him. He does not seem to have had even a taste for its literature or its lessons of human wisdom. In every great English writer, passages, similes, or illustrations from Scripture are plentiful in almost every page, interweaving themselves in the happiest sentences of our most brilliant orators and our most finished essayists; but in all Hume's philosophical writings we have marked only two references to the Scriptures. One of them is about the treasures of Hezekiah. It is introduced in a political essay, and with the indifferent words, *if I remember right.* In the whole history of his life there is but one occasion where he ever manifests the least sense for religious feeling. When in London he learned of the death of his mother. His sorrow was overwhelming. His friend Mr. Boyle said to him, "You owe this uncommon grief to having thrown off the principles of religion, for if you had not, you would have been consoled with the firm belief that the good lady, who was not only the best of mothers, but the most pious of Christians, was completely happy in the realms of the just." To which Hume answered, "Though I throw out my speculations to entertain the learned and metaphysical world, yet in other things I do not think so differently from the rest of the world as you imagine." This is a solitary instance, and, if really genuine, is altogether exceptional. When he drew near his own end, with all his faculties entire, he amused himself and his friends with jests about crossing the Styx, and how he would banter old Charon, and detain him as long as he could on this side of the river before he entered the ferry-boat.[5]

Hume's principles, of necessity, made him many enemies. We may praise the zeal of those who opposed him, but we can also admire the calm, self-possessed spirit which bore the opposition with meekness and patience. There is a story, well authenticated, that when an old man, and very heavy, he fell into the swamp at the bottom of the wall that surrounded Edinburgh Castle. He was unable to get out, and in great dread of there ending his life, he called to an old woman for assistance. The old woman told him that he was "Mr. Hume the Deist, and she would help none of him." "But, my good woman," said Hume, piteously, "does not your religion teach you to do good even to your enemies?" "That may be," she replied, "but ye shall'na come out o' that till ye become a

---

[5] A saying of Bishop Horne to Hume illustrates this defect in the sceptic's character. Hume had used it as an argument against the alleged consolatory effect of religion, that all the religious men he had met with were melancholy persons. "The sight of you," replied Horne, "is enough to make a religious man melancholy at any time." – ED.

Christian yoursel', and repeat the Lord's Prayer and the Belief." He performed the task, and got the promised assistance. David Hume is not the first whom ability to say the Creed has helped out of a ditch.

PREFACE
Anonymous

"Among the sayings of Homer mark well this one too and improve upon it; he says: – *A good messenger brings the greatest credit on every transaction.*" – Pindar's *Pythian*, iv. 277–78.

IF ever Truth sent "a good messenger" to the human race, it was in the person of David Hume, who was born at Edinburgh, on the 7th May 1711, N. S. But Hume did not receive his message from Truth written, as it were, on a sheet of paper. No: like Pindar's messenger of old, Hume had to acquire by labour and care the knowledge which enabled him to learn and deliver the message which he conveyed to mortals. Moreover, he was obstructed by two obstacles, which few men, prosecuting such studies as he laboured in, succeed in surmounting.

His first obstacle was poverty.

In his delightful little autobiography, ("My Own Life,") he informs us that his fortune was "very slender." How he surmounted this obstacle he tells us thus: – "I resolved to make a very rigid frugality supply my deficiency of fortune, to maintain unimpaired my independency, and to regard every object as contemptible, except the improvement of my talents in literature."

His second obstacle was Christianity.

It is not permitted to mortal man, in his present state of existence, to be by nature free from the prejudices which arise from his education, and the prepossessions imperceptibly springing from it. These adhered to Hume for a long time. He sent the manuscript of his "Dialogues concerning Natural Religion" to his friend, Sir Gilbert Elliott, with whom he corresponded on the subject. Writing to Sir Gilbert Elliott in March 1751, Hume says,

"The general progress of my thoughts began with an anxious search after arguments to confirm the common opinion

– doubts stole in – dissipated – returned – were again dissipated – returned again, and it was a perpetual struggle of a restless imagination against inclination – perhaps against reason."

Most probably this is virtually the true inner history of every honest thinker.

It was about the year 1730 that Hume commenced his "anxious search." Before that time, the inductive philosophy, or rather the logic of induction, first given to the world in a scientific shape by Bacon in his *Novum Organum*, 1620, had been applied solely to the phenomena of the physical world, especially by Flamsteed, James Gregory, Boyle, and Sir Isaac Newton.[1] But the application of that logic to the so-called world of spirit had been scarcely thought of. It is true, indeed, that Locke in his "Essay concerning Human Understanding," and more particularly in his subsequent letters in defence of that work, had maintained that matter might possess the quality of thinking power as well as the qualities of extension and solidity. But that matter contained the principle of its order within itself, and had of itself arranged the material universe, was an idea which had long ceased to influence the world of Thinkers: alas! a very small world

---

[1] It may be explained here that the Logic of induction consists in dealing with facts, not words. Thus, to prove that John, or any other man, is mortal, a disciple of Aristotle would say, "All men are mortal; John is a man; therefore John is mortal." To this a disciple of Bacon would object that the mortality of all men had been begged not proved. This objection is fatal to the argument; for we cannot prove that all men are mortal. We may believe that such is the case; but all we can prove regarding it amounts to this, namely, "So well as we know all men preceeding those now alive have died; we do not know that any man now living has any element of immortality in him; therefore we *infer* that all men are mortal – probably." The truth is that this inference is grounded on instinct rather than on reason: in the words of Hume, "'tis certain, that the most ignorant and stupid peasants, nay infants, nay even brute beasts, improve by experience, and learn the qualities of natural objects, by observing the effects which result from them. When a child has felt the sensation of pain from touching the flame of a candle, he will be careful not to put his hand near any candle; but will expect a similar effect from a cause which is similar in its sensible qualities and appearance." That we cannot prove to demonstration any matter of fact is the chief principle of Hume's philosophy. If the reader will reflect on the idea contained in the word *probability* he will thereby more clearly perceive the value of the inductive logic, and the truth of Hume's philosophy, than by anything that can be written by the editor.

indeed, and possessing very few inhabitants. Even if before Hume any of those "happy few" entertained that idea, it is very probable that he would have been deterred from publishing it; for by so doing he ran the risk of acquiring something more than fame from those Christians who chose to prosecute him, under the provisions contained in the mild "Act of Toleration," and other "tender mercies" of the Christians; and so, when Hume began his "anxious search," prudence required him to shew its results primarily on objects not generally calculated to excite suspicion.

So, his first effort was in his essay "Of the Idea of Necessary Connexion." In this essay he shews that we cannot assign a cause to any single phenomenon without having the opportunity of comparing it and its cause with other similar phenomena. He shews also that even when we perceive an instance of cause and effect we cannot tell why or how the cause produces the effect. Of course here he suppresses (although he doubtless perceived) the further inference that since Divine Providence never, for instance, was seen by any man in the act of creating a planet like our own, we have not sufficient proof, on even the ground of an argument from cause and effect, to shew that this planet, called the Earth, is not self-created.

But he hinted at this inference in his essay "Of a Particular Providence and of a Future State." There he says,

"I much doubt whether it be possible for a cause to be known only by its effect, or to be of so singular and particular a nature as to have no parallel, and no similarity with any other cause or object, that has ever fallen under our observation. 'Tis only when two species of objects are found to be constantly conjoined, that we can infer the one from the other; and were an effect presented, which was entirely singular, and could not be comprehended under any known species, I do not see that we could form any conjecture, or inference at all concerning its cause. If experience and observation and analogy be, indeed, the only guides which we can reasonably follow in inferences of this nature; both the effect and the cause must bear a similarity and resemblance to other effects and causes which we know, and which we have found, in many instances, to be conjoined with each other. As the antagonists of Epicurus always suppose the universe, an effect quite singular and unparalleled, to be proof of a Deity, a cause no less singular and unparalleled; reasonings, upon that supposition, seem, at least, to merit our attention. There is some difficulty, how we can ever return from the cause to the effect, and, reasoning from our ideas of the former, infer any alteration on the latter, or any addition to it."

To human beings this Earth is a singular performance. We do not know anything of what goes on in the other planets and stars. Consequently, from what we know of our own planet we cannot logically infer anything decided and definite regarding the other heavenly bodies, or prove whether or not they even shew marks of design.

In his "Dialogues concerning Natural Religion," Hume has brought forward almost every argument for and against the existence of Divine Providence that has been adduced on that subject from the days of Anaxagoras to those of Professor Tyndall. Hume says, "all religious systems, it is confessed, are subject to great and insuperable difficulties. Each disputant triumphs in his turn; while he carries on an offensive war, and exposes the absurdities, barbarities, and pernicious tenets of his antagonist. But all of them, on the whole, prepare a complete triumph for the Sceptic, who tells them that no system ought ever to be embraced with regard to such subjects; for this plain reason, – that no absurdity ought ever to be assented to with regard to any subject. A total suspense of judgment is here our only reasonable resource."

Nevertheless, so far as the human mind can judge, the material universe probably shews traces of design. But if so it is a design very different in its nature from that shewn in human works of art. Consequently the weight of probability is in favour of the supposition that the present material universe has been arranged by some *Intelligence* capable of the task, but who is in all other respects utterly unknown to us, and, probably, unknowable by us. In the words of Hume, "The whole of Natural Theology, as some people seem to maintain, resolves itself into one simple, though somewhat ambiguous, at least undefined proposition, *that the cause or causes of order in the universe probably bear some remote analogy to human intelligence.*"

One great merit of this doctrine is that it is consistent with all the phenomena in the moral as well as in the physical world. Instead of trying to force Philosophy to fit into beds and boxes far too small for the purpose, this doctrine leaves Philosophy free either to make or find for herself a suitable resting-place. Moreover, by shewing that *all we can know is only a very small amount of knowledge*, this doctrine proves to demonstration the uselessness and the immorality of bigotry and persecution. It is melancholy to think that the masses of mankind are nearly as ignorant of the practical worth of this invaluable doctrine in the present day as they were a century ago, in the days of Hume. Our object is now to republish it in a form accessible to every one able and willing to read and study it; and its inestimable value to mankind justifies us in expecting that its republication will receive the blessing of Divine Providence.

Hume's opinions excluded him from the professorships in the universities of Scotland, and, in fact, from all places in the state and in literature: just as they would exclude any one who professed them in the present day. He died at Edinburgh on Sunday the 25th August 1776, after having triumphantly surmounted all the miseries arising from both poverty and Christianity. The scope of this edition of the "Dialogues" precludes the Editor from entering upon the details of Hume's life. These the reader will find in Mr. John H. Burton's admirable work on that subject, which will well repay its perusal. For the history of David Hume affords a lesson of the utmost value, as an example, to the courageous Student and Thinker in this and probably many future ages.

POSTSCRIPT
Anonymous

A SHORT account of the "Dialogues" will probably be acceptable to the reader.

It has been stated, in the Preface to this edition of them,
that they were laid in manuscript before Sir Gilbert Elliott in
the year 1751. Hume was most anxious to publish them,
but his friends always dissuaded him from doing so, knowing
how dangerous to his personal and social peace the experiment might prove. So, by his will, he appointed his friend
Dr. Adam Smith his literary executor, with full power over
all his papers except the "Dialogues," which, however, Dr.
Smith was directed to publish. As an inducement to Dr. Smith
to comply with this direction, Hume added the following
clause: – "Though I can trust to that intimate and sincere
friendship which has ever subsisted between us for his faithful
execution of this part of my will, yet as a small recompense
of his pains in correcting and publishing this work, I leave
him £200 to be paid immediately after the publication of it."

Although there is not the least reason to call in question
the sincerity of the friendship above referred to, yet Hume
foresaw that Dr. Smith would not comply with the direction,
couched in such affectionate language, and followed by a
substantial legacy; for by a codicil bearing date the 7th August
1776, only a few days before Hume's death, he made the
following provision: – "I do ordain that if my Dialogues,
from whatever cause, be not published within two years and
a half after my death, as also an account of my life, the
property shall return to my nephew, David, whose duty in
publishing them, as the last request of his uncle, must be
approved of by all the world."

Almost immediately after Hume's death, his friend, Dr.
Smith, edited the autobiography, "My own Life," alluded to
in the codicil; and in a letter addressed to William Strahan,
Esq., dated 9 Nov. 1776, Dr. Smith gave an account "of the
behaviour of our late excellent friend, Mr. Hume, during his

last illness." That letter concludes thus: – "Upon the whole, I have always considered him, (Hume) both in his lifetime, and since his death, as approaching as nearly to the idea of a perfectly wise and virtuous man, as perhaps the nature of human frailty will permit." But Dr. Smith was afraid to publish the "Dialogues," and, although both they and the legacy of £200 were offered to him independently of any condition that might be implied in the terms of the bequest, he refused both. So it was left to be seen what "my nephew, David," would do.

This David Hume was an advocate at the Scotch bar, and subsequently a baron in the Court of Exchequer. He was a true Christian, a very bad writer, a staunch supporter of terrorism, and a bigoted upholder of all the arbitrary oppressions exercised by the English government during the period from 1793 to 1830. He was very unwilling to publish the "Dialogues." However, in the year 1779, he *printed* them, but without the name of any publisher, printer, or even place of printing attached to the volume. The editor has in his possession a copy of this first and merely printed edition of the "Dialogues." Its title page stands thus: – "Dialogues concerning Natural Religion, by David Hume, Esq.; Printed in 1779." – On the fly leaf there is written, "From the Author's Nephew," indicating that the merely printed copies were not exposed for sale, and were circulated only privately. But as *delivery* of any written or printed matter to only one person is "publication" in the eye of the law, perhaps the baron persuaded himself that he had complied with "the last request of his uncle" – in the eye of the law.

So intense was Baron Hume's dread of the social persecution which hitherto has always been suffered by those persons who have sided with the plaintiff in the good old cause of "*Truth* v. *Christianity.*" A cause not yet decided against the plaintiff, notwithstanding the atrocities which the defendant inflicts, almost every year on those who side with the plaintiff. The late Dr. John P. Nichol of Glasgow University, says, "It is at once unjust and unwise to consider errors and crimes of this sort (persecutions) as exclusive attributes of the Romish Church; on the contrary, their root lies deep in the heart of man. The domain of physical inquiry is now wholly safe from the disorders of intolerance; but there are large departments of knowledge within which Reason is not yet free; where authority abides on its throne, and *popular prejudice stores its thunderbolts.*"

THEISM; EVOLUTION OF THEOLOGY
Thomas Huxley

HUME seems to have had but two hearty dislikes: the one to the English nation, and the other to all the professors of dogmatic theology. The one aversion he vented only privately to his friends; but, if he is ever bitter in his public utterances, it is against priests[1] in general and theological enthusiasts and fanatics in particular; if he ever seems insincere, it is when he wishes to insult theologians by a parade of sarcastic respect. One need go no further than the peroration of the *Essay on Miracles* for a characteristic illustration.

"I am the better pleased with the method of reasoning here delivered, as I think it may serve to confound those dangerous friends and disguised enemies to the *Christian religion* who have undertaken to defend it by the principles of human reason. Our most holy religion is founded on *Faith*, not on reason, and it is a sure method of exposing it to put it to such a trial as it is by no means fitted to endure ... the Christian religion not only was at first attended with miracles, but even at this day cannot be believed by any reasonable person without one. Mere reason is insufficient to convince us of its veracity: And whoever is moved by *Faith* to assent to it, is conscious of a continual miracle in his own person, which subverts all the principles of his understanding, and gives him a determination to believe what is most contrary to custom and experience." – (IV. pp. 153, 154.)

It is obvious that, here and elsewhere, Hume, adopting a

---

[1] In a note to the Essay on Superstition and Enthusiasm, Hume is careful to define what he means by this term. "By priests I understand only the pretenders to power and dominion, and to a superior sanctity of character, distinct from virtue and good morals. These are very different from *clergymen*, who are set apart to the care of sacred matters, and the conducting of our public devotions with greater decency and order. There is no rank of men more to be respected than the latter." – (III. p. 83.)

popular confusion of ideas, uses religion as the equivalent of dogmatic theology; and, therefore, he says, with perfect justice, that "religion is nothing but a species of philosophy" (iv. p. 171). Here no doubt lies the root of his antagonism. The quarrels of theologians and philosophers have not been about religion, but about philosophy; and philosophers not unfrequently seem to entertain the same feeling towards theologians that sportsmen cherish towards poachers. "There cannot be two passions more nearly resembling each other than hunting and philosophy," says Hume. And philosophic hunters are given to think, that, while they pursue truth for its own sake, out of pure love for the chase (perhaps mingled with a little human weakness to be thought good shots), and by open and legitimate methods; their theological competitors too often care merely to supply the market of establishments; and disdain neither the aid of the snares of superstition, nor the cover of the darkness of ignorance.

Unless some foundation was given for this impression by the theological writers whose works had fallen in Hume's way, it is difficult to account for the depth of feeling which so good natured a man manifests on the subject.

Thus he writes in the *Natural History of Religion*, with quite unusual acerbity: –

> "The chief objection to it [the ancient heathen mythology] with regard to this planet is, that it is not ascertained by any just reason or authority. The ancient tradition insisted on by heathen priests and theologers is but a weak foundation: and transmitted also such a number of contradictory reports, supported all of them by equal authority, that it became absolutely impossible to fix a preference among them. A few volumes, therefore, must contain all the polemical writings of pagan priests: And their whole theology must consist more of traditional stories and superstitious practices than of philosophical argument and controversy.
>
> But where theism forms the fundamental principle of any popular religion, that tenet is so conformable to sound reason, that philosophy is apt to incorporate itself with such a system of theology. And if the other dogmas of that system be contained in a sacred book, such as the Alcoran, or be determined by any visible authority, like that of the Roman pontiff, speculative reasoners naturally carry on

their assent, and embrace a theory, which has been instilled into them by their earliest education, and which also possesses some degree of consistence and uniformity. But as these appearances are sure, all of them, to prove deceitful, philosophy will very soon find herself very unequally yoked with her new associate; and instead of regulating each principle, as they advance together, she is at every turn perverted to serve the purposes of superstition. For besides the unavoidable incoherences, which must be reconciled and adjusted, one may safely affirm, that all popular theology, especially the scholastic, has a kind of appetite for absurdity and contradiction. If that theology went not beyond reason and common sense, her doctrines would appear too easy and familiar. Amazement must of necessity be raised: Mystery affected: Darkness and obscurity sought after: And a foundation of merit afforded to the devout votaries, who desire an opportunity of subduing their rebellious reason by the belief of the most unintelligible sophisms.

Ecclesiastical history sufficiently confirms these reflections. When a controversy is started, some people always pretend with certainty to foretell the issue. Whichever opinion, say they, is most contrary to plain reason is sure to prevail; even when the general interest of the system requires not that decision. Though the reproach of heresy may, for some time, be bandied about among the disputants, it always rests at last on the side of reason. Any one, it is pretended, that has but learning enough of this kind to know the definition of *Arian, Pelagian, Erastian, Socinian, Sabellian, Eutychian, Nestorian, Monothelite,* &c., not to mention *Protestant,* whose fate is yet uncertain, will be convinced of the truth of this observation. It is thus a system that becomes absurd in the end, merely from its being reasonable and philosophical in the beginning.

To oppose the torrent of scholastic religion by such feeble maxims as these, that *it is impossible for the same thing to be and not to be,* that *the whole is greater than a part,* that *two and three make five,* is pretending to stop the ocean with a bulrush. Will you set up profane reason against sacred mystery? No punishment is great enough for your impiety. And the same fires which were kindled for heretics will serve also for the destruction of philosophers." – (IV. pp. 481–3.)

Holding these opinions respecting the recognised systems of theology and their professors, Hume, nevertheless, seems to have had a theology of his own; that is to say, he seems to have thought (though, as will appear, it is needful for an expositor of his opinions to speak very guardedly on this point) that the problem of theism is susceptible of scientific treatment, with something more than a negative result. His opinions are to be gathered from the eleventh section of the *Inquiry* (1748); from the *Dialogues concerning Natural Religion*, which were written at least as early as 1751, though not published till after his death; and from the *Natural History of Religion*, published in 1757.

In the first two pieces, the reader is left to judge for himself which interlocutor in the dialogue represents the thoughts of the author; but, for the views put forward in the last, Hume accepts the responsibility. Unfortunately, this essay deals almost wholly with the historical development of theological ideas; and, on the question of the philosophical foundation of theology, does little more than express the writer's contentment with the argument from design.

> "The whole frame of nature bespeaks an Intelligent Author; and no rational inquirer can, after serious reflection, suspend his belief a moment with regard to the primary principles of genuine Theism and Religion. – (IV. p. 435.)
>
> Were men led into the apprehension of invisible, intelligent power, by a contemplation of the works of nature, they could never possibly entertain any conception but of one single being, who bestowed existence and order on this vast machine, and adjusted all its parts according to one regular plan or connected system. For though, to persons of a certain turn of mind, it may not appear altogether absurd, that several independent beings, endowed with superior wisdom, might conspire in the contrivance and execution of one regular plan, yet is this a merely arbitrary supposition, which, even if allowed possible, must be confessed neither to be supported by probability nor necessity. All things in the universe are evidently of a piece. Everything is adjusted to everything. One design prevails throughout the whole. And this uniformity leads the mind to acknowledge one author; because the conception of different authors, without any distinction of attributes or oper-

ations, serves only to give perplexity to the imagination, without bestowing any satisfaction on the understanding." – (IV. p. 442.)

Thus Hume appears to have sincerely accepted the two fundamental conclusions of the argument from design; firstly, that a Deity exists; and, secondly, that He possesses attributes more or less allied to those of human intelligence. But, at this embryonic stage of theology, Hume's progress is arrested; and, after a survey of the development of dogma, his "general corollary" is, that –

> "The whole is a riddle, an enigma, an inexplicable mystery. Doubt, uncertainty, suspense of judgment, appear the only result of our most accurate scrutiny concerning this subject. But such is the frailty of human reason, and such the irresistible contagion of opinion, that even this deliberate doubt could scarcely be upheld; did we not enlarge our view, and opposing one species of superstition to another, set them a quarrelling; while we ourselves, during their fury and contention, happily make our escape into the calm, though obscure, regions of philosophy." – (IV. p. 513.)

Thus it may be fairly presumed that Hume expresses his own sentiments in the words of the speech with which Philo concludes the *Dialogues*.

> "If the whole of natural theology, as some people seem to maintain, resolves itself into one simple, though somewhat ambiguous, at least undefined proposition, *That the cause or causes of order in the universe probably bear some remote analogy to human intelligence*: If this proposition be not capable of extension, variation, or more particular explication: If it affords no inference that affects human life or can be the source of any action or forbearance: And if the analogy, imperfect as it is, can be carried no further than to the human intelligence, and cannot be transferred, with any appearance of probability, to the other qualities of the mind; if this really be the case, what can the most inquisitive, contemplative, and religious man do more than give a plain, philosophical assent to the proposition, as often as it occurs, and believe that the arguments on which it is established exceed the objections which lie against it? Some astonishment indeed will naturally arise from the

greatness of the object; some melancholy from its obscurity; some contempt of human reason, that it can give no solution more satisfactory with regard to so extraordinary and magnificent a question. But believe me, Cleanthes, the most natural sentiment which a well-disposed mind will feel on this occasion, is a longing desire and expectation that Heaven would be pleased to dissipate, at least alleviate, this profound ignorance, by affording some more particular revelation to mankind, and making discoveries of the nature, attributes, and operations of the Divine object of our faith."[2] – (II. pp. 547–8.)

Such being the sum total of Hume's conclusions, it cannot be said that his theological burden is a heavy one. But, if we turn from the *Natural History of Religion,* to the *Treatise,* the *Inquiry,* and the *Dialogues,* the story of what happened to the ass laden with salt, who took to the water, irresistibly suggests itself. Hume's theism, such as it is, dissolves away in the dialectic river, until nothing is left but the verbal sack in which it was contained.

Of the two theistic propositions to which Hume is committed, the first is the affirmation of the existence of a God, supported by the argument from the nature of causation. In the *Dialogues,* Philo, while pushing scepticism to its utmost limit, is nevertheless made to say that –

" . . . where reasonable men treat these subjects, the question can never be concerning the *Being,* but only the *Nature,* of the Deity. The former truth, as you will observe, is unquestionable and self-evident. Nothing exists without a cause, and the original cause of this universe (whatever it be) we call God, and piously ascribe to him every species of perfection." – (II. p. 439.)

The expositor of Hume, who wishes to do his work

[2] It is needless to quote the rest of the passage, though I cannot refrain from observing that the recommendation which it contains, that a "man of letters" should become a philosophical sceptic as "the first and most essential step towards being a sound believing Christian," though adopted and largely acted upon by many a champion of orthodoxy in these days, is questionable in taste, if it be meant as a jest, and more than questionable in morality, if it is to be taken in earnest. To pretend that you believe any doctrine for no better reason than that you doubt everything else, would be dishonest, if it were not preposterous.

thoroughly, as far as it goes, cannot but fall into perplexity[3] when he contrasts this language with that of the sections of the third part of the *Treatise*, entitled, *Why a Cause is Always Necessary*, and *Of the Idea of Necessary Connexion*.

It is there shown, at large, that "every demonstration which has been produced for the necessity of a cause is fallacious and sophistical" (I. p. 111); it is affirmed, that "there is no absolute nor metaphysical necessity that every beginning of existence should be attended with such an object" [as a cause] (I. p. 227); and it is roundly asserted, that it is "easy for us to conceive any object to be non-existent this moment and existent the next, without conjoining to it the distinct idea of a cause or productive principle" (I. p. 111). So far from the axiom, that whatever begins to exist must have a cause of existence, being "self-evident," as Philo calls it, Hume spends the greatest care in showing that it is nothing but the product of custom, or experience.

And the doubt thus forced upon one, whether Philo ought to be taken as even, so far, Hume's mouthpiece, is increased when we reflect that we are dealing with an acute reasoner; and that there is no difficulty in drawing the deduction from Hume's own definition of a cause, that the very phrase, a

---

[3] A perplexity which is increased rather than diminished by some passages in a letter to Gilbert Elliot of Minto (March 10, 1751). Hume says, "You would perceive by the sample I have given you that I make Cleanthes the hero of the dialogue; whatever you can think of, to strengthen that side of the argument, will be most acceptable to me. Any propensity you imagine I have to the other side crept in upon me against my will; and 'tis not long ago that I burned an old manuscript book, wrote before I was twenty, which contained, page after page, the gradual progress of my thoughts on this head. It began with an anxious scent after arguments to confirm the common opinion; doubts stole in, dissipated, returned; were again dissipated, returned again; and it was a perpetual struggle of a restless imagination against inclination – perhaps against reason ... I could wish Cleanthes' argument could be so analysed as to be rendered quite formal and regular. The propensity of the mind towards it – unless that propensity were as strong and universal as that to believe in our senses and experience – will still, I am afraid, be esteemed a suspicious foundation. 'Tis here I wish for your assistance. We must endeavour to prove that this propensity is somewhat different from our inclination to find our own figures in the clouds, our faces in the moon, our passions and sentiments even in inanimate matter. Such an inclination may and ought to be controlled, and can never be a legitimate ground of assent." (Burton, *Life*, I. pp. 331–3.) The picture of Hume here drawn unconsciously by his own hand, is unlike enough to the popular conception of him as a careless sceptic loving doubt for doubt's sake.

"first cause," involves a contradiction in terms. He lays down that, –

> "'Tis an established axiom both in natural and moral philo-
> sophy, that an object, which exists for any time in its full
> perfection without producing another, is not its sole cause;
> but is assisted by some other principle which pushes it from
> its state of inactivity, and makes it exert that energy, of
> which it was secretly possessed." – (I. p. 106.)

Now the "first cause" is assumed to have existed from all eternity, up to the moment at which the universe came into existence. Hence it cannot be the sole cause of the universe; in fact, it was no cause at all until it was "assisted by some other principle"; consequently the so-called "first cause," so far as it produces the universe, is in reality an effect of that other principle. Moreover, though, in the person of Philo, Hume assumes the axiom "that whatever begins to exist must have a cause," which he denies in the *Treatise*, he must have seen, for a child may see, that the assumption is of no real service.

Suppose Y to be the imagined first cause and Z to be its effect. Let the letters of the alphabet, *a, b, c, d, e, f, g,* in their order, represent successive moments of time, and let *g* represent the particular moment at which the effect Z makes its appearance. It follows that the cause Y could not have existed "in its full perfection" during the time *a–e*, for if it had, then the effect Z would have come into existence during that time, which, by the hypothesis, it did not do. The cause Y, therefore, must have come into existence at *f*, and if "everything that comes into existence has a cause," Y must have had a cause X operating at *e*; X, a cause W operating at *d*; and, so on, *ad infinitum*.[4]

If the only demonstrative argument for the existence of a Deity, which Hume advances, thus, literally, "goes to water" in the solvent of his philosophy, the reasoning from the evidence of design does not fare much better. If Hume really knew of any valid reply to Philo's arguments in the following

---

[4] Kant employs substantially the same argument: – "Würde das höchste Wesen in dieser Kette der Bedingungen stehen, so würde es selbst ein Glied der Reihe derselben sein, und eben so wie die niederen Glieder, denen es vorgesetzt ist, noch fernere Untersuchungen wegen seines noch höheren Grundes erfahren." – *Kritik.* Ed. Hartenstein, p. 422.

passages of the *Dialogues*, he has dealt unfairly by the reader in concealing it: –

"But because I know you are not much swayed by names and authorities, I shall endeavour to show you, a little more distinctly, the inconveniences of that Anthropomorphism, which you have embraced; and shall prove, that there is no ground to suppose a plan of the world to be formed in the Divine mind, consisting of distinct ideas, differently arranged, in the same manner as an architect forms in his head the plan of a house which he intends to execute.

It is not easy, I own, to see what is gained by this supposition, whether we judge the matter by *Reason* or by *Experience*. We are still obliged to mount higher, in order to find the cause of this cause, which you had assigned as satisfactory and conclusive.

If *Reason* (I mean abstract reason, derived from inquiries *a priori*) be not alike mute with regard to all questions concerning cause and effect, this sentence at least it will venture to pronounce: That a mental world, or universe of ideas, requires a cause as much as does a material world, or universe of objects; and, if similar in its arrangement, must require a similar cause. For what is there in this subject, which should occasion a different conclusion or inference? In an abstract view, they are entirely alike; and no difficulty attends the one supposition, which is not common to both of them.

Again, when we will needs force *Experience* to pronounce some sentence, even on those subjects which lie beyond her sphere, neither can she perceive any material difference in this particular, between these two kinds of worlds; but finds them to be governed by similar principles, and to depend upon an equal variety of causes in their operations. We have specimens in miniature of both of them. Our own mind resembles the one; a vegetable or animal body the other. Let experience, therefore, judge from these samples. Nothing seems more delicate, with regard to its causes, than thought: and as these causes never operate in two persons after the same manner, so we never find two persons who think exactly alike. Nor indeed does the same person think exactly alike at any two different periods of time. A difference of age, of the disposition of his body, of weather, of food, of company, of books, of passions; any of these particulars, or others more minute, are sufficient to alter the curious machinery of thought, and communicate to it very different movements and operations. As far as we can judge, vegetables and animal bodies are not more delicate in their motions, nor depend upon a greater variety or more curious adjustment of springs and principles.

How, therefore, shall we satisfy ourselves concerning the cause of that Being whom you suppose the Author of Nature, or, according to your system of anthropomorphism, the ideal world in which you trace the material? Have we not the same reason to trace the ideal world into another ideal world, or new intelligent principle? But if we stop and go no farther; why go so far? Why not stop at the material world? How can we satisfy ourselves without going on *in infinitum*? And after all, what satisfaction is there in that infinite progression? Let us remember the story of the Indian philosopher and his elephant. It was never more applicable than to the present subject. If the material world rests upon a similar ideal world, this ideal world must rest upon some other; and so on without end. It were better, therefore, never to look beyond the present material world. By supposing it to contain the principle of its order within itself, we really assert it to be God; and the sooner we arrive at that Divine Being, so much the better. When you go one step beyond the mundane system you only excite an inquisitive humour, which it is impossible ever to satisfy.

To say, that the different ideas which compose the reason of the Supreme Being, fall into order of themselves and by their own natures, is really to talk without any precise meaning. If it has a meaning, I would fain know why it is not as good sense to say, that the parts of the material world fall into order of themselves, and by their own nature. Can the one opinion be intelligible while the other is not so?" – (II. pp. 461–4.)

Cleanthes, in replying to Philo's discourse, says that it is very easy to answer his arguments; but, as not unfrequently happens with controversialists, he mistakes a reply for an answer, when he declares that –

"The order and arrangement of nature, the curious adjustment of final causes, the plain use and intention of every part and organ; all these bespeak in the clearest language one intelligent cause or author. The heavens and the earth join in the same testimony. The whole chorus of nature raises one hymn to the praises of its Creator." – (II. p. 465).

Though the rhetoric of Cleanthes may be admired, its irrelevancy to the point at issue must be admitted. Wandering still further into the region of declamation, he works himself into a passion:

"You alone, or almost alone, disturb this general harmony. You start abstruse doubts, cavils, and objections: You ask me what is the cause of this cause? I know not: I care not: that concerns not me. I have found a Deity; and here I stop my inquiry. Let those go further who are wiser or more enterprising." – (II. p. 466.)

In other words, O Cleanthes, reasoning having taken you as far as you want to go, you decline to advance any further; even though you fully admit that the very same reasoning forbids you to stop where you are pleased to cry halt! But this is simply forcing your reason to abdicate in favour of your caprice. It is impossible to imagine that Hume, of all men in the world, could have rested satisfied with such an act of high-treason against the sovereignty of philosophy. We may rather conclude that the last word of the discussion, which he gives to Philo, is also his own.

"If I am still to remain in utter ignorance of causes, and can absolutely give an explication of nothing, I shall never esteem it any advantage to shove off for a moment a difficulty, which, you acknowledge, must immediately, in its full force, recur upon me. Naturalists[5] indeed very justly explain particular effects by more general causes, though these general causes should remain in the end totally inexplicable; but they never surely thought it satisfactory to explain a particular effect by a particular cause, which was no more to be accounted for than the effect itself. An ideal system, arranged of itself, without a precedent design, is not a whit more explicable than a material one, which attains its order in a like manner; nor is there any more

---

[5] *I.e.* Natural philosophers.

difficulty in the latter supposition than in the former." – (II. p. 466.)

It is obvious that, if Hume had been pushed, he must have admitted that his opinion concerning the existence of a God, and of a certain remote resemblance of his intellectual nature to that of man, was an hypothesis which might possess more or less probability, but was incapable on his own principles of any approach to demonstration. And to all attempts to make any practical use of his theism; or to prove the existence of the attributes of infinite wisdom, benevolence, justice, and the like, which are usually ascribed to the Deity, by reason, he opposes a searching critical negation.[6]

The object of the speech of the imaginary Epicurean in the eleventh section of the *Inquiry*, entitled *Of a Particular Providence and of a Future State*, is to invert the argument of Bishop Butler's *Analogy*.

That famous defence of theology against the *a priori* scepticism of Freethinkers of the eighteenth century, who based their arguments on the inconsistency of the revealed scheme of salvation with the attributes of the Deity, consists, essentially, in conclusively proving that, from a moral point of view, Nature is at least as reprehensible as orthodoxy. If you tell me, says Butler, in effect, that any part of revealed religion must be false because it is inconsistent with the divine attributes of justice and mercy; I beg leave to point out to you, that there are undeniable natural facts which are fully open to the same objection. Since you admit that nature is the work of God, you are forced to allow that such facts are consistent with his attributes. Therefore, you must also admit, that the parallel facts in the scheme of orthodoxy are also consistent with them, and all your arguments to the contrary fall to the ground. Q.E.D. In fact, the solid sense of Butler left the Deism of the Freethinkers not a leg to stand upon. Perhaps, however, he did not remember the wise saying that "A man seemeth right in his own cause, but another cometh after and judgeth him." Hume's Epicurean philosopher adopts the main arguments of the *Analogy*, but unfortunately drives them home to a conclusion of which the good Bishop would hardly have approved.

---

[6] Hume's letter to Mure of Caldwell, containing a criticism of Leechman's sermon (Burton, I. p. 163), bears strongly on this point.

"I deny a Providence, you say, and supreme governor of the world, who guides the course of events, and punishes the vicious with infamy and disappointment, and rewards the virtuous with honour and success in all their undertakings. But surely I deny not the course itself of events, which lies open to every one's inquiry and examination. I acknowledge that, in the present order of things, virtue is attended with more peace of mind than vice, and meets with a more favourable reception from the world. I am sensible that, according to the past experience of mankind, friendship is the chief joy of human life, and moderation the only source of tranquillity and happiness. I never balance between the virtuous and the vicious course of life; but am sensible that, to a well-disposed mind, every advantage is on the side of the former. And what can you say more, allowing all your suppositions and reasonings? You tell me, indeed, that this disposition of things proceeds from intelligence and design. But, whatever it proceeds from, the disposition itself, on which depends our happiness and misery, and consequently our conduct and department in life, is still the same. It is still open for me, as well as you, to regulate my behaviour by my experience of past events. And if you affirm that, while a divine providence is allowed, and a supreme distributive justice in the universe, I ought to expect some more particular reward of the good, and punishment of the bad, beyond the ordinary course of events, I here find the same fallacy which I have before endeavoured to detect. You persist in imagining, that if we grant that divine existence for which you so earnestly contend, you may safely infer consequences from it, and add something to the experienced order of nature, by arguing from the attributes which you ascribe to your gods. You seem not to remember that all your reasonings on this subject can only be drawn from effects to causes; and that every argument, deduced from causes to effects, must of necessity be a grows sophism, since it is impossible for you to know anything of the cause, but what you have antecedently not inferred, but discovered to the full, in the effect.

But what must a philosopher think of those vain reasoners who, instead of regarding the present scene of things as the sole object of their contemplation, so far reverse the whole course of nature, as to render this life merely a passage to something further; a porch, which leads to a greater and vastly different building; a prologue which serves only to introduce the piece, and give it more grace and propriety? Whence, do you think, can such philosophers derive their idea of the gods? From their own conceit and imagination surely. For if they derive it from the present phenomena, it would never point to anything further, but must be exactly adjusted to them. That the divinity may *possibly* be endowed with attributes which we have never seen exerted; may be governed by principles of action which we cannot discover to be satisfied; all this will freely be allowed. But still this is mere *possibility* and hypothesis. We never can have reason to *infer* any attributes or any principles of action in him, but so far as we know them to have been exerted and satisfied.

Are there any marks of a distributive justice in the world? If you answer in the affirmative, I conclude that, since justice here exerts itself, it is satisfied. If you reply in the negative, I conclude that you have then no reason to ascribe justice, in our sense of it, to the gods. If you hold a medium between affirmation and negation, by saying that the justice of the gods at present exerts itself in part, but not in its full extent, I answer that you have no reason to give it any particular extent, but only so far as you see it, *at present,* exert itself." (IV. pp. 164–6.)

Thus, the Freethinkers said, the attributes of the Deity being what they are, the scheme of orthodoxy is inconsistent with them; whereupon Butler gave the crushing reply: Agreeing with you as to the attributes of the Deity, nature, by its existence, proves that the things to which you object are quite consistent with them. To whom enters Hume's Epicurean with the remark: Then, as nature is our only measure of the attributes of the Deity in their practical manifestation, what warranty is there for supposing that such measure is anywhere transcended? That the "other side" of nature, if there be one, is governed on different principles from this side?

Truly on this topic silence is golden; while speech reaches not even the dignity of sounding brass or tinkling cymbal, and is but the weary clatter of an endless logomachy. One can but suspect that Hume also had reached this conviction;

and that his shadowy and inconsistent theism was the expression of his desire to rest in a state of mind, which distinctly excluded negation, while it included as little as possible of affirmation, respecting a problem which he felt to be hopelessly insoluble.

But, whatever might be the views of the philosopher as to the arguments for theism, the historian could have no doubt respecting its many-shaped existence, and the great part which it has played in the world. Here, then, was a body of natural facts to be investigated scientifically, and the result of Hume's inquiries is embodied in the remarkable essay on the *Natural History of Religion*. Hume anticipated the results of modern investigation in declaring fetishism and polytheism to be the form in which savage and ignorant men naturally clothe their ideas of the unknown influences which govern their destiny; and they are polytheists rather than monotheists because, –

" . . . the first ideas of religion arose, not from a contemplation of the works of nature, but from a concern with regard to the events of life, and from the incessant hopes and fears which actuate the human mind. . . . in order to carry men's attention beyond the present course of things, or lead them into any inference concerning invisible intelligent power, they must be actuated by some passion which prompts their thought and reflection, some motive which urges their first inquiry. But what passion shall we have recourse to, for explaining an effect of such mighty consequence? Not speculative curiosity merely, or the pure love of truth. That motive is too refined for such gross apprehensions, and would lead men into inquiries concerning the frame of nature, a subject too large and comprehensive for their narrow capacities. No passions, therefore, can be supposed to work on such barbarians, but the ordinary affections of human life; the anxious concern for happiness, the dread of future misery, the terror of death, the thirst of revenge, the appetite for food and other necessaries. Agitated by hopes and fears of this nature, especially the latter, men scrutinize, with a trembling curiosity, the course of future causes, and examine the various and contrary events of human life. And in this disordered scene, with eyes still more disordered and astonished, they see the first obscure traces of divinity." – (IV. pp. 443, 4.)

The shape assumed by these first traces of divinity is that of the shadows of men's own minds, projected out of themselves by their imaginations: –

"There is an universal tendency among mankind to conceive all beings like themselves, and to transfer to every object those qualities with which they are familiarly acquainted, and of which they are intimately conscious . . . . The *unknown causes* which continually employ their thought, appearing always in the same aspect, are all apprehended to be of the same kind or species. Nor is it long before we ascribe to them thought, and reason, and passion, and sometimes even the limbs and figures of men, in order to bring them nearer to a resemblance with ourselves." – (IV. pp. 446–7.)

Hume asks whether polytheism really deserves the name of theism.

"Our ancestors in Europe, before the revival of letters, believed as we do at present, that there was one supreme God, the author of nature, whose power, though in itself uncontrollable, was yet often exerted by the interposition of his angels and subordinate ministers, who executed his sacred purposes. But they also believed, that all nature was full of other invisible powers: fairies, goblins, elves, sprights; beings stronger and mightier than men, but much inferior to the celestial natures who surround the throne of God. Now, suppose that any one, in these ages, had denied the existence of God and of his angels, would not his impiety justly have deserved the appellation of atheism, even though he had still allowed, by some odd capricious reasoning, that the popular stories of elves and fairies were just and well grounded? The difference, on the one hand, between such a person and a genuine theist, is infinitely greater than that, on the other, between him and one that absolutely excludes all invisible intelligent power. And it is a fallacy, merely from the casual resemblance of names, without any conformity of meaning, to rank such opposite opinions under the same denomination.

To any one who considers justly of the matter, it will

appear that the gods of the polytheists are no better than the elves and fairies of our ancestors, and merit as little as any pious worship and veneration. These pretended religionists are really a kind of superstitious atheists, and acknowledge no being that corresponds to our idea of a Deity. No first principle of mind or thought; no supreme government and administration; no divine contrivance or intention in the fabric of the world." – (IV. pp. 450–51.)

The doctrine that you may call an atheist anybody whose ideas about the Deity do not correspond with your own, is so largely acted upon by persons who are certainly not of Hume's way of thinking and, probably, so far from having read him, would shudder to open any book bearing his name, except the *History of England*, that it is surprising to trace the theory of their practice to such a source.

But on thinking the matter over, this theory seems so consonant with reason, that one feels ashamed of having suspected many excellent persons of being moved by mere malice and viciousness of temper to call other folks atheists, when, after all, they have been obeying a purely intellectual sense of fitness. As Hume says, truly enough, it is a mere fallacy, because two people use the same names for things, the ideas of which are mutually exclusive, to rank such opposite opinions under the same denomination. If the Jew says, that the Deity is absolute unity, and that it is sheer blasphemy to say that He ever became incarnate in the person of a man; and, if the Trinitarian says, that the Deity is numerically three as well as numerically one, and that it is sheer blasphemy to say that He did not so become incarnate, it is obvious enough that each must be logically held to deny the existence of the other's Deity. Therefore; that each has a scientific right to call the other an atheist; and that, if he refrains, it is only on the ground of decency and good manners, which should restrain an honourable man from employing even scientifically justifiable language, if custom has given it an abusive connotation. While one must agree with Hume, then, it is, nevertheless, to be wished that he had not set the bad example of calling polytheists "superstitious atheists." It probably did not occur to him that, by a parity of reasoning, the Unitarians might justify the application of the same language to the Ultramontanes, and *vice versa*. But, to return from a digression which may not be wholly unprofitable, Hume proceeds to show in what manner polytheism incorporated physical and moral allegories, and naturally accepted hero-worship; and he sums up his views of the first stages of the evolution of theology as follows: –

"These then are the general principles of polytheism, founded in human nature, and little or nothing dependent on caprice or accident. As the *causes* which bestow happiness or misery, are in general very little known and very uncertain, our anxious concern endeavours to attain a determinate idea of them: and finds no better expedient than to represent them as intelligent, voluntary agents, like ourselves, only somewhat superior in power and wisdom. The limited influence of these agents, and their proximity to human weakness, introduce the various distribution and division of their authority, and thereby give rise to allegory. The same principles naturally deify mortals, superior in power, courage, or understanding, and produce hero-worship; together with fabulous history and mythological tradition, in all its wild and unaccountable forms. And as an invisible spiritual intelligence is an object too refined for vulgar apprehension, men naturally affix it to some sensible representation; such as either the more conspicuous parts of nature, or the statues, images, and pictures, which a more refined age forms of its divinities." – (IV. p. 461.)

How did the further stage of theology, monotheism, arise out of polytheism? Hume replies, certainly not by reasonings from first causes or any sort of fine-drawn logic: –

"Even at this day, and in Europe, ask any of the vulgar why be believes in an Omnipotent Creator of the world, he will never mention the beauty of final causes, of which he is wholly ignorant: He will not hold out his hand and bid you contemplate the suppleness and variety of joints in his fingers, their bending all one way, the counterpoise which they receive from the thumb, the softness and fleshy parts of the inside of the hand, with all the other circumstances which render that member fit for the use to which it was destined. To these he has been long accustomed; and he beholds them with listlessness and unconcern. He will tell you of the sudden and unexpected death of such-a-one; the fall and bruise of such another; the excessive drought of this season; the cold and rains of another. These he ascribes to the immediate operation of Providence: And such events as, with good reasoners, are the chief difficulties in admitting a Supreme Intelligence, are with him the sole arguments for it. . . .

We may conclude therefore, upon the whole, that since the vulgar, in nations which have embraced the doctrine of theism, still build it upon irrational and superstitious grounds, they are never led into that opinion by any process of argument, but by a certain train of thinking, more suitable to their genius and capacity.

It may readily happen, in an idolatrous nation, that though men admit the existence of several limited deities, yet there is some one God, whom, in a particular manner, they make the object of their worship and adoration. They may either suppose, that, in the distribution of power and territory among the Gods, their nation was subjected to the jurisdiction of that particular deity; or, reducing heavenly objects to the model of things below, they may represent one god as the prince or supreme magistrate of the rest, who, though of the same nature, rules them with an authority like that which an earthly sovereign exerts over his subjects and vassals. Whether this god, therefore, be considered as their peculiar patron, or as the general sovereign of heaven, his votaries will endeavour, by every art, to insinuate themselves into his favour; and supposing him to be pleased, like themselves, with praise and flattery, there is no eulogy or exaggeration which will be spared in their addresses to him. In proportion as men's fears or distresses become more urgent, they still invent new strains of adulation; and even he who outdoes his predecessor in swelling the titles of his divinity, is sure to be outdone by his successor in newer and more pompous epithets of praise. Thus they proceed, till at last they arrive at infinity itself, beyond which there is no further progress; And it is well if, in striving to get further, and to represent a magnificent simplicity, they run not into inexplicable mystery, and destroy the intelligent nature of their deity, on which alone any rational worship or adoration can be founded. While they confine themselves to the notion of a perfect being, the Creator of the world, they coincide, by chance, with the principles of reason and true philosophy; though they are guided to that notion, not by reason, of which they are in a great measure incapable, but by the adulation and fears of the most vulgar superstition. (IV. pp. 463–6.)

Nay, if we should suppose, what never happens, that a popular religion were found, in which it was expressly declared, that nothing but morality could gain the divine favour; if an order of priests were instituted to inculcate this opinion, in daily sermons, and with all the arts of persuasion; yet so inveterate are the people's prejudices, that, for want of some other superstition, they would make the very attendance on these sermons the essentials of religion, rather than place them in virtue and good morals. The sublime prologue of Zaleucus' laws inspired not the Locrians, so far as we can learn, with any sounder notions of the measures of acceptance with the deity, than were familiar to the other Greeks." – (IV. p. 505.)

It has been remarked that Hume's writings are singularly devoid of local colour; of allusions to the scenes with which he was familiar, and to the people from whom he sprang. Yet, surely, the Lowlands of Scotland were more in his thoughts than the Zephyrean promontory, and the hard visage of John Knox peered from behind the mask of Zaleucus, when this passage left his pen. Nay, might not an acute German critic discern therein a reminiscence of that eminently Scottish institution, a "Holy Fair"? where as Hume's young contemporary sings: –

"... opens out his cauld harangues
On practice and on morals;
An' aff the godly pour in thrangs
To gie the jars and barrels
A lift that day.

What signifies his barren shine
    Of moral powers and reason?"

INTRODUCTION TO DIALOGUES
CONCERNING NATURAL RELIGION
Bruce McEwen

In professing to call attention to this often forgotten work of
the great Scottish philosopher, one cannot help noticing how
very similar the reception accorded to it by the outside world
has been to its treatment at the hands of the author himself.
During his lifetime he kept it in the safe obscurity of his study
drawer, where it lay until the day of his death. The plan of
the Dialogues had been clearly thought out by Hume as
early as 1750, and the active period of his contribution to
philosophy proper having closed almost in the same year, this
excursion of his into natural theology might most fitly have
been presented to his readers at once, especially if, as it seems
to us now, it may be rightly regarded as the crown and
consummation of his earlier speculations. Indeed some such
conception of the relation of the Dialogues to his other works
underlies the outlining of his scheme upon its first page,
where he founds his method "on the saying of an ancient
[Chrysippus], That students of philosophy ought first to learn
Logics, then Ethics, next Physics, last of all the nature of the
Gods."

From that year onwards, however, his literary activity was
directed into other and less speculative channels, and though
the book undoubtedly existed in manuscript, and was from
time to time submitted to his philosophical friends for their
opinion, it was as good as lost for the estimating of his whole
position by his contemporaries. In the inner circle of savants,
who were vaguely aware of its existence, considerable fear
prevailed as to what approaching cataclysm the appearance
of the "terrible David" upon the theological horizon might
portend; and as year after year passed safely by, their distrust
of the threatened publication of his meaning only increased
the more. When a book has such a history behind it, there
is naturally every reason to expect that its contents may

have been varied considerably by corrections, omissions, and insertions from the author's own hand. But provided always that the manuscript copy (now preserved in the library of the Royal Society of Edinburgh) from which it was first published in 1779, was the original draft, there can have been only the most trivial amendments, and the main lines of the argument were left untouched. Mr. Hill Burton's verdict[1] on this point is that, "while the sentiments appear to be substantially the same as when they were first set down, the alterations in the method of announcing them are a register of the improvements in their author's style for a period apparently of twenty-seven years." From what I have seen of the manuscript I should say, first, that the alterations upon the face of it are largely verbal; and secondly, that this particular copy is of later date than that which Hume invited his friend, Sir Gilbert Elliott, to criticise in 1751.

The question whether the whole work was ever substantially recast in the years during which Hume kept it by him cannot be definitely answered here. If, however, in at least one letter, the author asks for assistance and advice in the endeavour to render the argument on one side or the other "quite formal and regular," the possibility of a more or less thorough redaction having taken place must not be overlooked.[2] So much is certain, that by retaining the book unpublished he had opportunity of bringing it to a higher pitch of perfection, and that, accordingly, its sentiments may safely be regarded as the mature expression of his religious and theological opinions in strict accordance with his empirical philosophy.

The motive that prevailed with him to hinder publication seems to have been a strong sense of the incompleteness of his arguments, and, more particularly, the feeling often voiced by him that he had not done justice to that "genuine Theism, the most agreeable reflection which it is possible for human imagination to suggest." He speaks of the "natural propensity of the mind" towards the theistic argument from design in terms as warm as those of Kant, who called it the "oldest, the clearest argument, and most in conformity with the common reason of humanity." He had played the sceptic too long in

---

[1] Life of Hume, i. 328.

[2] Dugald Stewart's Works, i. 603.

the public eye to care very much for the popular verdict, or to share his friends' fear that he might incur increasing odium and obloquy. He knew that any orthodox conclusions he could offer in this theological essay of his would appear to zealous defenders of the faith only as Greek gifts; any that might seem in the light of current opinions to be unorthodox could make him no new enemies. His abstract speculations on the logical methods of reason had ended in his advocating "a *mitigated* scepticism," or, as it is also designated, "an academical philosophy,"[3] and when himself was forced to become the pioneer cultivator of the broad field of human knowledge with the untried implement which he had long chosen for his own, the promise of a harvest of positive results seems to have been difficult of realisation. Whether Hume feared that the Dialogues would offend his readers need not be discussed when we know, beyond doubt, that they disappointed his own expectations. Many an *opus magnum* has been utterly lost to the history of literature from considerations exactly similar to those which weighed heavily upon Hume.

So much is conjecture, but whatever the reason may have been, publication was delayed until death overtook the author in 1776. In his will it was found that careful directions were given, first to Adam Smith, Professor of Moral Philosophy in Glasgow, and afterwards by a codicil to William Strahan, Publisher in London, to secure the bringing of the book to the light – a sum of £200 being set aside for the necessary expenses. Both these gentlemen were so much averse to accepting the charge, that finally Hume's nephew, as residuary legatee, took it in hand. "His testamentary injunction directing their publication was declined by Adam Smith. But it was too peremptory not to be obeyed by a kinsman whom he had in some measure adopted."[4] And so in 1779 these long matured Dialogues at last became part of the common inheritance of philosophers.

It is not necessary in this present Introduction to give either particular or general details of Hume's life and philosophy; enough has been said to show how precarious a chance of existence this posthumous literary child of his had, and how

[3] Enquiry, XII., iii.

[4] Edinburgh Review, lxxxv. 4.

tedious the labour was that gave it birth. And the place it was to take in the history of philosophy subsequent to 1779 was entirely in accordance with its past.

The first edition, appearing early in that year from the press of Robinson in London, was rapidly followed by another reprint, with corrections. In 1788 the book was appended to a new edition of Hume's collected Essays printed for Cadell and Elliot, and thereafter it has been frequently republished along with these or other parts of his writings. As a separate work it has appeared once in England, in 1875, when it was used as one of a series of brochures issued privately in London by a Mr. T. Scott in the interests of a Society of Free-thinkers. It is not too much to say that, with the exception of this reprint, unworthy in itself, and by reason of the strongly biassed remarks which introduce it "to the reading public," it has been completely ignored by those who have undertaken to supply English libraries of the past century with ready means of access to Hume's far-reaching speculations. In the standard edition of Hume's Works by Green and Grose the only analytic notice of the Dialogues is contained in one singularly unsatisfactory sentence:[5] "Although perhaps the most finished of its author's productions, it has not excited general attention. There seems to be a deep-seated reluctance to discuss such fundamental questions." This curt dismissal of the Dialogues constitutes a verdict upon students of Hume rather than upon their master, but as a verdict it has ample justification in history. In England it has been generally felt that there is pressing need of an "answer to Hume" in this particular connection, but the temper of the early nineteenth century inclined to be impatient of such a thorough investigation of the deepest principles of natural theology as was necessary after the sifting criticism to which they had been subjected by the great Scottish sceptic. The watch-dogs of the orthodox temple often bark at friends as well as foes; and to express sympathy with the sentiments of Hume, even those admittedly unanswerable, was to incur popular suspicion such as always clings to the name of inquiry. In works professing to be animated with the genuine positive spirit, the easy, well-worn way of dealing with Hume's theology has been to rank his speculations as a side issue, to dub them

[5] Vol. iii. p. 80 (1898).

"Absolute Agnosticism" or "Universal Scepticism," and the reader, having been safely conducted up to the end of this philosophical cul-de-sac, is invited to retrace his steps and pursue his light-hearted journey by some other route.

The attack upon the Dialogues we shall have to consider later, but the curious reader may observe here of the timorous method of grappling with Hume's problems, that it prevails as much with his friends as his foes. Thus in 1818 a series of "Dialogues on Natural and Revealed Religion," with the avowed object of defending, supplementing, and enlarging the conclusions of Hume on principles similar to his, was advertised to appear in "Blackwood's Magazine"[6] for the month of April. These Dialogues are represented as being conducted by the same Cleanthes, Philo, and Demea who figure in Hume's work. The anonymous author is described (falsely) as one "who died in youth, not without high distinction among his contemporaries." His papers have come into the editor's hands, and it is promised that their publication "shall be continued regularly through twelve numbers of the Magazine." Only two parts had appeared, when, on account of the uneasiness they caused, the editor saw fit to retract his promise, and, without one word of explanation or apology to his readers, their place in the next issue of the periodical was filled up with other matter. Twelve years later the subterfuge of anonymity was cast aside, and the Rev. Dr. Robert Morehead[7] published these supplementary dialogues complete in book form, with his own name on the title-page.

When Hume's Dialogues appeared in 1779 his philosophy

---

[6] Blackwood, 1818: April and May.

[7] "Dialogues on Natural and Revealed Religion," by Robert Morehead, D. D., Edin., 1830. (In twelve parts: Nos. I. and II. almost literally from "Blackwood," April and May 1818.) This book deserves notice as a good commentary upon Hume's Dialogues, the only attempt of the kind known to the present writer. The scope of the argument from design is greatly extended. To the data allowed by Hume there are added as evidencing design "the laws of the procedure of the knowing mind as well as the laws visible in creation," "the formation of general notions and associations," and even the bare facts of what Dr. Morehead calls "external perception." While with Hume there is evidence for the "natural attributes" of God and little or none for the moral, the Philo and Cleanthes of this later book are made to agree "to lay the foundations of the argument for the moral attributes of the Divine Nature in the moral perceptions of the human mind." A few years later further Dialogues appeared from the same pen, but their tone is entirely apologetic and not at all convincing.

had already found many admirers in Germany and interrupted other slumbers than those of Kant. To quite a large circle of thinkers there this posthumous book was an unexpected but most welcome revelation. One in particular, Professor Ernst Platner, afterwards best known for his pungent criticisms of the Kantian doctrines, undertook a translation into the German language immediately, and published it with the explanation that it had been forwarded to him anonymously in 1781. The air of mystery so unfortunately associated with this book was increased by his following it in 1783 with a Discourse on Atheism,[8] which is intended to mitigate the consequences of his translation. In the meantime another translation of importance in the history of philosophy had been prepared by J. A. Hamann. From his correspondence with his publisher we learn that it[9] was begun on 21st July 1780 and finished on 8th August.

About this time, too, he heard of the other intended translation, and the news caused him to delay. Before September, however, of 1780, the manuscript of this translation had been submitted to Kant, who was greatly struck with it and urged the sending of it to press at once.[10] As time went on he wrote deploring its non-appearance, but now Hamann had taken fright at the prospect of his name being connected with such an infidel book, and after suggesting one or two fanciful descriptions of himself for the title-page, he finally intimated to Kant his withdrawal, because he felt another was undertaking "the difficult, dangerous, and unpopular task." Only a few days after the passing of this correspondence Kant began the composition of his "Critique of Pure Reason," and through the history of this suppressed manuscript, taken in conjunction with Kant's express references to the Dialogues in the Prolegomena,[11] the historical connection between Hume's "Sceptical Theology" and the famous criticism of "Rational Theology" in the Transcendental Dialectic of the great Critique is thoroughly well established. In this latter

---

[8] Gespräch über den Atheismus, E. Platner, 1783. The preface runs: The occasion of this Dialogue is the publication of Hume's Dialogues: its intention, to provide a reply and perhaps to reply to atheism generally.

[9] Hamann's Schriften, edited by Roth, 1821–43, vi. 158.

[10] Hamann, vi. 190.

[11] Prolegomena, §§ 57, 58, 59, *et passim*.

we shall see how a great many of Hume's positions are restated and his conclusions accepted according to Kant's understanding of them, – only, however, to be circumvented in the peculiar fashion of his new philosophy. And although Kant's reconstruction of theology be considered ever so unsatisfactory, it is because of the thorough way in which he and Hume before him had cleared the ground and showed men the "real point at issue"[12] that the philosophy of either became the starting-point for theistic speculation in the subsequent century and a half. Therefore, just as it is possible in Germany for a cry to be raised from time to time of a "return to Kant," so in Scotland there is always opportunity for a return to Hume.[13] The result in the two cases will always be widely different, for this reason, that the Copernican revolution in thought, initiated by Kant, makes it possible to break entirely with the past. It opened up the way to a brilliant series of speculative deductions in metaphysics and theology which all proceed alike upon one and the same method – namely, a mapping out of the different spheres of consciousness, moral or theoretical, cognitive or religious, as the case may be.

With the "Critique of Pure Reason" an epoch begins for philosophy, in which every such investigation into the problems of natural theology as is contained in the Dialogues is at once pronounced to be incapable of producing any fruit, and the whole argument appears as a beating of the empty air of illusion. But however closely every positive result for theology may be whittled down before the edge of Hume's scepticism, he still stops short of Kant's Transcendentalism just in refusing to make that distinction in our cognitive faculties which places theology on a different plane from all other knowledge, and enables Kant to dismiss the question in its older form on the ground of its being misconceived and insoluble, even while in the same moment he addresses himself to its solution under his own restatement. Hume is concerned merely to sift the results of natural theology on his own principles, and not to enter upon what Kant, in

---

[12] Kant and Hume compared in this respect. Flint's Theism, p. 389.

[13] The question in Germany is, Was uns Kant sein kann? The popular question in English refers to the past rather than the present, What has Hume been?

contrasting his own treatment of the theological Idea with the Dialogues, calls "a careful critique guarding the bounds of our reason with respect to its empirical use and setting limits to its pretensions." To be sure, Hume's work limits the results of such use strictly enough; but Kant limits the use itself by denying it in theology altogether.

It is true that one of the interlocutors in the Dialogues contends directly for the inadequacy of human reason to the apprehension of God's Being.[14] But this, the extreme position, is attributed it seems designedly to the weakest of the three disputants, and it would be hermeneutically impossible to read the whole book as if it led up to an absolute negation in this form. For although, with the exception of the argument in the Dialogues, Hume does almost nothing to illustrate at length his already expressed idea of that system of "Divinity or Theology" which he would save from the flames when running over the libraries of the past, he prescribes the conditions of such a system in words which are perfectly definite, and which there is no good reason to regard otherwise than as sincere.[15] "It has a foundation in *reason* so far as it is supported by experience; but its best and most solid foundation is *faith* and divine revelation." It is only in strict accordance with the first of these conditions that in this later work of his we expect to find an honest endeavour to determine how great or how small is the residuum of theological truth to which Hume will admit that the natural reason working within the sphere of experience can attain. The second, again shadowed forth in its closing lines, remains altogether unfulfilled, and indeed the appeal to faith and revelation, which he more than once voices in passages where scepticism seems to hold undisputed sway over his formal reasonings on theological subjects, must only be taken to express just such "a natural sentiment" or "propensity" of feeling as may always maintain its place in the clearest mind along with an utterly opposed conviction of the understanding. The inconsistency from a logical point of view may be

---

[14] Demea: "The nature of God, I affirm, from the infirmities of human understanding, to be altogether incomprehensible and unknown to us;" "The infirmities of our nature do not permit us to reach any ideas which in the least correspond to the ineffable sublimity of the divine attributes."

[15] Enquiry, iv. 135.

admitted by others; it may be explicitly present with the author in person as it probably was with Hume.[16] But if that be so, it can hardly be set down as a futile concession to popular orthodoxy, least of all in the Dialogues, and it remains a fact to be reckoned with seriously in any comprehensive estimate of Hume's opinions. Still, in the book itself the action of the dialogue proper stands altogether apart from this short, ill-defined, and perhaps misleading reference to faith and a "revelation" of some sort beyond; it is a plain, painstaking attempt on Hume's part to discover what reasoned foundation, if any, he could allow for religion.

The literary form into which the argument is cast – that of dialogue – though once a favourite method of conveying philosophical instruction, has not always been imitated successfully in later times. Two reasons are stated by Hume for its adoption in the treatment of his subject: first, that the conversational method sheds a variety of lights upon a truth "so obvious," "so certain," and "so important" as that of "the Being of a God"; second, that it allows the utmost play to opposing sentiments in dealing with questions so obscure, doubtful, and uncertain as those of His nature and attributes. Both reasons can easily be illustrated and paralleled from numerous passages in Hume's writings. In the Dialogues all parties to the argument agree in holding that of the existence of God there is no question whatever. Even the sceptical Philo, following Lord Bacon, compares the atheists of his time unfavourably with David's fool, who said in his heart, "There is no God," for they are not contented to say it in their hearts, but they also utter that impiety with their lips, and are thereby guilty of multiplied indiscretion and imprudence. "Such people, though they were ever so much in earnest, cannot methinks be very formidable."[17] After the same fashion the friend "who loves sceptical paradoxes," and takes the burden of maintaining the antitheistic argument in Hume's Enquiry, says,[18] "The chief or sole argument for a divine existence (which I never questioned) is derived from

---

[16] Enquiry, iv. 154, on Faith as a miracle "which subverts all the principles of a man's understanding and gives him a determination to believe what is most contrary to custom and experience."

[17] Dialogues, Part II.

[18] Works, iv. 112.

the order of nature." In a private letter as early as 1744 he had defined his conception of religion as being,[19] "The practice of morality and the assent of the understanding to the proposition that God exists." That may be culpably scanty as a definition, but in all his writings, without exception, this one proposition is always adhered to and often affirmed to be, in Hume's view, a possibly sufficient foundation for religion. For example, in a comparison of historical religions he says, "The only point of theology in which we shall find a consent of mankind almost universal, is that there is invisible intelligent power in the world."[20] This last quotation rounds off the other references by introducing a new point of view; but many other parallel passages drawn from Hume's writings might be used to show how firmly rooted is his purpose of making no question of the Being of a God.   The theory of existence which underlies them all was first propounded in the "Treatise of Human Nature": "'Tis evident that all reasonings from causes or effects terminate in conclusions concerning matter of fact: that is, concerning the existence of objects or of their qualities. 'Tis also evident that the idea of existence is nothing different from the idea of any object, and that when after the simple conception of anything we would conceive it as existent, we in reality make no addition to or alteration on our first idea. Thus, when we affirm that God is existent we simply form the idea of such a being as He is represented to us . . . . When I think of God, when I think of Him as existent, and when I believe Him to be existent, my idea of Him neither increases nor diminishes."[21] In thus distinguishing all other attributes from the one attribute of existence on the ground that the latter is no new or

[19] Burton's Life, i. 162.

[20] Natural History of Religion, sect. 4; cf. also sect. 15, "The universal propensity to believe in invisible intelligent power."

[21] Works, i. 394, 395. The word God occurs twice in the text of the whole Treatise, – in the two sentences given above, – and once in a note. The phrases Deity, Divine Being, and Supreme Being are used only in discussing the Cartesian certainty of perception, and Spinoza's Pantheism. A great deal of comment on the Treatise can be cast away at once by remembering this fact – *e.g.*, Green's Introduction, 339, beginning "From the point that our enquiry has reached we can anticipate the line which Hume could not but take in regard to self and God." The truth is, a discussion of the theology of the Treatise would be quite conjectural and always has been such.

distinct idea in the object, Hume may be understood to minimise the theoretical importance of every proposition concerning existence.   When therefore the distinction is applied
specially to the Being and attributes of God, it undoubtedly
lessens the positive significance of the assurance so often
reaffirmed in his latest work that at least there *is* a God.   But
whatever explanation Hume might have at hand to place
upon these simple words, his first reason for using the form
of Dialogue is amply justified within his own philosophy.

While then our author postulates in this way the validity
of a belief in God's existence, he finds that questions of
His attributes and His plan of providence in the world lend
themselves most easily to argument and discussion.   "These,"
he says, "have been always subjected to the disputations of
men." This historical reflection forms the second reason for
his composing the Dialogues.   Its sting lies in the truth of it.
It came in the middle of a century fruitful in "proofs" of the
Divine attributes, from the pen of one who had made a
careful comparison of the religious tenets of men in ancient,
in classical, and in modern times.   The conclusion of his
"Natural History of Religion" shows how Hume grasped the
fact of a widespread divergence of opinion, so that it is
possible, by "opposing one species of superstition to another,
to set them a-quarrelling: while we ourselves, during their
fury and contention, happily make our escape into the calm
though obscure regions of philosophy." Perhaps there is a
strain of malicious mockery in these words, but they point
to the possibility of such contrary views as had come under
Hume's notice being set forth just as they are in the Dialogues
with himself to pronounce a judicial verdict upon the merits
of each.

These then are the fundamental presuppositions of the
whole book: first, the certainty of God's existence; and secondly, the right of philosophy to discuss questions of His
attributes.[22]   The two are perfectly consistent with his attitude
to both points in his other works, and at the same time they
are in themselves complementary to each other.   In a note
added in the Appendix to the "Treatise of Human Nature"

---

[22] Cf. the two presuppositions of Butler's Analogy: "Taking for proved that
there is an intelligent Author of Nature and natural Governor of the
world;" "My design is to apply analogy to the subject of religion both
natural and revealed." – Introduction.

both principles may be clearly traced, already present with the author and enabling him, after a fashion peculiarly satisfactory to himself, to claim to be a believer even in his most agnostic attitude towards God's attributes, "The order of the universe proves an omnipotent mind. Nothing more is requisite to give a foundation to all the articles of religion, nor is it necessary we should form a distinct idea of the force and energy of the Supreme Being."[23]

For the task of advancing from these presuppositions to the systematic criticism of natural theology, Hume introduces to his reader no fewer than three imaginary friends – Philo, Cleanthes, and Demea – whose conversation upon the theme of natural religion he records. Whatever classical reference there may originally have been in the names is entirely lost in the essentially modern drama in which they play their part.[24] In form, also, the Dialogues have diverged widely from any classical model. Though an echo of Cicero's "De Natura Deorum" is occasionally heard in Hume's language,[25] and the subjects are really akin, Hume's plan of having each of the disputants to unfold at length a tenable and complete system precludes the use of that characteristic device by which the Greek and Latin dialecticians punctuate the arguments of their leading figures with the assents and simple questions of a learner, whose experience of being led on irresistibly from point to point by the master-mind is supposed to represent the reader's own. In Hume's book Cleanthes, Philo, and Demea do not yield to one another indiscriminately on the essential points of the argument. When they agree in their views they say so, when they differ they expound their differences, but

---

[23] Works, i. 456. Green and Grose.

[24] Thus Cleanthes has nothing in common with Zeno's pupil of that name, who presided over the Stoic School in the third century, BC. Almost the only allusion to the nomenclature of the Dialogues occurs in a playful passage of Hamann's "Golgotha" (1784), where he speaks of "Philo the Pharisee" having conspired with "Cleanthes the Hypocrite, to deny all possibility of understanding God's nature. They looked for a new Paraclete, the "adventitious instructor," to dispel their ignorance by Revelation."

[25] Cicero sums up thus: "Velleius held Cotta's arguments to be the truest; to me those of Balbus seemed more probable." And Hume's closing sentence is similar: "I confess that upon a serious review of the whole, I cannot but think that Philo's principles are more probable than Demea's, but that those of Cleanthes approach still nearer to the truth."

none of them succeeds altogether in convincing either of the others; and therefore at the close of the Dialogues the reader is left with an uneasy feeling that none of the great questions raised have really received an answer. When many diverse views are propounded, each so powerfully and all with so little agreement, it is difficult to say precisely which is meant to carry conviction. In consequence of this fact, many critics of the Dialogues have not hesitated to ascribe to its author only some mischievous purpose of casting all fixed religious opinions into inextricable confusion, and avoiding every expression of his own. Thus Professor Huxley, whose weakness for fathering his own agnosticism upon the great Scottish philosopher is predominant in his analysis of the Dialogues, says,[26] "One can but suspect that Hume's shadowy and inconsistent theism was the expression of his desire to rest in a state of mind which distinctly excluded negation, while it included as little as possible of affirmation respecting a problem which he felt to be hopelessly insoluble."

There can be no doubt that the Dialogues contain materials for constructing three perfectly distinct schemes of reflection on the Nature of God, each more or less exclusive of the others; and inasmuch as it is, humanly speaking, impossible for them all to spring from one brain without their having thoughts and ideas in common, it is easy to see that "the author had a certain amount of sympathy with all the characters, and that each of them alternately mirrored his own ever-changing mood." Parts, too, of his general doctrines are worked in at length into the utterances of all three, as was indeed unavoidable. Hume himself, however, helps the inquisitive reader somewhat farther than this. He invites him at the outset to contrast "the accurate philosophical turn of Cleanthes" with "the careless scepticism of Philo," and both of these "with the rigid inflexible orthodoxy of Demea." At the close in the passage already quoted (note, p. xxx) he puts into the mouth of Pamphilus, who reports the whole conversation, an explanatory statement that he agrees with Cleanthes rather than Philo, and with Demea least of all. Still it is only by following the argument from point to point, and noting just how much is distinctly admitted on each side,

[26] Hume, p. 157.

that the question of interpretation can ever be satisfactorily solved.

From the very first it has been the usual view of critics to identify the author's theological position with Philo's scepticism, and perhaps only with the most virulently sceptical parts of it. The notice of the book in the "Gentleman's Magazine" of October 1779, after mentioning the names of the characters, runs: "We need not say on which side this sceptical metaphysician inclines the balance, but must observe that the weapons with which Philo attacks the moral attributes of the Deity are the same with those which were employed by Lord Bolingbroke, and were most ably parried by Bishop Warburton." The polemical Priestley, in Letter IX. of his "Letters to a Philosophical Unbeliever," published in 1780, quotes "Philo who evidently speaks the sentiment of the writer." Kant, in his Prolegomena of 1784, regards Hume as speaking "in the person of Philo against Cleanthes," and holds that view throughout. And a passage[27] from a once popular book may be quoted at length to show as early as 1781 how strongly preconceived ideas of Hume's agnosticism had influenced current verdicts on the Dialogues. "In his dialogues concerning natural religion we have the substance of all his sceptical essays, and notwithstanding his declaration at the close in favour of Cleanthes, the natural religionist, it is evident from the whole tenor of the book, and still more so from the entire scepticism of his former publications, that Philo is his favourite. Sincerity constitutes no part of a philosopher's virtue." This is in that same vein of rejecting Hume's own evidence which prevails generally in criticisms of the self-revealed declarations of his position that abound in his writings and letters. Mr. Balfour, in his "Foundations of Belief," considers him an absolute sceptic, and when confronted with utterances that point the other way, he summarises in one sentence the difficulty a whole century of philosophers have experienced in trying to believe him, – "I think too well of Hume's speculative genius and too ill of his speculative sincerity." The meaning read into the Dialogues by an exclusive identification of Hume with Philo has maintained its place in the history of philosophy, and may safely be said to be the only one that finds acceptance to-day. Once

[27] Milner, Answer to Gibbon and Hume (1781).

or twice a voice has been raised to protest against it. Dugald Stewart aptly remarks that "the reasonings of Philo have often been quoted as parts of Hume's philosophical system, although the words of Shylock or Caliban might with equal justice be quoted as speaking the real sentiments of Shakespeare."[28] Professor Campbell Fraser also finds in the Dialogues a groping after a final theistic faith such as he himself advocates.[29] But these partial acknowledgments of the unfairness of prejudging the effect of Hume's latest and most mature philosophical work stand in almost complete isolation from all other references to him and his speculations: they may serve here as a preliminary warning to the reader that, along with much matter easily recognised to be a recapitulation of the author's earlier opinions, he may find in the Dialogues considerable modifications in their restatement.

The three characters introduced in the Dialogues can be easily defined and classified without identifying any of them with any particular philosophical system known in history. Demea belongs to the class of orthodox theologians who distrust or discredit all attempts to rationalise the existence of God. He praises piety and disparages philosophy. He can cite all the divines, almost, from the foundation of Christianity to support the adorably mysterious and incomprehensible nature of the Supreme Being. Human minds are finite, weak, and blind, and therefore with regard to reason he is a Sceptic holding fast always to a peculiar religious Sense which alone gives us Truth. With Malebranche he calls God a spirit, not so much in order to express positively what he is, as in order to signify that he is not Matter. Language which has a plain reference to the state and situation of man ceases to have its earthy meaning when applied to the Deity, and therefore in religion he is a Mystic. He accepts the ontological proof of an infinite Deity in the form which proceeds by analysing the idea of necessary existence, and he accepts also the cosmological proof in that attenuated form which Kant rightly reduced to the same elements as the other. In his presentation of both there is no specification of the world that actually exists: the premises of his arguments are the abstract ideas of existence in general, which lead the mind

---

[28] Dissertation note, CCC

[29] Theism, pp. 7–10, 115 ff.

back irresistibly, in Demea's logic, to first ideas as blank and colourless as themselves. For on his view the present actual order of things could not possibly serve as premise for any reasonable argument. It is nothing but vanity, imbecility, and misery; it exists only to be rectified under other dispensations and in some future period of existence, and so with regard to it he is a Pessimist.

This character is perhaps the most perfectly delineated of all three; nevertheless, it is not the favourite by any means with the author, and indeed it serves "mainly as a foil to the other two disputants."[30] Hume chooses to regard Demea as a type of the popular philosophiser of his own day, and the pictures drawn of him in that *rôle* may safely be taken to be historically accurate. With consummate literary skill Hume lays special emphasis upon point after point of his self-complacent orthodoxy, in which he is implicitly a complete agnostic.

Cleanthes is a rationalist in the sense that he has confidence in the natural operations of reason, and believes in its capacity of attaining truth, provided it confines itself to the sphere of ordinary experience and the interpretation of that experience. When he is confronted, as he inevitably is in Hume's plan of the drama, with the sceptical theory that all human knowledge is nescience, that "our senses are fallacious," "our understanding erroneous," "our ideas full of absurdities and contradictions," he reverts to the commonsense point of view that its refutation must be sought by an appeal to the procedure of ordinary life and practice. For such speculative reasoning undermines all positive scientific truths alike. It is sceptical of every received maxim whatever. Therefore Cleanthes brushes it aside in the present task of examining the grounds of a natural theology. For him any system is better than no system at all. At every stage of knowledge belief must be proportioned to the precise degree of evidence available, and "natural propensity" will always incline his assent towards an affirmation when there are some reasonable grounds for making it, rather than towards a suspense of judgment recommended only by an abstract and general distrust in reason. Having thus grasped the nettle firmly, he turns away from these preliminary questions with an obvious

---

[30] Orr, *Hume's Influence on Theology and Philosophy*, p. 201.

measure of confidence to consider the outside world. In its workmanship he finds evidence of design clear and distinct, not dependent upon or needing demonstration, because it is as immediately given as the most vivid impression of the senses. He considers it proof of the existence of a designing mind, which is a sufficient object to satisfy his religious wants. He has found a Deity, and therefore he claims to be a theist.[31] His natural desire is to predicate infinite benevolence and love of his God, and to this end, when he surveys the present order of things, he would fain close his eyes and deny absolutely the misery and wickedness of man. By choice, therefore, he would, if possible, be a thorough-going optimist, but the facts are too hard for him, and in the end he modifies his conception of God's goodness in creation, and falls back upon the pious hope that in other scenes the ills of the present may be rectified, and the full fruition of human happiness and good may be attained. Throughout the book the speeches of Cleanthes are touched by a genuine emotion and enthusiasm for his cause, which apparently reflect the feelings with which Hume himself professes to regard him.

For constructing the character of Philo, Hume, in the first place, has recourse to all the more sceptical elements which characterise his analysis of the human mind in his earlier works. To him the natural reason is an object of distrust: it furnishes invincible arguments against itself and all its own conclusions. It has especial difficulties in theology, because arguments there run wide of common life, get beyond the reach of our faculties, and strive after conclusions which, unlike those of political economy, ethics, and "criticism" – the topics of Hume's later life, be it noted – cannot be verified and tested by the senses and experience. A natural theology, therefore, is impossible. Moreover, it is meaningless. For it claims to make intelligible in the divine mind an ordering power which, as far as our knowledge of human reason goes, is not known to be inherent in reason itself, but may be derived from external principles of orderly arrangement. Other natural powers too, that are altogether irrational are observed daily to issue in order, so that it smacks of partiality to ascribe the origin and maintenance of the universe to any one of them rather than to the others. To Philo it appears at

---

[31] Cleanthes' Theism is really a form of Deism.

times that the order in Nature is much more easily explicable by natural powers than the design in reason by rational powers, and an orderly system therefore leads us to seek its cause in itself, not in a designing mind. So far he is a "naturalist," and the question of a theology does not arise for him. Neither does that of a theodicy. For in viewing the created world he holds the balance evenly between regarding it as good or as evil. He leans to no extreme view either of itself or its causes. Morally they are indifferent, right and wrong are illusions; goodness or malice cannot be affirmed of either one or the other.

But this description of Philo's position is quite insufficient to account for the conclusions to which he eventually comes, it may be inconsistently. Throughout the last three sections of the argument, he expressly makes repeated admissions that there is evidence for a design, purpose, or intention in Nature. "It strikes everywhere the most careless, the most stupid thinker." "The suspense of judgment," which is the triumph of scepticism, "is in this case impossible." "All the sciences almost lead us insensibly to acknowledge a first intelligent author, and their authority is often so much the greater as they do not directly profess that intention." "Here, then, the existence of a DEITY is plainly ascertained by reason." These and other sentences are not the strictly logical result of Philo's original position: in the Dialogues, considered as a single book, they plainly signify his partial acquiescence in the contentions of Cleanthes. They are not the results we should naturally expect to be propounded by Hume from the standpoint of the Treatise or the Inquiry; therefore, in his general philosophy, if they are to be taken as the sincere expression (and I think they must be) of his last word in developing his own doctrine, they denote in Hume a slackening of his earlier scepticism – whether through the mellowing influence of time, or natural inclination, or reasoned conviction, it is hard to say. In any case, both Cleanthes and Philo converge upon this measure of positive assertion and agreement – of course from opposite sides, – and to Philo it is the maximum he will allow in natural religion. With the popular faith of his own time Philo has no sympathy whatever, and in this respect, too, he has Cleanthes with him, both again representing the life-long attitude of Hume to what he always terms "false religion."

From what has just been said, the Dialogues obviously afford a very pretty question of interpretation. The problem, however, is simplified in the end by Demea's abrupt disappearance from the stage, leaving the argument between Cleanthes and Philo. The initial alliance between Demea and Philo was one that could only endure so long as the former remained blind to the consequences which his friend would infer from their common principles. A theology which starts from a doctrine of human ignorance, adds to that the doctrine that the present order is one of unmitigated evil and illusion, and then concludes by affirming the Deity to be absolutely transcendent, is reduced at once under Hume's canons of truth to absolute scepticism. It is usually unaware of its own implications, and Hume represents it so; therefore, in any philosophical writing it would naturally be regarded as an imperfect and incomplete variation of a more reasoned theory: in dialogue it can be developed into its final form with especial ease. This is exactly what happens in Hume's treatment of the subject: Demea is a mere puppet in the hands of the more systematic sceptic, and the issue of the whole argument may be said to lie between Philo and Cleanthes.

From this general statement there must always be excepted that section of the Dialogues which deals with the *a priori* proofs of God's Nature. Part IX. of the book is an interlude in the dramatic action, much shorter than the other parts, and quite distinct from them in every way. Its omission would not detract in the least degree from the continuity of the argument; it is complete in itself, and may properly be considered and disposed of separately. The *a priori* proofs are put into Demea's mouth, and on this one point he receives no support whatever from Philo. He is left alone to defend what is even for him an obviously ill-grounded inconsistency. And in a very few, clear, and pithy sentences Hume makes Cleanthes and Philo give the whole substance of all the criticisms that have since been directed against the use of *a priori* reasoning in speculative theology.

Of the usefulness of such reasoning could it be validly admitted there is no real doubt, and two points with regard to it are absolutely determined in Hume's analysis. It proves the unity of God's Nature and the infinity of His attributes with a directness not to be found in any other topic. At the same time, it requires a habit of thinking so special that it neither commands general assent nor awakens strictly religious feeling. Accordingly, there are advantages and conveniences in it for theology, if the solidity of its argument be left out of question; nevertheless, even on that supposition, it is too much out of touch with ordinary life to be very convincing or to buttress up practical religion.

Hume leaves the dissection of the *a priori* arguments in the hands of Cleanthes. In the speech of Demea, setting them forth, two lines of proof are inextricably jumbled together, one from the contingency of existence which impels the mind to trace back the series of causes to a first, which is its own cause; and another, expounding the implications of the idea of a first cause, who carries the reason of His existence in Himself, whose non-existence, therefore, is expressly contradictory. This conjoining of the arguments, commonly distinguished as the cosmological and the ontological proofs of God's existence, foreshadows the Kantian procedure, the ways of stating them being identical, and the criticisms passed upon them having considerable analogy in the two philosophers of Scotland and Germany.[32] Hume, however, so far from introducing any particular preconstituted theory of the causal nexus into his argument, as Kant does, treats the question in the Dialogues without reference to his own analysis of causes and effects, or to any other. On the path of all causal reasoning, which abstracts from the particular and seeks to predicate a cause for existence (or its equivalent the world), he establishes one grand dilemma which bars that path effectually and finally. Two metaphysical presuppositions are possible to him who would prepare premises for the cosmological argument, and each is an abstraction from experience. Let that pass. On the first the world is conceived as an eternal succession of objects, linked together temporally by a chain of relation in which each is at once effect of a preceding cause and cause of a succeeding effect. To this Hume objects that it leaves no room for a prius, and therefore it seems absurd to inquire for a primum. The regular process of tracing natural causes, which in the Dialogues at least is recognised as quite legitimate, is under this presupposition taken to have universal application, while at the same time

---

[32] *Vide* Caldecott and Mackintosh, Theism, pp. 193, 203. Also specially Kant's First and Fourth Antinomies.

it is for theological purposes abandoned; and the maxim, every effect must have a cause, is in the end pronounced self-contradictory.

On the other presupposition, what Hume calls an arbitrary act of the mind unites all the particular parts of the temporal succession into a *whole*, which is then said to want a cause. "Did I show you," says Cleanthes, "the particular causes of each individual in a collection of twenty particles of matter, I should think it very unreasonable should you afterwards ask me what was the cause of the whole twenty. That is sufficiently explained, in explaining the cause of the parts." This impugns directly the logical possibility of conceiving the world as a unity. It is the same argument as occurs in the Treatise.[33] "Twenty men *may be considered as an unite*. The whole globe of the earth, nay, the whole universe, *may be considered as an unite*. That term of unity is merely a fictitious denomination." For Hume, therefore, this form of cosmological argument begins by putting forward most questionable premises, and in addition to this objection, which is urged from his own peculiar standpoint, he proceeds to attack its method of drawing conclusions from them. The object of the argument expressly is to establish the Infinity and Unity of the Deity. But these two qualities are in the first instance surreptitiously ascribed to the created world, which, accordingly, might perfectly well be the only self-existent Being. Whatever argument for the existence of God adopts as its method the ordinary category of cause, is bound to assume for the world the very qualities it wishes to prove for the Deity; and to Hume, in his most agnostic mood, all such arguments appear reducible to pure naturalism or materialism.

In the Dialogues, therefore, the cosmological argument which, as Kant says, professes "to begin with experience and is not completely *a priori*," is shown to derive all its nerve and force not from its supposed solid basis in a reference to the real world, but from metaphysical presuppositions which have transformed that reference into abstractions that seem to Hume altogether apart from experience and imaginary. He is not content, however, with merely detecting this sophistical illusion in the argument, but proceeds to give it a turn that

[33] Works, i. 338, Part II. 2.

is distinctly antitheistical. In endeavouring to link God and the world together as cause and effect, the mind wavers between two views of that relationship as it is evidenced in creation. Either the present order is equated mechanically to its cause, in which case, being the better known, it merits the more adoration in itself, and can be so regarded as to exclude any inference to God, or else it is arbitrarily taken to be contingent and insufficient in its existence to be real; and then Hume holds that this arbitrary judgment may as easily be passed upon God's Being as upon that of the world. In both respects Hume's trenchant criticism is most effective, and while it will still be possible to inquire whether the more refined analysis of the concept of cause in modern times has enabled theology to rehabilitate such argument, it is necessary here once more to emphasise the fact that Hume's treatment of it is in no way dependent upon the limitations, either of his own outlook or of that of his time.

The remaining parts of Demea's argument make no pretence of appealing to our experience, and are purely *a priori*. In very few words his reasoning runs: "We must have recourse to a necessarily existent Being, who carries the REASON of His existence in Himself, and who cannot be supposed not to exist without an express contradiction. There is consequently such a Being – that is, there is a Deity." This process of speculation is dealt with in the most summary fashion by Cleanthes whose words so obviously express all that Hume has to say on the matter, that they may be quoted in full: "Nothing is demonstrable unless the contrary implies a contradiction. Nothing that is distinctly conceivable implies a contradiction. Whatever we conceive as existent we can also conceive as non-existent. There is no being, therefore, whose non-existence implies a contradiction. Consequently there is no being whose existence is demonstrable. I propose this argument as entirely decisive, and am willing to rest the whole controversy upon it."

The method, therefore, of such argument is rejected by Hume, almost contemptuously: he is altogether out of sympathy with the very possibility of it. But he also brings his own theory of "necessity" to bear upon the idea of necessary existence as it is predicated of the Deity, his purpose being to prove how naturally it affords an inference directly opposite to the religious hypothesis. Mathematical necessity depends upon ideal relations, and for Hume is more easily ascribed to the propositions of algebra (and arithmetic), where the mind deals with its own abstractions, than to those of geometry, for which Hume could account only with great difficulty.[34] And "necessity" in mathematics is so obviously independent of the question of the existence of objects, that the theological use of that idea to illustrate some occult quality in God involves an application of the term that is altogether new. Both Cleanthes and Philo take their stand upon the nature of mathematical necessity, which Kant in a parallel passage calls "this logical necessity, the source of the greatest delusions." Cleanthes is content to point out that "necessity" is a term valid only in defining the relations of ideas: "We lie under a necessity of always conceiving twice two to be four." Existence is a term used only in dealing with "matters of fact." The words, therefore, *necessary existence*, have no meaning, or, which is the same thing, none that is "consistent." Philo goes on to point out the danger of introducing the idea of necessity at all into our cosmology, where it may lead as easily to a naturalism of necessary laws as to a theism. In mathematics every theorem that is proved states a necessary property of the objects to which it applies, and therefore, however much regularity and order and beauty there may be in any of its problems, it is always possible to demonstrate that every appearance of design is in reality the work of blind necessity. It might easily be the case that just as the most complex arithmetical series to a skilled calculator is an immediate deduction from the simple uninspiring rule that one and one make two, so the whole economy of the universe, if we are to ask why it must be as it is and not otherwise, can be referred back to previous states which for natural science render it absolutely impossible that any other disposition than the present should ever have come to pass.

And because science has a perfect right to subject all its objects without exception to the power of thus deducing their necessity, it may, with some appearance of justice, convert this principle of its own method into a universally valid postulate. A mathematician who observes that the diagonal of a square or the circumference of a circle bear a fixed relation to the magnitude of the circle or the diameter respectively,

---

[34] Treatise, Part iii. sect. 1.

and are at the same time incommensurable with these latter, considers himself justified in taking this relation to be a neces- sary one, and sets about proving it without any further pre- liminaries. If, as in the *a priori* argument, this same idea of a necessary existence be introduced in a scientific view of the created world, Hume points out that no room whatever is left for a hypothesis of design. This hypothesis being all- important for an empirical or natural theology, Hume rejects the ontological argument on every point: his explanation of its common acceptance simply is that "a habit of thinking," appropriate in mathematics, has been "transferred to subjects where it ought not to have place."

Such is Hume's criticism of the cosmological and ontologi- cal arguments as he conceived either them or the principles on which they rest. The subsequent history of philosophy may be searched in vain for any attempt to meet it fairly and squarely. It is the final and irrevocable judgment of empiri- cism upon *a priori* arguments in theology, and even when his general principles, or even when other of his conclusions, have failed to commend themselves to a later age, it at least has never been formally appealed against. "Theism," says Professor Flint, "is not vitally interested in the fate of the so- called *a priori* or ontological arguments,"[35] and this remark well describes the resignation with which modern thought has viewed their disappearance.

Since Hume wrote his Dialogues, argument of an ontologi- cal type has been concerned with a question at once more comprehensive in its bearings and more definite in its formu- lation – namely, the investigation of the fundamental relations of all thought and all existence. The primary and necessary principles of knowledge have to be reconciled at every point with the self-existence of reality, if knowledge is to be accepted as true and not illusory. This question includes the older inquiry as to the existence of a Deity corresponding to the ideals of reason, and like it demands an answer from the analysis of the implications of thought itself, not from any- thing that is given in sense or comprehended by understand- ing. It is more concerned, however, to spiritualise the universe as an object of knowledge than to cognise an individual or personal spirit in it. Hume's difficulties for theistic specu-

---

[35] Theism, p. 267

lation are circumvented, therefore, by stating them on the grand scale as objections to the apprehension of the most simple matters of fact. When this is done a dilemma is established between our believing the mind to have a natural credibility in virtue of its own essence, and our affirming it dogmatically to be without relation to any real Being whatever. And so all the points touched upon by Hume receive one by one a solution in which his distinctions between "ideas" and "facts," between "principles of union among ideas" and "natural relations" disappear. Thus for Herbart causal connection reduces to a purely logical form; for Lotze it is the evidence directly given of a "supernatural sustaining power, immanent in all existence and operative in all change," in the revealing activity of one person to another: and so for these and all similar systems the whole of the theory of knowledge depends upon ontological argument. The idea of God, like other ultimate truths, is intuitive; it is the work of "objective reason"; it is a presupposition of thought; or it is the unity of thought and being on which all individual thought and existence rest. There are many possible alternatives for such speculation when it takes upon itself to become theological, but all are linked together through their common starting-point in the endeavour to prove consciousness and its real content to be a harmonious and indivisible whole. Suppose now that this basis be granted, and that it be found sufficiently trustworthy, then the argument to the existence of God does proceed upon the familiar lines of the old cosmological and ontological proofs, and resembles them closely enough to pass for a serious attempt at reconstruction. It proves God's existence by invoking the necessities of human reason; it deduces His Personality from the needed completion of all our conceptions; and it ascribes attributes to Him which are not by any means to be verified in our passive experience of any known objects (the created world), but are implied in our outgoing self-realising activity. And once this stream of *a priori* reasoning is in full flood, it were, in Hume's own vivid phrase, "to stop the ocean with a bulrush" to urge the considerations which had sufficed in the Dialogues for diverting its first course. Nevertheless, whenever any serious attempt is made to expound or illustrate or defend the unity and harmony of the ideal with the real, the argument cannot but take upon itself a teleological form. It can easily be classified under this heading, and probably such reasoning is invested with its peculiar charm for speculative thought solely through the considerations of design in mind and external reality which it undoubtedly contains.

In the Dialogues,[36] with the exception of the few sentences of Part IX., which deals expressly with the *a priori* arguments, the treatment of Hume's subject is concerned entirely with an analysis of the teleological argument. The *a priori* proofs being ruled out, the whole book is dominated by Cleanthes' steady insistence upon this one foundation for his theism. "By this argument *a posteriori*, and by this argument alone, do we prove at once the existence of a Deity, and His similarity to human mind and intelligence," (p. 31); accordingly the sole question is as to the possibility and accuracy of this proof. If, however, Cleanthes admits only one form of argument, he represents it to be so wide as to be all-inclusive. In different passages he appeals to "the whole world and every part of it" – "the image of mind reflected on us from innumerable objects," "our immeasurable desires of good," "the operations of reason," and in fact to all actual phenomena of experience, external and internal alike, as affording material for his hypothesis of design. To begin with, therefore, the scope of his proposed theme knows no limits.

Again, an obvious consequence of the book falling into the literary form of dialogue is, that the argument for a natural religion in it undergoes a process of gradual development and refinement in the course of the conversation. Simple and ill-defined conceptions are succeeded by others more complex and more accurate as the conversation proceeds, each of the speakers contributing something to the final result. On Cleanthes alone lies the burden of maintaining the positive conclusion. The other two are on the negative side. If there is any continuity in the book, an impartial analysis ought not to be adversely affected by the progressive restatement which naturally ensues of the position of each. Cleanthes, for example, gives up a notable part of his original scheme when he abandons the possibility of tracing design in the moral world. Philo in turn, by reason of the admission he makes to him at the close of the argument, cannot be supposed to

---

[36] From this point references to the Dialogues will be given to the paging in the present edition.

retain his scepticism unbroken. Each of the two is in many different points corrected by the other.

The drama opens with a very complete statement of the purely sceptical theory of human knowledge from Philo and Demea. Our natural reason is subject to "uncertainty and endless contrarieties," not only in science but "even in subjects of common life and practice" (p. 9). The science of quantity alone has any pretence of certainty, and even in it error and contradictions are more abundant than truth. These are the old commonplaces of Hume in the Treatise when he takes that *intense* view of reason to which he is impelled as a philosopher, and in opposition to it Cleanthes reminds him of the sentiments of his spleen and indolence which he had there confessed to govern his life as a man; how "it is impossible for him to persevere in this total scepticism or make it appear in his conduct for a few hours." The bent of his mind relaxes, and his conduct is so obviously subject to a necessity to believe, that his scepticism appears to others pretended and insincere.

Here, then, in the Dialogues the two opposing elements in which Hume's theory of knowledge had ended, the enthusiasm of abstract speculative negation and the instinctive determination to live and act by ordinary maxims, are restated exactly – almost in the same language – as in the last section of the Treatise on the Understanding. There Hume in his single person makes no choice, and indeed prides himself upon the fact that because it is a choice "betwixt a false reason and none at all," he can regard it with indifference. But here and now the choice is made definitely by Philo the sceptic himself, and the balance on which judgment formerly was suspended inclines ever so little to the side of belief "in common life." It is necessary to note exactly how much he will admit, because it is through the very first chink in the sceptical armour, so perfect before, that Cleanthes pushes home his thrusts. The words of Philo's present confession are: "To whatever length any one may push his speculative principles of scepticism, he must act, I own, and live, and converse; and for this conduct he is not obliged to give any other reason than the absolute necessity he lies under of so doing" (p. 14). "The sceptical reasonings" are "so refined and subtile that they are not able to counterpoise the more solid and more natural arguments derived from the senses and experience." Philo therefore lays aside the pretence of absolute scepticism for practical life and conduct, and also, what is more important, for his consideration of the sciences commonly called "natural." "So long as we confine our speculations to trade, or morals, or politics, or criticism, we make appeals every moment to common-sense and experience which strengthen our philosophical conclusions and remove (at least in part) the suspicion which we so justly entertain with regard to every reasoning that is very subtle and refined." And a few pages later, after Cleanthes had clinched this concession, he refers more boldly still to "those suggestions of the senses and common understanding by which the most determined sceptic must allow himself to be governed" (p. 24). One cannot help feeling that Hume is here allowing that very ground for an answer to himself which was almost simultaneously being occupied by Reid for his Philosophy of Common-Sense.

It is, however, unnecessary to ask how far this position differs from the doctrine of the Treatise, because it appears that Philo, having admitted this much positively in the Dialogues, is immediately carried one step farther. For a single moment he excludes theology from the favour yielded to other sciences. In theological reasonings we have not the advantage of an appeal to sense and experience. "We know not how far we ought to trust our vulgar methods of reasoning in such a subject, since even in common life and in that province which is peculiarly appropriated to them, we cannot account for them, and are entirely guided by a kind of instinct or necessity in employing them."

Cleanthes at once questions the validity of this distinction. For him a "natural religion" is bound to put itself strictly into line with all natural sciences whatever.

> "In vain would the sceptic make a distinction between science and common life, or between one science and another. The arguments employed in all, if just, are of a similar nature, and contain the same force and evidence. Or if there be any difference among them, the advantage lies entirely on the side of theology and natural religion."

He divides the various systems of scepticism that seem possible to him into three classes. One is fatal to "all knowledge," and not to religion specially. It is absolute agnosticism which discusses no evidence in any particular case, but dismisses everything as uncertain or insoluble. Without any breach of courtesy to his companions he can liken this way of thinking to the brutal and ignorant prejudice which the vulgar entertain to everything they do not easily understand. The most generally accepted results in science depend upon elaborate trains of minute reasoning, and yet because they are so abstruse, they are not one whit less securely established than the plainest experimental deduction. And for his own argument he promises by anticipation that it will be of the simplest and most obvious kind. If "the general presumption against human reason" be made a plea against natural religion, there is neither need nor opportunity to proceed further; but this is the very presumption which Philo has put away from himself, and therefore the only possible method for "the most refined and philosophical sceptics" is to consider each particular evidence "apart, and proportion their assent to the particular degree of evidence which occurs." To the general question of the bare credibility of our knowing faculties, Cleanthes has his own answer. If that be allowed to arise, a problem is set of which he says, "I have not capacity for so great an undertaking: I have not leisure for it: I perceive it to be superfluous." Superfluous it certainly was in the discussion between himself and Philo, if the latter was willing to abide by the statements he had already made.

Besides this form of total unbelief, Cleanthes, in considering the possibilities of scepticism, makes a distinction between two other forms of it, very aptly described by Philo as "religious" and "irreligious", or, as the modern phrase is, "anti-religious" scepticism. The first, which exalts the certainty of theology, and distrusts the common sciences, is the most objectionable to Hume. It lends itself easily to priestcraft, which he held in steady abhorrence, and so far as it is the motive of Demea's contentions in the Dialogues, it issues in irrational obscurantism and receives the full force of Hume's satire. Philo sums up the verdict for Cleanthes in one sentence, "If we distrust human reason, we have now no other principle to lead us into religion."

There now remains the third form, namely, that of "irreligious" scepticism, which may depend upon the most varied grounds, but must at least give its reasons when called for. To it Philo declares himself to adhere, and he states the considerations which determine him to it as plainly as possible. "In reality, Cleanthes, there is no need to have recourse to that affected scepticism, so displeasing to you, in order to come at this determination. Our ideas reach no farther than our experience. We have no experience of divine attributes and operations. I need not conclude my syllogism. You can draw the inference yourself" (p. 30). With this acknowledgment the preliminaries may be considered settled by mutual consent, and the ground is cleared between the two principal disputants. The question of the natural fallibility of human reason is waived and remains so, even when at various points later Philo indicates implicitly the possibility of reviving it. What remains to be argued is whether experience, the sole fountain of truth, yields any evidence whatever apposite to the theological inference, and the question if such evidence can be legitimately converted into proof.

For a starting-point in his construction of a teleological view of the world, Cleanthes adopts one of the popular deistical conceptions of the eighteenth century. The universe is "nothing but one great machine, subdivided into an infinite number of lesser machines, which again admit of subdivisions," apparently to an unlimited degree. This familiar figure of speech is not intended to express more than the fact of ubiquitous order, and because of its common use in contemporary theological essays, both Cleanthes and Philo set themselves to the task of stating the argument depending upon it before the discussion begins. Each gives a short summary, and each agrees that the other has not done injustice to its ordinary statement, Philo saying (p. 35), "I must allow that he [Cleanthes] has fairly represented that argument," while Cleanthes assents (p. 38) that Philo "has made a fair representation of it." We can therefore draw upon the speeches of both for a formal analysis of its successive steps. The fact of order in the world is admitted; but this is "not of itself any proof of design." We can only say that as it occurs throughout all nature, order or adaptation or adjustment resembles the productions of human contrivance. Only experience can inform us at all of the causes of such order; and as we find by experience that the plan of any work of human art – a watch, a ship, a house – is first formed in the mind, so we conclude that without this preparation such things would for ever remain uncreated and unknown.

Therefore by *analogy* we conclude that the original principle
of the universe lies in a designing mind. The causes in each
case must be of the same kind, only proportioned each to its
several effects.[37] The whole argument undergoes considerable
development in Hume's hands, and obviously it is stated only
as a convenient and easily recognised scheme upon which he
can graft his own criticisms. In particular, the questions of
the nature of "analogy" and of the "proportion" it involves
are left open, and admit discussion at once.

The unavoidable uncertainty of analogy in every science is
an immediate objection to its use. No stronger evidence than
perfect similarity in two cases of the same nature is "ever
desired or sought after," but wherever there is difference and
alteration analogy is weakened, and its conclusions do not
command confidence in the same degree. It demonstrates
only probabilities, and therefore it is essentially a method of
deduction to be entered upon with the slow and deliberate
step of philosophy, and not in uncritical haste. Philo questions its validity in the present case for three distinct reasons,
stated briefly in Part II. of the Dialogues. In the first place,
there is no proof offered of the similarity between the universe
and the productions of human contrivance, as there ought to
be in face of apparent dissimilitude. In the second place,
other natural powers than reason are observed at work in the
mechanism of the universe, and therefore, unless something
determines us in favour of one particular principle, we could
not pretend to draw an analogy from the operations of any
natural power in its own peculiar sphere, or infer it to be the
first cause of all. And lastly, our experience extends only to
a small part of the universe, and to a very short period of its
existence: the inference sought to be drawn in theology is one
as to the cause of the whole from the beginning of all time.

The second objection, very briefly stated here, contains the
nerve of all Philo's argument in Parts IV.–VIII., and if its

[37] This representation of analogy as involving "a proportion" is borrowed
from Butler. Kant also, speaking of the physico theological argument in
the Critique, says, "We infer from the order and design visible in the
universe as a disposition of a thoroughly contingent character the existence of a cause proportioned thereto." In a note to the prolegomena (§
58 dealing directly with the Dialogues), analogy is treated in a formal
illustration, "As the welfare of children (=*a*) is to the love of parents (=
b), so is the welfare of men (=*c*) to the unknown in God (=*x*) which we
call love.

consideration be deferred until we treat of them, we only follow Hume's own plan. The last objection receives its answer at once; for, as it is worded in the Dialogues, Hume describes it, quite justly, to be brought forward "somewhat between jest and earnest."

Philo has reached the point of saying that for his opponent "it were requisite that we had experience of the origin of worlds; it is not sufficient, surely, that we have seen ships and cities arise from human contrivance," and demanding how the theistic inference can be confirmed by repetition of instances and experiment. But the conditions imposed by this demand are obviously incapable of fulfilment: they put an impossible meaning upon the word experience, and Cleanthes points this out perfectly clearly in reply, "To prove by experience the origin of the world, is not more contrary to common speech than to prove the motion of the earth from the same principle." Our experience is limited in space and in time and in extent, – we cannot better it; but this fact alone cannot invalidate our right to infer a meaning in what we do know.

Philo, like Hume's imaginary opponent in the Essay on Providence and a Future State, has insisted that the singular and unparalleled nature of the act of creation bars all possibility of drawing any analogy between it and other events; and Hume, in the first person, had already met the difficulty by a direct negative.

> "In a word, I much doubt whether it is possible for a cause to be known only by its effect, or to be of so singular and particular a nature as to have no parallel and no similarity with any other cause or object that has ever fallen under our observation."

And accordingly, when stripped of the impossible demand for infinite experience, the third objection of Philo to the analogical argument returns upon the first, and becomes a call for further explanation of the alleged similarity between human productive activity, as we observe it, and the generation of an orderly universe. The "reasonings of too nice and delicate a nature," upon which Hume had declined to enter in the Inquiry, are forced upon him now, when the whole question is being treated expressly.

The method which Cleanthes adopts for overcoming his opponent's first objection is to minimise it.

"It is by no means necessary that theists should prove the similarity of the works of Nature to those of art, because this similarity is self-evident and undeniable."

The proof which Philo asks for is not one that can be reduced to the forms of logic: the first step towards the inference of design must be intuitive. The possibility of arguments of this logically irregular nature is proved, says Cleanthes, by their universal and irresistible influence. If, in the simplest inference from perception, – for example, if, when we infer from hearing a speech the fact that there was a speaker expressing his meaning in what we hear, – it then be objected that our inference cannot be expressed in accordance with the principles of logic, and must therefore be rejected, nothing remains but that form of absolute scepticism which both have already agreed to abjure. All conclusions concerning fact are founded upon experience, and accordingly the possible validity of intuitive deductions from it, such as are every day drawn in common life, must be admitted by all who take up the positions held by the two leaders in the Dialogues. Self-evident intuition always accompanies experience, and Cleanthes holds that his opponent's demand for proof of the similarity between creation and a work of human art implies a misapprehension of the essential nature of the only possible assurance on that point.

He gives two examples of immediate deductions which resemble the theistic inference. A voice being heard which is not mere sound, but is articulate with meaning and instruction, and rational, wise, coherent; we at once conclude that it proceeds from reason and intelligence, and in our conclusion it is a matter of indifference whether the sound be extraordinarily loud and widespread, or whether it be of the commonest kind. Again, we read a book, and find it conveys a meaning and intention; we conclude that it sprang from design. Let it be supposed that books could be propagated by natural generation and descent, as plants and animals are; even then our reading still justifies our conclusion. Nature is like a library of books addressed to our minds in a universal language. "When it reasons and discourses; when it expostulates, argues, and enforces its views and topics; when it applies sometimes to the pure intellect, sometimes to the affections; when it collects, disposes, and adorns every consideration suited to the subject: could you persist in asserting that all this at the bottom had really no meaning, and that the first formation of this volume in the loins of its original parent proceeded not from thought and design?" (p. 52). To demand "proof" of the similarity of the meaning of Nature to the meaning of language is to demand the impossible. The self-evident is indemonstrable. "Consider, anatomise the eye," says Cleanthes, "survey its structure and contrivance, and tell me, from your own feeling, if the idea of a contriver does not immediately flow in upon you with a force like that of sensation." And whatever object we set before ourselves teleologically, it is the same idea with the same force that it suggests. The crucial difficulty for Cleanthes is just the one to which this ultimate position is a complete answer in the Dialogues. So far, the general current of the conversation, as the present writer conceives it, has been concerned with the important question of the correct method in teleological argument. And Hume, in his treatment of the old well-worn demonstration of God's existence from the mechanism of the universe, represents one at least of the three disputants to have penetrated to the fundamental point on which it all depends. An immediate self-evident intuition with the same force as sensation cannot be demonstrated by the principles of logic, and Cleanthes seems to have grasped to the full all the bearings of his position, just as they were afterwards grasped, in treating of the theory of knowledge generally by those who replied to Hume. The power of conviction, where evidence of this kind is adduced, is so great that logic is required not to dispute it but to account for it, or admit it as best logic can. The only question applicable to such evidence as Cleanthes pins his faith to is that of its occurrence or non-occurrence in consciousness, and if we carry our survey of the development of the argument to the close of the whole book, we shall find that this particular question is always answered in an affirmative way. Cleanthes points out repeatedly that the hypothesis of design cannot be got rid of at any turn, and in the end Philo adopts it himself for his own conclusions. The conclusion to design is exceedingly plain and simple according to Cleanthes; it may only give foundation for a very slight fabric of superadded truth: but again, even on that supposition, both disputants declare themselves satisfied of its sufficiency.

At the point in the Dialogues where this position is reached (in the end of Part III.) Philo is represented "as a little embarrassed and confounded," and makes no reply to Cleanthes' final statement of his meaning: the questions which intervene between it and the resumption in the concluding part of the thread of argument here dropped deal with other issues. In the letter to Sir Gilbert Elliott already quoted, Hume himself divides the Dialogues at this point, and advises his friend that he need go no farther in order to apprehend his true meaning.

We have already seen that it is Demea who diverts the continuity of the argument at another point, by introducing as a side issue the discussion on the *a priori* proofs of God's Being; so, also, it is he who gives the opening later on to the consideration of the moral argument. And at the present juncture it was Demea again who "broke in upon the discourse" and saved Philo's countenance. The interruption which is put into his mouth revives Philo's second objection to the design argument, exactly as it had already been expressed by him, and to the exposition of it the sceptic naturally turns the whole course of the debate; but with Demea's disappearance at the close of Part XI. he joins hands again with Cleanthes upon the conclusions reached thus early in the book. If, then, we are to interpret the Dialogues as expressing any settled opinions at all of the author, we must infer that he considered the existence of design in Nature to be established either certainly, or at least sufficiently, by the appeal to what is self-evident.

So far, then, the author's procedure has been directed simply to prove that design is traced in Nature by one of the simplest and most direct inferences of which the human mind is capable. However, no sooner has Cleanthes gained this first and most essential point than the difficulties which follow it are brought up with all the force of the author's best style. They are many and very diverse, and some of them are so evidently true to Hume's general attitude on common subjects, they are treated at such length and with so much dialectical skill, that they do undoubtedly constitute a formidable attack from him upon the whole design argument, and thus far justify the view ordinarily taken that the Dialogues are directly antithetical in their tendency. Still, it is only by selecting the finest and most subtle doubts which the hypothesis of design suggests to Philo, by ignoring any positive truths that both he and Cleanthes profess to accept about creating intelligence, and by overlooking altogether the argument which leads up to them, that most of the references to the book in the history of philosophy interpret it in the purely sceptical sense. An impartial verdict ought to hold both the positive affirmations, at least so far as they seem agreed upon, and the negative criticisms together for a proper estimate of this contribution of Hume to the philosophy of theology.

For the teleological argument, as Hume conceived it, really involves two distinct movements of thought. The first is the argument to, or towards, design; which is meant to prove no more than that design, and a designing intelligence of some sort, must exist in the universe. The second is the argument from design; which follows the first and depends upon it, which seeks to define further the conception of designing intelligence by help of its works, and in particular proceeds to inquire whether or not such intelligence can legitimately have predicated of it such attributes as personality and unity, perfection and infinity, or self-existence and omnipotence. The first movement may be exceedingly simple, the second always is exceedingly involved. That Hume should have distinguished the two, and approved of the first while treating the second in a thoroughly sceptical manner, does not seem to have occurred even as a possibility either to friendly or unfriendly critics.

Accordingly, no sooner has Cleanthes expounded what he calls his "hypothesis of design" than Demea inquires whether it may not "render us presumptuous by making us imagine we comprehend the Deity, and have some adequate idea of His nature and attributes?" He restates Hume's own doctrine of the human mind just as Philo had done in the as yet undiscussed objection to the design argument which we have already noticed. The human mind is nothing more than a succession of ideas united in one subject yet distinct, arranged for one moment yet constantly fleeting away: if Hume can explain it at all, it is the product of natural forces. In its beginning it is observed daily to originate in generation and birth, in its course the machinery of thought is altered and even controlled by external causes and accidental impression; all that we know of its essence is that it seems dependent, and not original or self-supporting. If, then, Cleanthes maintains that there is evidence of the existence of a designing intelligence, both Demea and Philo are quite entitled, on Hume's principles, to ask how we can possibly suppose this divine mind of his to be "the model of the universe" (pp. 40 and 57). Cleanthes is quite willing to be tied down to affirming the similarity between the divine mind and the human, and says so with no uncertain voice. The creating intelligence is "like the human," and "the liker the better"; twice he declares "I know no other" (p. 74), and courageously taking up this position with all the difficulties attaching to it, he allows the epithet of anthropomorphism to be applied to his doctrine with indifference or even with his express approval. He holds fast to his "first inferences," as Philo terms them later (p. 92), and without reservation declares always for the positive consequences of the resemblance of the divine to the human, even to the length of affirming of God weaknesses and imperfections, and limitations by necessity, such as constantly are experienced in man.

Philo, on the other hand, has no difficult task on the negative side in showing "the inconveniences of that anthropomorphism" which his opponent has embraced. It is here that the destructive criticism of the Dialogues is really to be found, and here that it is based upon Hume's own settled opinions. It was Kant's accurate and most just verdict upon the book[38] that "all the arguments in it dangerous to theism centre round this one point of anthropomorphism," and yet the danger from Philo is not so much to Cleanthes' method of proof as to the meaning to be read into the conclusion. In the winding up of the argument, where Philo acknowledges that the "existence of a Deity is plainly ascertained by reason," he states quite clearly how much scope he will finally allow to the argument from design. "If we are not contented with calling the first and supreme cause a GOD or DEITY, but desire to vary the expression, what can we call Him but MIND or THOUGHT, to which He is justly supposed to bear a considerable resemblance?" (p. 170). This clearly is to admit the bare elements of his opponent's second contention that the designing intelligence is like in kind to the human mind, and Philo goes on to define the question between them as one of the degree of resemblance. This presents itself to him

---

[38] *Prolegomena*, § 57.

conveniently as a species of verbal controversy "which, from the very nature of language and of human ideas, is involved in perpetual ambiguity, and can never, by any precaution or any definitions, be able to reach a reasonable certainty or precision."[39] It is generally admitted that in the history of the teleological argument, the greatest error of its exponents has been their uncritical tendency to press the anthropomorphic analogy to unreasonable lengths, and in this respect their licence requires always to be curtailed. When Philo in the Dialogues undertakes this task, it is done thoroughly enough, the argument is confined within limits narrower than those it commonly is inflated to fill; but that process of compression is by no means one of annihilation, although by entering upon a question of degree as "incurably ambiguous" as those referred to by Hume, any one may easily persuade himself of the contrary. It is just in conceiving the Deity after the likeness of man that the strength of the teleological argument lies, and its weakness. For its proper treatment it is essential that both sides should be accurately displayed, and in this respect the Dialogues seem to afford an excellent example of systematic analysis.

The first inconvenience of the anthropomorphic explanation of order in the universe is that it need not be taken to be final or complete. Human reason itself is held by Philo not to be self-dependent. We may not know or be able to explain the causes why its ideas arrange themselves in order to form plans towards its ends, but we have no more right to attribute that power of arranging to a rational faculty inherent in mind than we have to attribute order to an orderly faculty in other natural powers. Philo, therefore, having no theory of reason as a real entity, independent of the ideas, passions, and sensations which "succeed each other" in it, has no theory to account for the falling into order of "the different ideas which compose the reason of the Supreme Being" (p. 67). Their order or arrangement require and demand an explanation just as much as the order in the visible world. "The first step we take leads us on for ever. When you go one step beyond the mundane system, you only

---

[39] For this doctrine in a modern form, cf. Bradley, "Appearance and Reality," p. 533. "It is better to affirm personality than to call the Absolute impersonal. But neither mistake should be necessary."

excite an inquisitive humour which it is impossible ever to satisfy." To him Cleanthes' explanation of the form of the world by a divine intelligence appears only "to shove off the difficulty" for a moment, and to account for what we observe by means of a cause itself unaccountable. It sets up an infinite series of deductions in which the same thing always remains unexplained. "If the material world rests upon a similar ideal world, this ideal world must rest upon some other, and so on without end."

Cleanthes, however, refuses to be drawn into this discussion of the possibility of an infinite tracing out of the causes of design. "Even in common life, if I assign a cause for any event, is it any objection that I cannot assign the cause of that cause, and answer every new question which may incessantly be started?" (p. 69). His first step is not the beginning of an endless journey from hypothesis to hypothesis "entirely in the air," as he terms such procedure in another connection (p. 137), – it is an immediate inference to design and a designing mind; and with an obvious hit at his opponent, he asks what philosophers could possibly insist upon demanding the cause of every cause, "philosophers who confess ultimate causes to be totally unknown." Cleanthes does not attempt to give a theory of reason in opposition to Philo's, – no doubt the author felt the impossibility of representing him in that *rôle*, – he only denies that there is any need for him to do so. "You ask me the cause of my intelligent cause." "I know not; I care not; that concerns not me. I have found a Deity, and here I stop my inquiry. Let those go farther who are wiser or more enterprising."

Philo therefore quits this ground of objection in the Dialogues, and a little later, in the course of his own attempt to give a naturalistic theory of order, when he is asked by Demea to offer some ultimate explanation of the vegetative principle which he prefers to the intelligent cause of all (p. 98), he explicitly refers to the nature of the agreement reached by Cleanthes and himself. For Cleanthes it was considered sufficient if the first step is supported by experience. He himself takes the same ground, and maintains that it is undeniable that vegetation and generation as well as reason are experienced to be principles of order in nature. "If I rest my system of cosmogony on the former preferably to the latter, 'tis at my choice. The matter seems entirely arbitrary. And when

Cleanthes asks me (which of course he has not done) the cause of my great vegetative or generative faculty, I am equally entitled to ask him the cause of his great reasoning principle. These questions we have agreed to forbear on both sides, and it is chiefly his interest on the present occasion to stick to this agreement." The dispute between pure naturalism and theism is not to be decided against, either by the respective difficulties of explaining the essential operations and internal structure of natural forces on the one hand, or of reason on the other. In both cases there is the same inconvenience; and while Philo is left to say that "an ideal system arranged of itself without a precedent design is not a whit more explicable than a material one," the dispute is not made one whit clearer by this particular method of comparing their merits.

The battle on this point, them, is left drawn, and a lasting truce called by mutual consent. But with the suggestion of the possibility of a naturalistic derivation of reason, the way is open for a pure naturalism to claim an equal right with the most refined spiritual interpretation of the world, and the discussion in the Dialogues gradually veers round to a balancing of these two alternatives.

The argument from design is, first of all, considerably reduced in its weight by the losses which its conception of the Deity undergoes in direct consequence of its anthropomorphic method of conceiving Him. Infinity, perfection, unity, and omnipotence, – in fact, all the transcendent attributes usually connected with the idea of God, – are implicitly denied in affirming His likeness to man; and in fact no part of the design argument is directed to prove them. It proceeds upon the strictly empirical method, and therefore is doomed from the first to fall short of attributes which apply to nothing we experience in observing real things. No combination of the evidences of design can ever prove the "unity" of the designer, that very term "unity" being a "fictitious denomination," and no addition of them can reach to His infinity. To all Philo's suppositions of possible ways of conceiving the Deity, or deities, without these attributes, Cleanthes accordingly has no answer, save to point out that none of them "get rid of the hypothesis of design." He never abuses his argument by pretending that it proves more than it can reach; indeed he has his own objections to using the word *infinite*, which savours more of panegyric than of philosophy, and should be replaced by more accurate and more moderate expressions (p. 142), in which our knowledge of God approximates to the comprehension of His perfection, representing His wisdom and power as greater than any other that we know, without proceeding to define them as infinitely great.[40] The argument from design reaches a conception of God that may be lofty, yet it can never attain to the conception of an Infinite. It defines His qualities by similarity with finite things, and that being its professed aim it accepts cheerfully those inconveniences which arise from its not attaining a fuller result than it actually seeks after. At this stage of the argument[41] Philo touches upon the alternative of having recourse to a pantheism, not so much as a possibility for himself as for his opponent. He expresses himself unwilling to defend any particular system of this nature, yet because it is "at least a theory that we must, sooner or later, have recourse to whatever system we embrace," it cannot be overlooked. The classical notion of the soul of the world is introduced because it has the apparent advantage of representing the form and order of the universe to be coeval and conterminous with the matter. It has, therefore, many points of kinship with Cleanthes' teleological theism, and is, indeed, as Philo remarks, "a new species of anthropomorphism." It excels just in emphasising the inherent nature of the eternal principles of order in the world, and in treating their connection with it organically rather than mechanically.

But Hume does not discuss the possibilities of a spiritual pantheism at any length; he makes Philo accept the suggestion of Cleanthes, that "the world seems to bear a stronger resemblance to a vegetable than to an animal"; and because it is to the former a matter of indifference whether we hold the original inherent principle of order to be in thought or in matter, he abandons at once the only part which, in the doctrine of a world-soul, attributes reason to it. A spiritual pantheism always suggests itself as an easy variation upon theism, and we may shrewdly suspect it was introduced in

---

[40] An empirical philosophy must always take the idea of infinity to be reached by way of approximation, – a method which derives confirmation from its use in Euclidean geometry.

[41] Part VI.

the Dialogues only as a temporary suggestion in order to lead up to pan-materialism.

Hitherto Philo has confined himself to pointing out "the inconveniences"[42] of his friend's anthropomorphism, but now, in expounding a purely naturalistic or materialistic hypothesis of order, he recognises that his attack is no longer upon "the consequences" of the design argument, but upon "the first inferences," from which it all depends. The real enemy of theism is naturalism. Both start from the same base in the observed fact of the presence of *order* in the world, but from this common point of agreement they derive principles that are altogether irreconcilable. For one party, the first step is to prove that order implies design; for the other, it is to point out that order is derived from purely irrational principles, and the divergence which commences with the first step leads on to complete opposition. The two views cannot possibly be combined – one must be allowed and the other denied; and yet the careful reader of the Dialogues will not find them brought forward with the aim of having their respective merits decided. Naturalism is not a system to which Philo is at all inclined to commit himself unreservedly, and his method of discussing it is to point out how very similar its analogies and inferences are to those of theism, and how little argument the adherents of one theory can bring against the other without destroying the validity of their own reasonings. In his conclusions on this point his inconsistency is more plainly marked than elsewhere in the whole book; for while in holding the balance even between naturalism and theism he maintains that "a total suspense of judgment is here our only reasonable resource" (112), and prides himself on having no fixed station or abiding city to defend, his judgment in the end is given, without further trial, in favour of one side.

The parallel which Philo draws between methods and grounds of the two opposing schemes is most complete. We have experience not only of reason as a principle of order in the world, but of other principles – such as instinct, generation, vegetation, and perhaps a hundred more, which undoubtedly exist, and also do certainly have some degree of a conserving and developing power, such as is required to maintain the great fabric of the whole. The universe

[42] pp. 64, 72.

resembles a machine, but it also resembles countless objects which are independent of human agency, – a spider's web spun by instinct, a vegetable sprouting up from its seed, an animal developing out of an egg. The resemblances in each case are striking: all of them have commended themselves to the judgment of mankind in history; who, then, shall decide between them? None of the analogies drawn from them pretend to be final, but stop short of defining the ultimate causes of the world. Reason, instinct, vegetation, even Nature, are all alike inexplicable, and no one principle can justly claim a preference to the others.

Philo, therefore, claims the right to be indifferent in choosing whether he will ascribe priority to thought or to matter. Experience can hardly decide the question: abstract reason is not to be trusted, because it is not an impartial judge; no possible touchstone can be brought to bear upon what we observe, and therefore we ought to ban all speculation, theistic and naturalistic alike.

This negative conclusion of itself sets limits to pure naturalism, but Hume proceeds to show how cautiously, even, in the most speculative mood, any advocate of naturalism must approach his questions, and how many dangers beset his most familiar paths. Philo undertakes for a moment to expound that evolutionary theory of order on which modern naturalism is most commonly based – one with which in every age naturalism has been so closely connected as even to be wholly identified with it. It is attempted to ascribe all the multiplicity and adjustment now observable in the world to an origin in the simplest elements possible, and while Philo allows only "a faint appearance of probability" to such a theory, he anticipates its most systematic statement so completely as to expound probably all the essential points in it.

Order is to be evolved out of disorder by blind unreasoning force, and if this can be done the grounds of the theistic inference from design disappear altogether, and only a naturalism or a materialism remains.

Only three elements are demanded for his new hypothesis of "cosmogony" – matter, motion, and eternity in time. The first two, all sciences hold to be constant in their quantity; we turn to experience, and "there is not probably, at present, in the whole universe, one particle of matter at absolute rest." An infinite duration in time is perhaps only a supposition, but it is a possible one. We turn again to experience, and find that there actually is a system, an order, "an economy of things by which matter can preserve that perpetual agitation which seems essential to it, and yet maintain a constancy in the forms which it produces." With the possibility of infinite transpositions all orders are possible, unstable positions pass away and decay, total or partial chaos ensues, "till finite, though innumerable, revolutions produce at last some forms whose parts and organs are so adjusted as to support the forms amidst a continued succession of matter": the present world, therefore, can be conceived as a stage in the history of matter-seeking form, and "by its very nature that order, when once established, supports itself for many ages, if not to eternity." Possibility and actuality therefore agree; the conclusion is simple. "Wherever matter is so poised, arranged, and adjusted as to continue in perpetual motion, and yet preserve a constancy in the forms, its situation must of necessity have all the same appearance of art and contrivance which we observe." If we turn from the inorganic to the organic in Nature, Hume has no theory such as later was used to account for the development of species; but Philo shadows forth that very idea which lies at the root of it, of order being "requisite for the subsistence" of the individual. "It is in vain to insist upon the uses of the parts in animals or vegetables and their curious adjustment to each other. I would fain know how an animal could subsist unless its parts were so adjusted? Do we not find that it immediately perishes whenever this adjustment ceases, and that its matter corrupting tries some new form?"

On this line of argument the theory of the evolution of order in the universe by natural laws of self-development must inevitably dispense with a reference to design, and probably would do so altogether in modern times were it not the case that modern teleology has widened her outlook upon creation, is willing to walk in imagination as far backward along the course of the world's development as the evolutionist is able to lead her, but only demands that he shall not minimise the nature of the primitive elements, nor ignore the fact that they really *involve* all the multiplicity of adjustment in themselves as truly as their latest combinations do. But whatever may be the true way of reconciling the evolutionary and naturalistic explanation of order with the inference to design, the Dialogues indicate one possible reply to the evolutionary theory by which the need for a reconciliation may be avoided altogether. And because the hypothesis of evolution in the Dialogues is admittedly "incomplete and imperfect," being a side issue "suggested on a sudden in the course of the argument," we have only to state Hume's partial reply to it, – a reply which is perfectly valid in its own place after a century and a half of steady advance in speculation.

The proposition that everything which exists must be subject to order is not convertible directly into this other, that the only purpose of order is to conserve existence. The first is obviously within experience; the second would require confirmation from an analysis of each individual instance of order, and could be disproved by one single case in which order is not an indispensable condition of bare life. Such cases, says Hume, though in general very frugal in Nature, "are far from being rare." He mentions only the physical conveniences and advantages which men possess, but one might add all the æsthetic and intellectual pleasures so profitable, so necessary for the perfection of man's nature, and then ask his question, Without all these "would human society and the human kind have been immediately extinguished?" And one proved instance of order where existence is not made more secure but rather more pleasurable and more complete by it, "is a sufficient proof of design, and of a benevolent design which gave rise to the order and arrangement of the universe." But the whole tenor of the evolutionary hypothesis is that all order, without exception, arises from the natural predisposition of all species that are generative towards the securing of life. Cleanthes does not question that such a power does operate in the world – he only denies that it is sufficient to account for all of the innumerable forms that are made known to us in experience; and Philo allows his contention without hesitation.

With this partial vindication of design against pure naturalism, Hume leaves the question between them apparently undecided. It is not further argued; indeed, Philo's view of it is that no amount of argument can ever completely prove the one or completely discredit the other. If it comes to a question of probability, of balancing the reasons for either side, if it is possible in his own phrase to "believe that the arguments on which a theory of design is established exceed the objections which lie against it," – if, in fact, a definite conclusion is demanded for common life, as conclusions are demanded every moment on questions less lofty than theology, – then Philo's judgment is not suspended, but becomes a "plain philosophical assent." But that the assent should be so plainly given from the sceptic's side, as it is in the Dialogues, is in itself proof of a distinct positive advance on the speculations of Hume's early years.

There is, however, one point on which the Dialogues yield only a negative result, and strangely enough it is the very argument from the idea of morality which Kant also excepted from the remainder of his critique of theology, treating it favourably, and endeavouring to give it a deeper setting among the necessary postulates of reason. Hume recognises quite fully the need for a conception of God which will harmonise with our highest ethical standards. Cleanthes is made to say expressly, "To what purpose establish the natural attributes of the Deity while the moral are still doubtful and uncertain?" In his desire to complete his theme he would willingly embrace the only method of supporting divine benevolence which he can conceive possible – namely, "to deny absolutely the misery and wickedness of men." But optimism is not a cloak that will fit Hume as it did Leibnitz. The world never presents itself to him at any time as a scene in which the good preponderates over the evil, even in the least degree, much less is it purely and unmixedly good. It is not a picture in which unpleasant shadows and jarring contrasts are used only in order to accentuate the brightness and harmony of the main subject, so that the whole work is one of beauty; it is rather an unfinished daub, parts of which might possibly be praised in isolation, but the greater proportion of its surface ought to be covered up. And therefore Cleanthes abandons all claim of moral perfection for God. He is "regulated by wisdom," desires to be benevolent, but is "limited by necessity." The natural operations that we observe at work in life might easily have been bettered by omnipotent goodness, and made more conformable to our conceptions of right without any loss to the other products of design. Four ways of morally amending the present order suggest themselves to our author. Pleasure might be employed to excite all creatures to self-preservation in every case where the present means is pain;[43] general laws might be made less rigid where their effects are cruel and unfair; the powers and faculties for good and happiness might be increased; excessive passions in man and unbridled power in Nature might be regulated and controlled so that all convulsions and revolutions should be impossible. As we read the pages of the Dialogues we seem to hear an echo of the ironical pessimism of Voltaire and Bolingbroke, and they evidently express Hume's confirmed and settled attitude to the worth of life in his mature as in his early years. And Hume saw in the light of dispassionate reason how little there is to suggest the existence of an indulgent fatherly love, ruling the universe with a direct interest in the welfare of its creatures: it is rather "a blind nature impregnated by a great vivifying principle, and pouring forth from her lap, without discernment or parental care, her maimed and abortive children." So far as our experience of reality goes, we cannot lean to any extreme theory of the moral qualities it expresses. We cannot suppose them perfectly good or perfectly bad; we dare not suppose them mixed and opposite, for that means conflict and contradiction; we can only suppose that good and evil are illusions, and that all real things are indifferent.

This antitheistic conclusion (for Hume admits it to be so) is entirely in accordance with his general theory of morals, and his contemporaries were not slow to lay their finger upon the point at issue. All moral judgments for Hume depend upon the natural psychology of man. In political and social ethics we conceive right and wrong only because certain ends are agreed upon, have been customary, and are accepted as such. Certain rules of conduct appear "useful" for these ends, and therefore we distinguish them as being right. In the ethics of the individual, also, we have no reason for making any judgment, except through the arbitrary constitution of the human mind; so that, as Reid says,[44] "by a change in our structure what is immoral might become moral, virtue might be turned into vice, and vice into virtue." The unessential

---

[43] Only a Paley could base any argument upon the inverse consideration that pleasure seems superadded for purposes which "might have been effected by the operation of pain." – Nat. Theol., chap. xxvi., which is small consolation for the ills of life.

[44] Active Powers, Essay V., chap. vii.

nature of moral distinctions for Hume had already been illustrated in his other writings, notably in that one which bears
the title "A Dialogue," and therefore Reid adds justly, "Mr.
Hume seems perfectly consistent with himself in allowing of
no evidence for the moral attributes of the Supreme Being,
whatever there may be for His natural attributes." And therefore it is to the nature of his theory of morals that we must
trace the motive of his main objection to natural religion.

If, then, in beholding the natural order of the world, Hume
is moved to despair, the inward moral order in man cannot
bring him relief. For it, according to him, is arbitrary and
fluctuating, and has no independent authority. "What I have
said concerning natural evil will apply to moral, with little
or no variation; and we have no more reason to infer that
the rectitude of the Supreme Being resembles human rectitude
than His benevolence resembles the human." And so his negative to the moral argument in natural religion is complete.
Probably had his scepticism here been less unmistakably his
own reasoned verdict, it might have been taken for a grand
satire upon the popular theology of his own day. In it the
wretchedness and wickedness of men were favourite topics,
and the darkest shadows in Hume's pessimism are bright in
comparison to the absolute blackness pictured by orthodox
divines when they referred to the estate of sin and misery
that resulted from the fall. It was only Hume's fearless
logic that warned them of the atheism implied in their moan-
ings: he himself seems content to rest in the conclusion he
had drawn from premises which at least were his own,
whether others shared them or not.

In whatever way it may be possible to restate the moral
argument, Hume's judgment of it in the form in which he
conceived it is unfavourable. Even the earliest direct reply to
the Dialogues, that of Milner in 1781, points out how far
Hume's general position in ethics is accountable for this phase
of his speculation. Conscience and the very intuitive nature of
the moral sense are not taken into his view at all, and yet
there are "final causes in the moral world as obvious as in
the administration of the natural world."[45] And with the
deepening sense of the reality of moral distinctions and moral
laws, the nature of the moral argument has changed rapidly

[45] Milner's Answer, sect. 12.

in modern times, and the ascription of ethical perfection to God is on every side considered to be an indispensable and essential condition of any expression of belief in Him.

With Hume the consciousness of such a necessity is not present, and in summing up briefly the net result of the Dialogues, we must bear his difficulty carefully in mind. The total of agreement between the two principals is not very great in extent. They both accept the argument from design, and it alone, for all we know of God. They find evidence everywhere of the presence of an active ordering intelligence, a creative reason, a mind. This is all we *know* of God, and therefore in this form it is we must worship Him. If we are pleased to call Him good, it is with this reservation, that goodness in God is less like goodness as we know it than His reason is like ours. "The moral qualities in man are more defective in their kind than his natural abilities." Analogy, which formerly enabled us to discover the admitted truth, fails us now to describe the moral qualities of God: there is no evidence for them as there undoubtedly is for His designing intelligence. Let us, therefore, call Him Mind, and for the rest keep silence and believe. This is the final message of Hume's latest utterance on the greatest question of the ages. We should be wrong if we claimed that it contained more – unjust if we supposed it contained less.

In their closing paragraphs the Dialogues call us away from the speculations of pure theology to the practical application of divine truth in life. He had as little sympathy as his contemporary, the poet Burns, with the awful doctrines of a God all power and fore-knowledge, ruling by terror of hell and hope of heaven, with "devils and torrents of fire and brimstone," in which "the damned are infinitely superior in number to the elect," – all the crude Calvinistic dogma, so prevalent among his fellow-countrymen, from which they hoped to derive some guidance for their conduct in the way. In his opinion it overlooked the importance of the ordinary virtues, neglecting them in order to concentrate attention upon eternal salvation, even holding that they are unessential and unmeaning. To him it serves only as an example of false religion, with consequences pernicious in society and utterly demoralising in the individual; only a little better than no religion at all; a superstition, with a kernel of truth encased in a shell of doctrines that can and ought to be cast away.

For the false Hume would substitute now as the true that conception of religion running through all his writings from the earliest to the latest, according to which we assent to the existence of God, and for the rest give all our energies to the practice of morality. "The proper office of religion is to regulate the heart of men, humanise their conduct, infuse the spirit of temperance, order, and obedience; and as its operation is silent, and only enforces the motives of morality and justice, it is in danger of being overlooked and confounded with these other motives. When it distinguishes itself, and acts as a separate principle over men, it has departed from its proper sphere, and has become only a cover to faction and ambition."[46] Not concerned with dogmatising about the many and mysterious attributes of God or the incomprehensible decrees of His Providence, as though some necessity lay upon us to profess complete knowledge of Him, religion is for Hume, in the first place, a simple faith and a present rule of conduct in the present life. It has a certain limited knowlege of God derived by reason working in the realm of experience. No doubts can take that much away; but out beyond there always lies for Hume, when he goes deepest in his search for truth, the realm of faith and revelation. The last word of the Dialogues is a cry for it, – the only refuge for human reason from its ignorance and imperfections. So also ends the Inquiry, so also the Essay on the Immortality of the Soul. For religion that has to do with concrete life, lived in the clear sense of God's existence, must surely end either in a claim of perfect knowledge or else in just such a cry. Though Hume nowhere defines these terms of faith and revelation, and nowhere gives an analysis of their use, I see no reason why, in choosing the second of these alternatives, he should be deemed inconsistent or insincere.

And if from the purely historical point of view the closing lines of the Dialogues be considered their author's last utterance in speculation, they may be taken to indicate how, to the very end, the natural man strove with the philosopher in Hume's thought and left him dissatisfied still.

---

[46] P. 176. Compare with this passage of the Dialogues the following from "The History of Great Britain," vii. 450: "The proper office of religion is to reform men's lives, to purify their hearts, to enforce all moral duties, and to secure obedience to the laws of the civil magistrate."

III. Natural History of Religion

A POSTSCRIPT ON MR. HUME'S NATURAL HISTORY OF RELIGION
A. Marvel

P.S. Mr. DAVID HUME, in *his natural history of religion,* allows its foundation in reason to be most obvious.

> "for no rational enquirer can, after serious reflexion, suspend his belief a moment with regard to the primary principles of genuine theism and religion."

But then he thinks it more difficult to shew, "its origin in human nature."[1] On these principles he grounds his enquiry. But what can he mean by religion admitting the clearest solution, concerning the foundation it has in reason; yet, not so concerning its origin in human nature? May reason then be separated from human nature in the religion of mankind? is this possible? How shall it be done, when no rational enquirer can, after serious reflexion, suspend his belief one moment with regard to the primary principles of genuine theism and religion?

To secure his distinctions,

> "Polytheism or idolatry was, and necessarily must have been the first and most ancient religion of mankind. For, the most ancient records of the human race still present us with Polytheism as the popular and established system."[2]

– Does it not seem more natural to conclude, that from the creation mankind clearly saw the invisible things of God? But that when they knew God, they glorified him not as God, became wanton in their imaginations, and so corrupted the primary principles of pure theism. If the history of *Moses* be authentic, men degenerated from true theism to idolatry; and by their debaucheries brought on the destructive deluge. The primary religion of the new world, peopled by *Noah* and his

[1] P. 1.

[2] P. 3.

family, surely could not be polytheism and idolatry. And certain we are, superstition, polytheism or idolatry could not be the primary profession of christians. Especially since Mr. H. has said,

> "nothing indeed would prove more strongly the divine origin of any religion, than to find, (and happily this is the case with christianity) that it is free from a contradiction, so incident to human nature."[3]

Whatever was his design, this is the true character of genuine christianity, untouched by the over-officious fingers of men. And to which, this elegant writer seems much indebted for that charming description of theism,[4]

> "a system which supposes one sole deity, the perfection of reason and goodness, which is justly prosecuted, will banish every thing frivolous, unreasonable, or inhuman from religious worship; and set before men the most illustrious example, as well as the most commanding motives of justice and benevolence."

It must be allowed a fine copy of the Gospel original; and could be taken from no other system.

This lively writer makes some very uncommon observations.

> "Men have a natural tendency to rise from idolatry to theism, and to sink again from theism into idolatry." And he concludes, "that religion and idolatry have one and the same origin."

See his 8th section.

But in his 10th, "the corruption of the best things give rise to the worst."[5] – Of this we have some conception. Not so of theism and polytheism having one origin. Nor of the natural tendency in men to rise from idolatry to theism. And we should be inclined to ask some proof, how it comes to pass, that in this natural tendency to both extremes, we see not the mechanical vibrations of the pendulum equal, or nearly equal? How can we read over Mr. HUME's *natural*

---

[3] P. 50.

[4] P. 59.

[5] Also p. 63. *Corruptio optimi pessima.*

history of religion, and give him credit, if this observation has any truth in it? Why such an universal polytheism, if there be this natural tendency in man to rise from idolatry to theism?

There is another discovery made by this Philosopher, and that is, "the origin of idolatry or polytheism, is, the active imagination of men, incessantly imployed, in cloathing the conception they have of objects, in shapes more suitable to its natural comprehensions."[6] Which if conclusive, then religion and idolatry, theism and polytheism are equally natural to man; and have alike a very fanciful origination. –

But in truth, his idea of the religion of mankind, does not intend more, than the superstition which has arisen from depravity. For, sais he, "one may safely affirm, that all popular theology, especially the scholastic, has a kind of appetite for absurdity and contradiction. If that theology went not beyond reason and common sense, her doctrines would appear too easy and familiar. Amazement must of necessity be raised: mystery affected: darkness and obscurity sought after: and a foundation of merit afforded the devout votaries, who desire an opportunity of subduing their rebellious reason, by the belief of the most unintelligible sophisms".[7] Is not this *Sir*, a fair specimen of what he means by the religion of mankind? But could this be the first and most ancient religion of mankind? Does he not explicitly own it could not?[8] "In short, all virtue, when men are reconciled to it by ever so little practice, is agreeable: all superstition is for ever odious and burthensome."[9] – and again, "after the commission of crimes, there arise remorses and secret horrors, which give no rest to the mind, but make it have recourse to religious rites and ceremonies, as expiations of its offences. Whatever weakens or disorders the internal frame, promotes the interests of superstition: and nothing is more destructive to them than a manly, steady virtue, which either preserves us from disastrous, melancholy accidents, or teaches us to bear them. During such calm sun-shine of the mind, these

6 P. 55.

7 P. 70.

8 P. 55.

9 P. 106.

spectres of false divinity never make their appearance. On the other hand, while we *abandon our selves* to the undisciplined suggestions of our timid and anxious hearts, every kind of barbarity is ascribed to the supreme Being, from the terror with which we are agitated; and every kind of caprice, from the methods which we embrace, in order to appease him."[10]

I would not mistake this writer, and therefore produce another of his descriptions of the popular religions; in which he is very express in shewing, that these superstitions have not their origin in human nature. "And that it may safely be affirmed, many popular religions are really, in the conception of these more vulgar votaries, a spirit of Dæmonism; and the higher the deity is exalted in power and knowledge, the lower of course is he frequently depress'd in goodness and benevolence; whatever epithets of praise may be bestowed on him by his amazed adorers. Amongst idolaters, the words may be false, and belie the secret opinions: but amongst more exalted religionists, the opinion itself often contracts a kind of falsehood, and belies *the inward sentiment. The heart secretly detects such measures of cruel and implacable vengeance*; but the judgment dares not but pronounce them perfect and adorable. *And the additional misery of this inward struggle* aggravates all the other terrors, by which these unhappy victims to superstition are for ever bounded".[11]

From this citation, I would ask, whether Mr. *Hume* has not acknowledged, that idolatry and superstition are not natural to man? And that consequently, the principles of genuine theism and religion, must have their origin in human nature. – Superstition, the gloomy dread of deity, is no primary principle in the heart of man.[12] The opinion belies the inward sentiment: there is a secret detestation of it in the heart!

I presume to make the following conclusions.

Mr. *Hume*'s fundamental principles are manifestly wrong. He has called the superstition of the world, *a natural history of the religion of mankind.* He has affirmed, a natural tendency in man to rise out of idolatry into religion. He has strangely declared, that religion and superstition, theism and polytheism have one and the same origin; and this no better

[10] P. 109.

[11] P. 98

[12] Though it is affirmed to be so in the 13th Proposition.

than the imagination. – Whereas, religion and reason in man, are inseparable. Religion could not arise out of superstition, theism out of polytheism. The universal spread of idolatry, by his own history, as universally confronts the proposition: and will not suppose it to have the least foundation in nature. For superstition has its origin in the disordered passions and imaginations of mankind; religion has its origin in a natural sovereignty which the reason of man exercises over these faculties. And from the nature of the thing, idolatry or polytheism could not be the primary profession of mankind; but must have been a corruption of pure theism and religion. Notwithstanding these sophisms, Mr. *Hume* has finely exposed superstition and popery: professeth himself an advocate of pure theism. And so far as he is a theist, he cannot be an enemy to genuine christianity.

HUME'S FOUR DISSERTATIONS
Anonymous

Source: The Monthly Review, vol. 16, 1757

THERE are but few of our modern Writers, whose works are so generally read, as those of Mr. Hume. And, indeed, if we consider them in one view, as sprightly and ingenious compositions, this is not at all to be wondered at: there is a delicacy of sentiment, an original turn of thought, a perspicuity, and often an elegance, of language, that cannot but recommend his writings to every Reader of taste. It is to be regretted, however, that such a genius should employ his abilities in the manner he frequently does. In his attacks upon the religion of his country, he acts not the part of an open and generous enemy, but endeavours to weaken its authority by oblique hints, and artful insinuations. In this view his works merit little, if any, regard; and few Readers, of just discernment, we apprehend, will envy him any honours his acuteness, or elegance, can possibly obtain, when they are only employed in filling the mind with the uncomfortable fluctuations of scepticism, and the gloom of infidelity. But leaving general reflections, let us proceed to give an account of the Dissertations now before us; the first of which is entitled, *The Natural History of Religion.*

    This Dissertation Mr. Hume introduces with observing, that there are two questions in regard to religion, which challenge our principal attention, viz. that concerning its foundation in reason, and that concerning its origin in human nature. The first question, which is the most important, admits, he says, of the clearest solution. The whole frame of nature bespeaks an intelligent Author; and no rational enquirer can, after serious reflection, suspend his belief a moment with regard to the primary principles of genuine theism and religion. But the other question, concerning the origin of religion in human nature, admits of some more difficulty. The belief of invisible intelligent power, has been very generally diffused over the human race, in all places, and in all ages; but it has neither, perhaps, been so universally, we are told, as to admit of no exceptions, nor has it been, in any degree, uniform in the ideas which it has suggested. Some nations have been discovered, who entertained no sentiments of religion, if travellers and historians may be credited; and no two nations, and scarce any two men, have ever agreed precisely in the same sentiments.

"It would appear, therefore," continues Mr. Hume, "that this pre-conception springs not from an original instinct, or primary impression of nature, such as gives rise to self-love, affection betwixt the sexes, love of progeny, gratitude, resentment; since every instinct of this kind has been found absolutely universal in all nations and ages, and has always a precise, determinate object, which it inflexibly pursues. The first religious principles must be secondary; such as may easily be perverted by various accidents and causes, and whose operation too, in some cases, may, by an extraordinary concurrence of circumstances, be altogether prevented. What those principles are, which give rise to the original belief, and what those accidents and causes are, which direct its operation, is the subject of our present enquiry."

Mr. Hume is of opinion, that if we consider the improvement of human society, from rude beginnings to a state of greater perfection, it will appear, that Polytheism or Idolatry, was, and necessarily must have been, the first and most antient religion of mankind. In order to support this opinion, he observes, that the farther we mount up into antiquity, the more we find mankind plunged into Idolatry. The North, the South, the East, the West, give their unanimous testimony to this fact: As to the doubtful and sceptical principles of a few Philosophers, or the Theism, and that too not entirely pure, of one or two nations, these form no objection worth regarding. According to the natural progress of human thought too, he says, the ignorant multitude must first entertain some groveling and familiar notion of superior powers, before they stretch their conception to that perfect Being, who bestowed order on the whole frame of nature: and we may as reasonably imagine, that men inhabited palaces before huts and cottages, or studied geometry before agriculture, as assert, that the Deity appeared to them a pure spirit, omniscient, omnipotent, and omnipresent, before he was apprehended to be a powerful, though limited Being, with human passions and appetites, limbs, and organs. In a word, our Author thinks it impossible, that theism could, from reasoning, have been the primary religion of the human race, and have afterwards, by its corruption, given birth to Idolatry, and to all the various superstitions of the Heathen world.

If we would therefore indulge our curiosity, he says, in enquiring concerning the origin of religion, we must turn our thoughts towards Idolatry or Polytheism, the primitive religion of uninstructed mankind. And here he observes, that if men were led into the apprehension of invisible, intelligent power, by a contemplation of the works of nature, they could never possibly entertain any conception but of one single Being, who bestowed existence and order on this vast machine, and adjusted all its parts, according to one regular plan, or connected system. On the other hand, if, leaving the works of nature, we trace the footsteps of invisible power, in the various and contrary events of human life, we are necessarily led into Polytheism, and to the acknowlegement of several limited and imperfect Deities. Storms and tempests ruin what is nourished by the sun; the sun destroys what is fostered by the moisture of dews and rains. War may be favourable to a nation, whom the inclemency of the seasons afflicts with famine: sickness and pestilence may depopulate a kingdom, amidst the most profuse plenty. In short, the conduct of events, or what we call the plan of a particular Providence, is so full of variety and uncertainty, that if we suppose it immediately ordered by any intelligent Being, we must acknowlege a contrariety in their designs and intentions, a constant combat of opposite powers, and a repentance, or change of intention in the same power, from impotence or levity.

It may be concluded therefore, Mr. Hume imagines, that in all nations which have embraced Polytheism, or Idolatry, the first ideas of religion arose not from a contemplation of the works of nature; but from a concern with respect to the events of life, and from the incessant hopes and fears which actuate the human mind. Accordingly we find, it is said, that all Idolaters, having separated the provinces of their Deities, have recourse to that invisible agent, to whose authority they are immediately subjected, and whose province it is to superintend that course of actions, in which they are at any time engaged. Juno is invoked at marriages; Lucina at births; Neptune receives the prayers of seamen; and Mars of warriors. Each natural event is supposed to be governed by some intelligent agent; and nothing prosperous, or adverse, can happen in life, which may not be the subject of peculiar prayers or thanksgivings.

In further treating of this subject, Mr. Hume observes, that we are placed in this world as in a great theatre, where the true springs and causes of every event, are entirely unknown to us; nor have we either sufficient wisdom to foresee, or power to prevent, those ills with which we are continually threatened. We hang in perpetual suspence betwixt life and death, health and sickness, plenty and want; which are distributed amongst the human species by secret and unknown causes, whose operation is oft unexpected, and always unaccountable. These *unknown causes* then, we are told, become the constant object of our hope and fear; and while the passions are kept in perpetual alarm by an anxious expectation of the events, the imagination is equally employed in forming ideas of those powers, on which we have so entire a dependence. No wonder then, Mr. Hume says, that mankind being placed in such an absolute ignorance of causes, and being at the same time so anxious concerning their future fortunes, should immediately acknowlege a dependance on invisible powers, possessed of sentiment, and intelligence. The *unknown causes*, which continually employ their thought, appearing always in the same aspect, are all apprehended to be of the same kind or species. Nor is it long before we ascribe to them thought, and reason, and passion, and sometimes even the limbs and figures of men, in order to bring them nearer to a resemblance with ourselves.

Our Author goes on to consider the gross Polytheism and Idolatry of the vulgar, and to trace all its various appearances in the principles of human nature, whence they are derived. Whoever learns by argument, he observes, the existence of invisible, intelligent power, must reason from the admirable contrivance of natural objects, and must suppose the world to be the workmanship of that Divine Being, the original cause of all things. But the vulgar Polytheist, so far from admitting that idea, deifies every part of the universe, and conceives all the conspicuous productions of nature to be themselves so many real Divinities. The sun, moon, and stars, are all Gods, according to his system: fountains are inhabited by nymphs, and trees by hamadryads: even monkies, dogs, cats, and other animals, often become sacred in his eyes, and strike him with a religious veneration. And thus, however strong men's propensity to believe invisible, intelligent power, in nature, their propensity is equally strong to rest their attention on sensible, visible objects; and in order to reconcile these opposite inclinations, they are led to unite the invisible power with some visible object.

Mr. Hume observes further, that the Deities of the vulgar are so little superior to human creatures, that where men are affected with strong sentiments of veneration or gratitude, for any hero, or public benefactor, nothing can be more natural than to convert him into a God, and fill the Heavens after this manner, with continual recruits from amongst mankind. Most of the Divinities of the antient world are supposed to have once been men, and to have been beholden for their *apotheosis* to the admiration and affection of the people. And the real history of their adventures, corrupted by tradition, and elevated by the marvellous, became a plentiful source of fable; especially in passing through the hands of Poets, Allegorists, and Priests, who successfully improved upon the wonder and astonishment of the ignorant multitude.

Polytheism, or idolatrous worship, he says, being founded entirely in vulgar traditions, is liable to this great inconvenience, that any practice, or opinion, however barbarous or corrupted, may be authorized by it; and full scope is left for knavery to impose on credulity, till morals and humanity be expelled from the religious systems of mankind. At the same time he observes, Idolatry is attended with this evident advantage, that, by limiting the powers and functions of its Deities, it naturally admits the Gods of other sects and nations to a share of divinity, and renders all the various Deities, as well as rites, ceremonies, or traditions, compatible with each other.

Theism is opposite, both in its advantages and disadvantages, as it supposes one sole Deity, the perfection of reason and goodness, it should, our Author says, if justly prosecuted, banish every thing frivolous, unreasonable, or inhuman, from religious worship, and set before men the most illustrious example, as well as the most commanding motives of justice and benevolence. These mighty advantages are not, indeed, over balanced, (for that is not possible) but somewhat diminished, we are told, by inconveniences, which arise from the vices and prejudices of mankind. While one sole object of devotion is acknowledged, the worship of other Deities is regarded as absurd and impious. Nay, this unity of object seems naturally to require the unity of faith and ceremonies, and furnishes designing men with a pretext for representing their adversaries as prophane, and the objects of divine, as well as human, vengeance. For as each sect is positive, that its own faith and worship are entirely acceptable to the Deity; and as no one can conceive, that the same Being should be pleased with different and opposite rites and principles; the several sects fall naturally into animosity, and mutually discharge on each other, that sacred zeal and rancour, the most furious and implacable of all human passions.

The tolerating spirit of Idolaters, both in ancient and modern times, Mr. Hume says, is very obvious to any one, who is the least conversant in the writings of historians, or travellers; and the intolerance of almost all religions, which have maintained the unity of God, is as remarkable as the contrary principle in Polytheists. The implacable narrow spirit of the Jews, we are told, is well known. Mahommdeism set out with still more bloody principles, and even to this day deals out damnation, though not fire and faggot, to all other sects. And if, amongst Christians, the English and Dutch have embraced the principles of toleration, this singularity has proceeded from the steady resolution of the civil magistrate, in opposition to the continued efforts of priests and bigots.

"I may venture to affirm," continues our Author, "that few corruptions of Idolatry and Polytheism are more pernicious to political society, than this corruption of Theism, when carried to the utmost height. The human sacrifices of the Carthaginians, Mexicans, and many barbarous nations, scarce exceed the Inquisition, and persecutions of Rome and Madrid. For besides, that the effusion of blood may not be so great in the former case, as in the latter; besides this, I say, the human victims, being chosen by lot, or by some exterior signs, affect not in so considerable a degree, the rest of the society. Whereas virtue, knowledge, love of liberty, are the qualities which call down the fatal vengeance of Inquisitors; and when expelled, have the society in the most shameful ignorance, corruption, and bondage. The illegal murder of one man by a tyrant, is more pernicious than the death of a thousand by pestilence, famine, or any undistinguishing calamity."

From the comparison of Theism and Idolatry, our Author proceeds to form some other observations, in order to confirm the vulgar saying, that the corruption of the best things gives rise to the worst. He tells us, that where the Deity is represented as infinitely superior to mankind, this belief, though altogether just, is apt, when joined with superstitious terrors, to sink the human mind into the lowest submission and abasement, and to represent the monkish virtues of mortification, pennance, humility, and passive suffering, as the only qualities which are acceptable to him. But where the Gods are conceived to be only a little superior to mankind, and to have been many of them advanced from that inferior rank, we are more at our ease in our addresses to them; and may even, without profaneness, aspire sometimes to a rivalship, and emulation of them. Hence activity, spirit, courage, magnanimity, love of liberty, and all the virtues which aggrandize a people.

He observes further, to the same purpose, that if we examine, without prejudice, the antient Heathen Mythologyas contained in the Poets, we shall not discover in it any such monstrous absurdity, as we may be apt at first to apprehend. Nay, so natural does Mr. Hume think the whole mythological system, that in the vast variety of planets and worlds contained in this universe, he thinks it more than probable, that, somewhere or other, it is really carried into execution.

"The chief objection to it," says he, "with regard to this planet, is, that it is not ascertained by any just reason or authority. The antient tradition insisted on by the Heathen Priests and Theologers, is but a weak foundation, and transmitted also such a number of contradictory reports, supported, all of them, by equal authority, that it became absolutely impossible to fix a preference among them. A few volumes therefore must contain all the Polemical writings of Pagan Priests, and their whole theology must consist more of traditional stories, and superstitious practices, than of philosophical argument and controversy.

But where Theism forms the fundamental principle of any popular religion, that tenet is so conformable to sound reason, that philosophy is apt to incorporate itself with such a system of theology. And if the other dogmas of that system be contained in a sacred book, such as *the Alcoran*[1]; or be determined by any visible authority, like that of the Roman Pontiff; speculative reasoners naturally carry on their assent, and embrace a theory which has been instilled into them by their earliest education, and which also possesses some degree of consistence and uniformity. But as these appearances do often, all of them, prove deceitful, philosophy will soon find herself very unequally yoked with her new associate; and instead of regulating each principle as they advance together, she is at every turn perverted to serve the purposes of superstition: for, besides the unavoidable incoherencies which must be reconciled and adjusted, one may safely affirm, that all popular theology, especially the scholastic, has a kind of appetite for absurdity and contradiction. If that theology went not beyond reason and common sense, her doctrines would appear too easy and familiar. Amazement must of necessity be raised. Mystery affected, darkness and obscurity sought after; and a foundation of merit afforded the devout votaries who desire an opportunity of subduing their rebellious reason, by the belief of the most unintelligible sophisms.

Ecclesiastical history sufficiently confirms these reflections. When a controversy is started, some people pretend always with certainty, to conjecture the issue. Which ever opinion, say they, is more contrary to plain sense, is sure to prevail; even where the general interest of the system requires not that decision. Though the reproach of heresy may for some time be bandied about amongst the disputants, it always rests on the side of reason. Any one, it is pretended, that has but learning enough to know the definition of *Arian, Pelagian, Erastian, Socinian, Sabellian, Eutychian, Nestorian, Monothelite, &c.* not to mention *Protestant*, whose fate is yet uncertain, will be convinced of the truth of this observation. And thus a system becomes

[1] *The Koran*, Mr. Hume should have said.

more absurd in the end, merely from its being reasonable and philosophical in the beginning.

To oppose the torrent of scholastic religion, by such feeble maxims as these, that *it is impossible for the same thing to be and not to be*; that *the whole is greater than a part*; that *two and three make five*; is pretending to stop the ocean with a bull-rush. Will you set up profane reason against sacred mystery? No punishment is great enough for your impiety. And the same fires which were kindled for heretics, will serve also for the destruction of philosophers."

After several other reflections on this subject, Mr. Hume goes on to observe, that notwithstanding the dogmatical imperial style of all superstition, the conviction of the religionists, in all ages, is more affected than real, and scarce approaches, in any degree, to that solid belief and persuasion which governs us in the common affairs of life. Men dare not avow, even to their own hearts, the doubts, which they entertain on such subjects; they make a merit of implicit faith, and disguise to themselves their real infidelity, by the strongest asseverations, and most positive bigotry. But nature is too hard for all their endeavours, and suffers not the obscure, glimmering light, afforded in those shadowy regions, to equal the strong impressions made by common sense, and by experience. The usual course of men's conduct belies their words, and shews, that the assent in these matters is some unaccountable operation of the mind, betwixt disbelief and conviction, but approaching much nearer to the former than the latter.

"Since therefore," continues Mr. Hume, "the mind of man appears of so loose and unsteady a contexture, that even at present, when so many persons find an interest in continually employing on it the chissel and the hammer, yet are they not able to engrave theological tenets with any lasting impression; how much more must this have been the case in antient times, when the retainers to the holy function were so much fewer in comparison? No wonder that the appearances, were then very inconsistent, and that men, on some occasions, might seem determined infidels, and enemies to the established religion, without being so in reality; or at least without knowing their minds in that particular."

In the further prosecution of this subject, our Author observes, that in every religion, however sublime the verbal definition which it gives of its divinity, many of the votaries, perhaps the greatest number, will still seek the divine favour, not by virtue and good morals, which alone can be acceptable to a perfect Being, but either by frivolous observances, by intemperate zeal, by rapturous extasies, or by the belief of mysterious and absurd opinions. Nay, if we should suppose, he says, what seldom happens, that a popular religion were found, in which it was expresly declared, that nothing but morality could gain the Divine favour; if an order of Priests were instituted to inculcate this opinion, in daily sermons, and with all the arts of persuasion; yet so inveterate are the people's prejudices, that for want of some other superstition, they would make the very attendance on these sermons the essentials of religion, rather than place them in virtue and good morals. The manner in which he accounts for this, is as follows:

The duties, he says, which a man performs as a friend or parent, seem merely owing to his benefactor, or children; nor can he be wanting to these duties, without breaking through all the ties of nature and morality. A strong inclination may prompt him to the performance: a sentiment of order and moral beauty joins its force to these natural ties; and the whole man, if truly virtuous, is drawn to his duty without any effort or endeavour. Even with regard to the virtues which are more austere, and more founded on reflection, such as public spirit, filial duty, temperance, or integrity; the moral obligation, in our apprehension, removes all pretence to religious merit; and the virtuous conduct is esteemed no more than what we owe to society, and to ourselves. In all this a superstitious man finds nothing which he has properly performed for the sake of his Deity, or which can peculiarly recommend him to the divine favour and protection. He considers not, that the most genuine method of serving the Divinity, is by promoting the happiness of his creatures. He still looks out for some more immediate service of the Supreme Being, in order to allay those terrors with which he is haunted. And any practice recommended to him, which either serves to no purpose in life, or offers the strongest violence to his natural inclinations; that practice he will more readily embrace, on account of those very circumstances, which should make him absolutely reject it. It seems the more purely religious, that it proceeds from no mixture of any other motive or consideration. And if, for its sake, he sacrifices much of his ease and quiet, his claim of merit appears still to rise upon him, in proportion to the zeal and devotion which he discovers. In restoring a loan, or paying a debt, his Divinity is no way beholden to him; because these acts of justice are what he was bound to perform, and what many would have performed, were there no God in the universe. But if he fast a day, or give himself a sound whipping, this has a direct reference, in his opinion, to the service of God. No other motive could engage him to such austerities. By these distinguished marks of devotion, he has now acquired the Divine favour; and may expect, in recompence, protection and safety in this world, and eternal happiness in the next.

Mr. Hume concludes this long Dissertation, which takes up near half the volume, in the following manner.

"Though the stupidity of men, barbarous and uninstructed, be so great," says he, "that they may not see a sovereign Author in the more obvious works of nature, to which they are so much familiarized; yet it scarce seems possible, that any one of good understanding should reject that idea, when once it is suggested to him. A purpose, an intention, a design, is evident in every thing; and when our comprehension is so far enlarged, as to contemplate the first rise of this visible system, we must adopt, with the strongest conviction, the idea of some intelligent cause or author. The uniform maxims too, which prevail through the whole frame of the universe, naturally, if not necessarily, lead us to conceive this intelligence as single and undivided, where the prejudices of education oppose not so reasonable a theory. Even the contrarieties of nature, by discovering themselves every where, become proofs of some consistent plan, and establish one single purpose or intention, however inexplicable and incomprehensible.

Good and ill are universally intermingled and confounded; happiness and misery, wisdom and folly, virtue and vice. Nothing is pure, and entirely of a piece. All advantages are attended with disadvantages. An universal compensation prevails in all conditions of Being and Existence. And it is scarce possible for us, by our most chimerical wishes, to form the idea of a station or situation altogether desirable. The draughts of life, according to the Poet's fiction, are always mixed from the vessels on each hand of Jupiter. Or if any cup be presented altogether pure, it is drawn only, as the same Poet tells us, from the left-hand vessel.

The more exquisite any good is, of which a small specimen is afforded us, the sharper is the evil allied to it; and few exceptions are found to this uniform law of nature. The most sprightly wit borders on madness; the highest effusions of joy produce the deepest melancholy; the most ravishing pleasures are attended with the most cruel lassitude and disgust; the most flattering hopes make way for the severest disappointments. And, in general, no course of life has such safety (for happiness is not to be dreamed of) as the temperate and moderate, which maintains, as far as possible, a mediocrity, and a kind of insensibility, in every thing.

As the good, the great, the sublime, the ravishing, are found eminently in the genuine principles of Theism, it may be expected, from the analogy of nature, that the base, the absurd, the mean, the terrifying, will be discovered equally in religious fictions and chimeras.

The universal propensity to believe in invisible, intelligent power, if not an original instinct, being at least a general attendant of human nature, it may be considered as a kind of mark or stamp, which the Divine Workman has set upon his work; and nothing, surely, can more dignify mankind, than to be thus selected from all the other parts of the creation, and to bear the image or impression of the universal Creator. But consult this image, as it commonly appears in the popular religions of the world, how is the Deity disfigured in our representations of him! What caprice, absurdity, and immorality are attributed to him! How much is he degraded, even below the character which we should naturally, in common life, ascribe to a man of sense and virtue!

What a noble privilege is it of human reason, to attain the knowledge of the Supreme Being; and, from the visible works of nature, be enabled to infer so sublime a principle as its supreme Creator? But turn the reverse of the medal, survey most nations and most ages. Examine the religious principles, which have in fact prevailed in the world; you will scarcely be persuaded, that they are other than sick men's dreams: or perhaps will regard them more as the playsome whimsies of monkeys in human shape, than the serious, positive, dogmatical observations of a Being, who dignifies himself with the name of rational.

Hear the verbal protestations of all men: nothing they are so certain of as their religious tenets. Examine their lives, you will scarcely think they repose the smallest confidence in them.

The greatest and truest zeal gives us no security against hypocrisy: the most open impiety is attended with a secret dread and compunction.

No theological absurdities so glaring, as have not, sometimes, been embraced by men of the greatest and most cultivated understanding. No religious precepts so rigorous, as have not been adopted by the most voluptuous and most abandoned of men.

Ignorance *is the mother of devotion.* A maxim that is proverbial, and confirmed by general experience. Look out for a people entirely devoid of religion: if you find them at all, be assured that they are but a few degrees removed from brutes.

What so pure as some of the morals included in some theological systems? What so corrupted, as some of the practices to which these systems give rise?

The comfortable views exhibited by the belief of a futurity, are ravishing and delightful: but how quickly vanish on the appearance of its terrors, which keep a more firm and durable possession of the human mind?

The whole is a riddle, an ænigma, an inexplicable mystery. Doubt, uncertainty, suspence of judgment, appear the only result of our most accurate scrutiny, concerning this subject. But such is the frailty of human reason, and such the irresistable contagion of opinion, that even this deliberate doubt could scarce be upheld, did we not enlarge our view, and opposing one species of superstition to another, set them a quarrelling, while we ourselves, during their fury and contention, happily make our escape into the calm, though obscure, regions of philosophy."

Thus have we given a pretty full view of what is contained in Mr. Hume's first Dissertation; which abounds with shrewd reflections, and just observations, upon human nature: mixed with a considerable portion of that sceptical spirit, which is so apparent in all his works; and with some insinuations, artfully couched, against the Christian religion.

REMARKS ON MR. DAVID HUME'S ESSAY ON THE NATURAL HISTORY OF RELIGION
Addressed to the Reverend Dr. Warburton
Anonymous

Source: The Monthly Review, vol. 17, 1757

THESE Remarks are addressed to Dr. Warburton, as to the supposed Author of the *Four Letters on Lord Bolingbroke's Philosophy*, and under this character, our Author says, the Doctor has a right to them as being little more than his own Remarks, only transferred from a Patrician to a Plebeian Naturalist.

It might have been expected, this Remarker tells us, that after so complete a conquest as Dr. Warburton had gained over Lord Bolingbroke, the rabble of the enemy, after their Chieftain was subdued, would have dispersed, at least, that they would not have rallied again, till in future times some other Champion of their cause, as illustrious by his name and quality, should arise to reconduct them to the charge.

"But, alas!" continues he, "the irreligious spirit, tho' it may be disgraced, is not so easily suppressed. Ere the public had time to celebrate your triumphs, behold a puny Dialietician from the North (for as Erasmus long since observed, *Scoti* DIALECTICIS ARGENTIIS *sibi blandiuntur*), all over armed with doubts and disputation, steps forth into his place, and, with the same beggarly troop of routed Sophisms, comes again to the attack.

But now, as the enemy is so contemptible, and the danger so little pressing, you may well enjoy your repose, and leave it to some inferior hand to chastise his insolence. And the very weakest may be equal to this attempt. For nothing remains but to employ against them the weapons which you have furnished; in a word, to draw again that Sword of the Spirit, which you had borrowed from the Sanctuary, and whose resistless splendour flashes, if not conviction, yet confusion in every face.

To this office I presume to devote myself. I have a portion, at least of your zeal to animate my endeavours. And if my talents should be found as mean as those of my adversary, this circumstance would not discourage me. The contest would only be more equal; and in such a quarrel the serious advocate for religion would be sorry to owe his success to any thing but the goodness of his cause."

After this introduction, and a page or two concerning himself, addressed to Dr. Warburton, he proceeds to his Remarks, which, he tells us, are such as occurred to him on a single reading of the Essay; were entered hastily on the margin, as he went along; and are now transcribed, with little or no variation, for the public use. He entreats the public not to be offended with this appearance of neglect, and acquaints us, that he never designed his animadversions for an elaborate piece of instruction or entertainment to the learned Reader, being only the employment of a vacant hour, to expose to the laughter of every man, that can read, the futility, licence, and vanity of Mr. DAVID HUME.

Such is the account our Author gives of his Remarks, which are written in a smart lively manner; pretty much in the spirit of Dr. Warburton; and are intended to point out the contradictions and inconsistencies that are to be met with in Mr. Hume's Essay. The religion which Mr. Hume means to recommend in his Natural History, our Remarker says, is *Naturalism*, or the belief of a Creator and physical Preserver, but not moral Governor. Of the truth of this every Reader of the Essay must be left to judge for himself.

REMARKS UPON THE NATURAL
HISTORY OF RELIGION
by S. T.

Letter to Theophilus

I HAVE lately met with a treatise entitled, *The Natural History of Religion*, in which the author proposes to enquire into the primary religion of mankind upon the principles of reason, unassisted with revelation, and has produced a series of arguments to prove that it was polytheism. I do not pretend to be a judge of the merits of this performance; but must confess, that the air of freedom which enlivens every part of it, delighted me extremely. You know, Theophilus, that I am a friend to liberty in the literary, as well as civil world, since tyrannical authority in either will equally depress the writer, and enslave the subject; to *think* is the prerogative of every rational creature, and freely to declare its sentiments, its happiest privilege. This liberty indeed, you will say, is designed for the investigation of truth, so should be safely preserved from the abuses of the *freethinker* when he endeavours to pervert or corrupt this advantage, as well as from the attacks of the *bigot*, when he wants to destroy it; and, if you read this pamphlet, will think perhaps, that its ingenious author should be ranked under the first class, and that he may be suspected of some such intention, as he has advanced an opinion entirely repugnant to the profession of the Mosaic history. I should be glad then if you would carefully examine it, and tell me whether Mr. Hume has given us a true delineation of human nature in its primitive state, or whether he hath not unjustly depreciated its dignity, by describing our ancient ancestors as altogether *rude, ignorant* and *barbarous*; for as they wore the same frame, possessed the same rational faculty, and were actuated by the same passions with myself, so I am desirous of being acquainted with their civil and religious constitution soon after they were placed upon this beautiful theatre. That affection, which you call benevolence, uninfluenced either by the interest, or connection of relations, friends, or countrymen, uninterrupted with those passions of envy or malice, which are too apt to engage themselves in a party towards our contemporaries, now glows with the purest ardor, and makes me wish to find that advantageous characters are given of the human race, even in the remotest ages of antiquity.

ACASTO.

Letter to Acasto

I Sat down with a full expectation of being highly entertained with the perusal of the pamphlet which you recommended to me in your letter; for the character of its author, and the plan he proposes to pursue, gave me great hopes of finding some new light flung upon the obscure parts of antiquity: but you may judge of the satisfaction it afforded me in this respect by the following abstract.

"It appears to me (says Mr. Hume,) that if we consider the improvement of human society, from rude beginnings to a greater state of perfection, polytheism or idolatry was, and necessarily must have been the first and most ancient religion of mankind. This opinion I shall endeavour to confirm by the following arguments.

'Tis a matter of fact uncontestable, that about 1700 years ago all mankind were idolaters. – Behold then the clear testimony of history. The farther we mount up into antiquity, the more we do find mankind plunged into idolatry. No marks, no symptoms of any more perfect religion. The most ancient records of human race still present us with polytheism, as the popular and established system. As far as writing or history reaches, mankind in ancient times appear universally to have been polytheists. Shall we assert, that in more ancient times, before the knowledge of letters, or the discovery of any art or science, men entertained the principles of pure theism? That is, while they were ignorant and barbarous they discovered truth: but fell into error as soon as they acquired learning and politeness. But in this assertion you not only contradict all appearance of probability, but also our present experience concerning the principles and opinions of barbarous nations. The savage tribes of America, Africa, and Asia, are all idolaters."

The meaning of this argument is, that as far as history reaches, the popular religion of most countries is found to have been polytheism; and as mankind were altogether ignorant and barbarous before the knowledge of letters, or the discovery of any art or science, so unable in such a state to find out the principles of theism, therefore polytheism must have been their first and most ancient religion.

But the incapacity of a people unacquainted with the arts and sciences, to find out the principles of theism, should be demonstrated, before this argument can have any weight or validity whatever; otherwise mankind may reasonably be supposed to have made this discovery, long before the arts and sciences were known. For the works of the creation are the certain, and have been the perpetual testimony of the existence of a God, and reason is the medium with which the human creature, from the very first period of its being, hath been furnished to discover it: it always saw the sun enlivening every part of the creation, the earth bringing forth provision for its use, the seasons returning in the utmost regularity and order; it must always have observed itself to be surrounded by an innumerable species of creatures, and could not help perceiving its own inability to form or give life to the meanest insect: and from that reflection must have been immediately led to conclude, that this beauteous scene of things must certainly have been created by a being infinitely superior in wisdom and power to man. But the mind did not want the irradiation of the arts, to enable it to discover this truth; for neither the utmost perfection in architecture, sculpture, painting, or statuary, would lead it to such contemplation as these. In succeeding ages indeed, when mankind were acquainted with the sciences, they might have acquired more refined proofs of a deity: as the beautiful symmetry of parts which is conspicuous in the human frame, is an infallible conviction to the anatomist of the wisdom of its author; the laws of gravity in the heavenly bodies will afford the astronomer the most august idea of that being who first put them into motion. But it will be too peremptory to affirm, that the illiterate *ancient* might not from pure intellect contemplate this scence of things, with the same rapture of admiration, with the same emotions of gratitude towards his Creator, as the cultivated *modern*. Education indeed may polish the reflections of mankind, but it cannot generate them;

and you must necessarily suppose the seeds of knowledge to be planted in the peasant, before they can be expanded into the arts and sciences in the philosopher. So mankind were as able to discover the existence of a God in the remotest ages of antiquity, as at present; and consequently it neither contradicts any appearance of probability to assert, that notwithstanding as far as history reaches, mankind in ancient times appear to have been polytheists; yet in more ancient times, before the knowledge of letters, or the discovery of any art or science, men entertained the principles of theism. That is, while they were ignorant of these accomplishments, they discovered truth, but were afterwards compelled to embrace idolatry, for political purposes (as it will appear in the sequel). Neither doth such an assertion contradict our experience of barbarous nations, who are not all idolaters: the natives of New England believe in a supreme power, that created all things, whom they call Kichtan[1], and those of Canada believe in the existence of a God[2].

The Peruvians called the first cause of all things, Pachacamac; by which word they meant the quickener of the universe; or the great soul of the world. This name was so very sacred, and venerable amongst them, that they never mentioned it but upon extreme necessity; and then not without all the signs of devotion imaginable, as bowing the body and head, lifting up the eyes to heaven, and spreading out their hands[3].

The idolatrous Indians of Asia acknowledge only one infinite God, almighty, and only wise, the creator of heaven and earth, whom they call Permessar, and represent by an oval figure, as the most perfect[4].

The Africans of Negroland likewise worship Guihimo, i.e. the Lord of heaven[5].

But to confirm this opinion: Mr. H – proceeds to tell us, that

"a barbarous necessitous animal (such as man is on the

---

[1] L. 5. c. 30. Harris's coll. of voyages.

[2] L. 5. c. 18. Ibid.

[3] L. 5. c. 14. Ibid.

[4] L. 2. c. 7. Tavernier's trav. from Harris.

[5] L. 3. c. 1. Harris's coll. of voyages.

very first origin of society) pressed by such numerous wants and passions, has no leisure to admire the regular face of nature, or make enquiries concerning the cause of objects, to which from his infancy he had been gradually accustomed. – Imagine not that he will so much as start the question, whence the whole system, or united fabric of the universe arose[6]."

This is a notable observation indeed, and indisputably proves, that as long as man continued to be a *barbarous, necessitous animal*, he was most certainly *a barbarous*, and *necessitous animal*; but it by no means follows from thence, that he was a *polytheist*. A creature starving with hunger would be anxious only of conquering its immediate wants, and not yet curious of enquiring into the order of the universe, or what relation it might have to a superior being; and so, in such a state as this, would be of no religion whatever. Therefore the society must necessarily be supposed to have been amply supplied with the conveniencies of life, and that different stations were allotted to its several members, before curiosity excited any of them, whose employments might engage them the least in their worldly affairs, to enquire from whence they sprung; and man must have been a civilized, contemplative, and reflecting creature, before he could have been a religious one; must be supposed to have argued, and reasoned upon his own nature, to have been sensible of his dependence on a superior power, before he could think of applying to that power for relief.

The question is, whether the human creature, after having exercised its intellectual faculties, and considered the different parts of nature, after having surveyed the stupendous furniture of the heavens, and admired the exquisite order and harmony of this beauteous scene, it would suppose it to be the effect of infinite power, perfect wisdom, and goodness, and so be led to adore its supreme Creator; or whether, (as Mr. H – asserts) it imagined, *each element to be subjected to its invisible power and agent; the province of each god to be separated from that of another; and that its first ideas of*

---

[6] Lord Bolingbroke argues in the same manner. Sect. II. Essay II. Phil. Works.

*religion arose from the incessant hopes and fears which actu-
ate the human mind; so invoked Juno at marriages, Lucina
at births.*

In short, the question is, whether the primary religion of a
rational creature, was the offspring of its reason, or the
monster of its fears. This latter opinion Mr. H – has borrowed from the poet's observation, that *primus in orbe deos
fecit timor*[7]: an assertion which deserves rather to be ridiculed, than to be seriously confuted.

To proceed. The author observes,

> "it must necessarily be allowed, that, in order to carry men's
> attention beyond the visible course of things, or lead them
> into any inference concerning invisible, intelligent power,
> they must be actuated by some passion, which prompts
> their thought, and reflection, some motive which urges their
> first enquiry. But what passion shall we have recourse to,
> for explaining an effect of such mighty consequence? not
> speculative curiosity, or the pure love of truth. That motive
> is too refined for such gross apprehensions, and would
> lead them into enquiries concerning the frame of nature,
> a subject too large, and comprehensive for their narrow
> capacities. No passions therefore can be supposed to work
> upon such barbarians, but the ordinary affairs of human
> life: the anxious concern for happiness, the thirst of revenge,
> the appetite for food, and other necessaries."

Such is Mr. H–'s opinion of our ancient ancestors. He thinks,
that they were senseless of every emotion, but *fear, revenge,*
and *hunger*; qualities indeed more justly applicable to the
beasts of the forest, than to rational creatures. But it may
be asked; why was *speculative curiosity, or the pure love of
truth, too refined for their apprehensions?* Doth he imagine
that nature did not bestow her talents in so liberal a manner
amongst her ancient sons, as amongst us? Doth he suppose
that no inquisitive genius, no philosophic mind ever prevailed
amongst them, but that reason and reflection are only of
modern growth? Why might not a *Bacon, Locke,* or *Newton,*
have existed in the remotest ages, since human nature hath

---

[7] Statius, Theb. 3.

always been the same from its first creation? perhaps as the poet observes[8],

> Before great Agamemnon reign'd
> Reign'd kings as great as he, and brave,
> Whose huge ambition's now contain'd
> In the small compass of a grave,
> In endless night they sleep unwept, unknown
> No *bard* had they to make all time their own.
>
> FRANCIS

But withall, we may demand what right he has to give them the appellation of *ignorant barbarians*, of having *gross apprehensions, narrow capacities*? for a deficiency of records must always deprive an impartial enquirer of that full conviction, by which alone he can be authorized to pronounce with any decision upon the state and condition of the ancient world. The very invention of letters did not precede the christian æra perhaps above 2000 years, being found out by Thoth in the reign of Tham[9], and the Greeks wrote nothing in prose before the conquest of Asia by Cyrus the Persian[10]; and consequently as mankind existed many ages before the use of letters, they had no means whatever (if we except hieroglyphicks, which were not to be depended upon, as being capable of various interpretations) of conveying any account of their lives to posterity; so one generation passed away and was but feintly remembered, or entirely forgotten by its succeeding one, and some edifice or column perhaps was the only evidence that mankind then had of the very existence of their ancestors. If a few centuries would thus obliterate the memory of people, and nations, before the use of letters, must not we call it presumption in this author, thus dogmatically to declare that

---

[8] Vixere fortes ante Agamemnona
Multi: fed omnes illacrymabiles
Urgentur, ignotique longâ
Nocte, carent quia vate sacro.
Hor. 1. 4. od. 9.

[9] Soc. Ηκθσα τοινυν περι Ναυκρατιν της Αιγυπτθ γενεζαι των εκει παλαιων τινα Θεων–αυτω δε ονομα τω δαιμονι ειναι Θευθ, τθτον δε πρωτον, αριθμον τε και λογσμον ευρειν–και γραμματα.
Platonis Phædrus.

[10] Newton's Chron.

they were altogether *rude, ignorant,* and *barbarous* in their manners, and that idolatry was their first religion?

So whether theism or polytheism was the primary religion of mankind, can be determined upon no other authority, than revelation; and if *that* is excluded by this author, then the solution of this question can be only founded on conjecture, and that side of it which is supported by the greatest degree of probability have a right to our assent.

Upon this principle alone must we argue, and let us consider the state of mankind in the remotest ages, upon the testimony of the most ancient monuments, and records, and endeavour from thence to form a reasonable idea of their manners and religion.

The pyramids of Egypt were built before the use of letters,[11] and have still survived the storms, and mouldering hand of time, to convince us, that its builders compounded the mechanical powers in a manner unknown to us at present[12]; and their situation likewise proves that they were acquainted with astronomy[13]. Architecture[14], sculpture[15], ship building[16], and embroidery[17] were brought to great perfection in Homer's time. Xenophon speaks of great masters in statuary, and painting[18]: and we find in Plutarch, a remarkable proof of the excellent administration of justice amongst the ancient Egyptians[19]. If we consider withal the descriptions which

---

[11] Pliny speaking of the pyramids says,
   "Qui de iis scripserunt, sunt Herodotus, Euhemerus, Duris Samius, Aristagoras, Dionysius, Artemidorus, Alexander Polyhistor, Butorides, Antisthenes, Demetrius, Demoteles, Apion, inter omnes eos non constat à quibus factæ sint." Nat. Hist. l. 36. c. 12.

[12] All the stones of the pyramid built by Cheops are 30 feet long, well squared, and jointed with the greatest exactness.
   Herod. l. 2. c. 124.

[13] Norden's travels into Ægypt.

[14] Homer's Iliad, l. 6. v. 242, &c.

[15] Ibid. l. 18. v. 483, &c.

[16] Ibid. l. 5. v. 62, &c.

[17] Ibid. l. 6. v. 289, &c.

[18] Xenophon's memorab. 1. 1. c. 4.

[19] "At Thebes the statues of the magistrates were carried without hands, and that of the chief judge with his eyes looking upon the ground, to signify that they should neither be prevailed upon by bribery, nor influenced by perswasion to act contrary to justice."
   de Iside & Osiride.

authors have given us of the magnificent cities of Thebes[20], Babylon[21], and Memphis[22]; of the temple of Diana at Ephesus[23], of the amazing works of the labyrinth[24], of the lake Mœris[25], or of the famous statue of Memnon[26]; can we help being astonished at the progress which the ancients had made in the mechanical arts? Is it then reasonable to suppose, with Mr. H–, that these people were *rude* and *ignorant*, and *that speculative curiosity was too refined for their gross apprehensions?* Is it to be imagined that these ancient philosophers, artists, and law-givers, were not curious to enquire from whence they sprung, and what being it is who endued them with that excellent faculty, by which they were enabled to measure time, to calculate the motions of the heavenly bodies, to plan the city and the pyramid; that faculty which taught them how to animate the block into a statue, and to enliven the canvass to a picture? Can we believe that these ingenious people, who by the greatest strength of mind had invented that amazing art of letters, and the noble science of mathematicks, who had improved their understanding to such a degree of excellence in every respect, were either unable to discover the existence of a God, by the plain evidence of his works, or could refrain from enquiring what power it was, which constituted such beautiful order through the whole creation? Or shall we think with Mr. H–, that they looked upon this scene of things with the same indifference and stupidity, as the irrational brute? No! we cannot, after such indisputable evidence of the ingenuity and wisdom of the remotest ages, believe otherwise, than that they discovered and adored the divine being; for these testimonies are matters of fact, which no prejudice can elude, and as indisputably demonstrate the ability of man, as the works of the creation demonstrate the power and wisdom of God. Permit me then to indulge myself in a conjecture, that my ancient

[20] Homer's Iliad, l. 9. v. 383.

[21] Herod. l. 1. c. 178.

[22] Ibid. l. 2. c. 99.

[23] Pliny's natural history, l. 16. c. 40.

[24] Herod. l. 2. c. 148.

[25] Ibid. l. 2. c. 149.

[26] Pliny's natural history, l. 36. c. 7.

ancestors often turned their eyes to the blue vault of heaven, and chanted to their Creator like Adam in his morning orison, (for they undoubtedly observed, reflected, and admired.)

These are thy glorious works, parent of good,
Almighty, thine this universal frame,
Thus wondrous fair; thyself how wondrous then!
Unspeakable, who sit'st above the heavens
To us invisible, or dimly seen
In these thy lowest works; yet these declare
Thy goodness beyond thought, and pow'r divine.

Mil. par. loft. l. v. 153, &c.

We have likewise great reason to believe that theism was the primary religion of mankind, as the sensible part of them in all ages were of this opinion.

Orpheus[27], Homer[28], Thales[29], Pythagoras[30], Anaxagoras[31], Socrates[32], Plato[33], and Aristotle[34] believed in the existence of a divine being. The Thebans believed in a self-existent and

---

[27] Εις εσ' αυτογενης ενος εκγονα παντα τετυκται.
Εν δ' αυτοις αυτος περινισσεται. βδε τις αυτον
Εισοραα θνητων, αυτος δε τε παντας ο αται
Ουτώς μεν δη Ορφευς.
Clem. Alex. admon. ad gentes.

[28] Agamemnon says to Achilles,
Ει μαλα καρτερος εσσι. Θεος πθ σοι τογ' εδωκεν.
Iliad l. I. v. 178.

[29] Πρεσβυτατον των οντων. Θεος, αγενητον γαρ, καλλιστον, χοσμος. πογμα γαρ θερ'Ι
Διογεν'Ι Δαερτιθσ ιν ωιτα Τηαλετισ'Ι

[30] Pythagoras censuit animum effe per naturam rerum omnem intentum, & comme antem. Cic. de nat. deorum, l. I. C. II.

[31] Ο δε Αγαξαγορας θησιν ως εισηκει κατ' αρχας τα σωματα, νβς δε αυτα διαχοσμησε θεγ, χαι τας γενεσεισ των ολων εποιησεν.
Plutarch. Plac. Philos. l. I.

[32] Xenophon's memorabilia, l. I. c. 4.

[33] Ο αυτος γαρ βτος χειροτεχνης, βμονον παντα οιος τε σκευη ποιησαι. αλλα χαι τα εκ της γης φυομενα απαντα ποιει, κχαι ζωα παντα εργαζ-εται, τα τε αλλα χαι εαυτον, χαι προς τβτοις γην χαι πρανον χαι θεθς χαι παιτατα εν θραιω χαι τα εν αδθ υπο γης απαντα ε γαζεται.
Plato de republica, 1. 10.

[34] Ο τε γαρ θεος δοκει το αιτιον πασιν ξινου χαι αζχη τις.
Arift. Metap.

immortal being, whom they called Kneph[35], and all the Egyptians in general esteemed God to be the cause of every creature that was generated, and of all the powers in nature, that he is superior to every thing, and that he is an immaterial, immortal, self-existent being, who governs and sustains every part of the creation[36]. The Ethiopians[37], the Persians[38], and Chinese[39], professed the same belief. Cicero observes, that there is no nation so savage and barbarous, which doth not believe in the being of a God, tho' it may be ignorant of the manner of his existence[40]. Dr. Warburton likewise says,

> "It is not only possible that the worship of the first cause of all things was prior to any idol worship, but in the highest degree probable; idol worship having none of the appearances of an original custom, and all the circumstances attending a depraved and corrupted institution[41]."

If we then impartially consider the evidence of probability on either side of this question, we shall certainly be induced to believe that theism was the primary religion of mankind. Nay, if these testimonies which have been produced in favour of this opinion be excluded, let me even then ask you, Acasto, whether it is not more consistent with reason, to suppose that the wise, ingenious, thinking creature which we call man, whom the supreme being hath so eminently distinguished from the rest of the animal creation, by reason and reflec-

---

[35] Τὸς Θηβαιδα κατοικθντες, ως θνηον θεν εδεν νομιζοντας, αλλα ον καλθσιν αυτοι Κνηφ, αγενητον οντα και αθανατον.

Plutarch. de If. & Ofir.

[36] Ο της γενενεως και φυσεως ολης, και των εν τοις στοιχειοις δυναμεων πασων, ωιτιος θεος, ατε δη υπεξεχων τβταν, αϋλος και ασωματος και υπεξευης, αγενητος τε και αμεριστος ολος εξ εαυτβ, και εν εαυτω αφανης πζοηγειται παντων τβτων, και εν εαυτω τα ολα περιεχει.

Jamblichus de mysteriis, sect. 7. c. 2.

[37] Strabo, l. 17.

[38] Hyde de religione vet. Pers.

[39] Tabula chronologicæ monarchiæ Sinicæ ante Christum juxta cyclos, *annorum* 60. ante Christum, 2697. Hoam Ti, hoc est flavus imperator fundator monarchiæ. Templum pacis Xam Ti, id est supremo imperatori feu deo.

Confucius.

[40] De legibus, l. I. c. 8.

[41] Divine Legation, l. 3. 6th sect.

tion[42], believed and adored his Creator, in the remotest ages
of antiquity, than (according to Mr. Hume's plan) that he
worshipped the ridiculous objects of idolatry? So I shall conclude this epistle with the words of Sir Isaac Newton;

"The believing that the world was framed by one supreme
God, and is governed by him, and the loving and worship-
ping him, and honouring our parents, and loving our neigh-
bours as ourselves, and being merciful even to brute beasts,
is the oldest of all religions[43]."

THEOPHILUS.

[42] Cicero de legibus, l. I. c. 7.

[43] Newton's Chron.

REMARKS UPON THE NATURAL HISTORY OF RELIGION BY MR. HUME. WITH DIALOGUES ON HEATHEN IDOLATORY, AND THE CHRISTIAN RELIGION BY S.T.

Anonymous

Source: The Monthly Review, vol. 19, 1758

THE Author of these Remarks, &c. appears to be a friend to religion and freedom of enquiry; but he has advanced nothing, in our opinion, that can give the judicious reader any high idea of his discernment or acuteness. His remarks upon Mr. Hume's Natural History of Religion are extremely superficial, and scarce contain any thing that deserves particular notice. Theism, he thinks, was the primary religion of mankind; since it is more consistent with our idea of a rational creature, to believe, that its religion, or the sense of its duty towards its Creator, at first arose from the conclusions of its reason, rather than from the suggestions of its fears: and though mankind in ancient times appear, as far as history reaches, to be Polytheists, yet in more ancient times, we are told, before the knowledge of letters, or the discovery of any art or science, it is probable that men entertained the principles of theism. If it be asked, To what cause was it owing that mankind so strangely degenerated? our Author answers, They were compelled to embrace idolatry for political purposes. This is the point he endeavours to prove in his dialogue on heathen idolatry, where we meet with many quotations from Greek and Latin authors; but nothing satisfactory upon the subject.

It was extremely difficult, he thinks, if not impossible, for a legislator, in the early ages of the world, to govern a community that was refined with the arts, without the assistance of idolatry; it was necessary therefore, he says, to apply to this institution for political purposes. The brutal worship of

the Egyptians he produces as a remarkable evidence in favour
of his assertion: hear what he says.

"The Egyptians were a sharp and sensible people by nature,
as born in a fine climate, and withal were very numerous.
They inhabited a country, whose soil was made extremely
fertile, by the annual sediment of the Nile, and were neither
much employed in agriculture, or commerce; so having
an opportunity of improving their understanding, would
gradually become refined by cultivation. They were governed by a king, priesthood, and soldiery, who were not only
vested with the whole legislative and executive power, but
had likewise the property of the whole kingdom in their
own possession. A state, thus exercising its tyrannical
authority over such a people, might reasonably be jealous
of their enquiring into their natural rights and privileges,
and that they would probably conspire to subvert a government, by which they were so unjustly deprived of them.
Therefore every expedient was to be tried, and most effectual laws to be instituted, in order to preserve such a powerful and injured people from rebellion; and no other
contrivance seemed so likely to secure them from uniting
in an alliance against the state, as keeping them in ignorance, and generating a mutual envy and malice amongst
them. The *first* they effected by concealing the sciences in
hieroglyphics, and confining it to the priesthood, and withal
by compelling the sons of the mechanics, husbandmen,
tradesmen, and shepherds, to follow the several vocations
of their fathers, from generation to generation, and pro-
hibiting them from meddling with the affairs of the state,
under the penalty of a severe punishment. The *other* was
likewise performed, by appointing different animals to be
worshipped in different cities, which being natural enemies
to each other, would necessarily engage their several votaries in disputes concerning them, and be a perpetual occasion
of quarrels and contention with each other. A people thus
divided in their opinions about these objects of their
worship, would be very effectually prevented from conspir-
ing against the establishment; and so the government, in
the mean time, remain secure in their illegal possessions."

This may serve as a sufficient specimen of our Author's abilities, for unfolding the policy of ancient states, and renders

any farther account of what is advanced upon this subject, unnecessary. In the Dialogue on the *Christian Religion*, there is nothing to be met with but what has been often repeated; nothing urged, but what has been often urged with much greater accuracy and strength of reasoning.

REMARKS ON MR. DAVID HUME'S ESSAY ON THE NATURAL HISTORY OF RELIGION (1777)
William Warburton

The bookseller to the reader

THE following is supposed to be the Pamphlet referred to by the late Mr. David Hume, in Page 21, of his Life, *as being written by* Dr. HURD. Upon my applying to the Bishop of Litchfield and Coventry for his permission to republish it, he very readily gave me his consent. His Lordship only added, he was sorry he could not take to himself the WHOLE infamy of the charge brought against him; but that he should hereafter, if he thought it worth his while, explain himself more particularly on that subject.

STRAND,
March, 1777.

T. CADELL.

Remark I

The writer, I have to do with, is a Veteran in the dark and deadly trade of Irreligion. But my concern at present is only with a volume of his, just now given to the public and entitled, FOUR DISSERTATIONS. And of these *Four*, I confine myself to the FIRST, which bears the portentous name of an Essay, *On the natural history of Religion*.

The purpose of it is to establish NATURALISM on the ruins of RELIGION; of which, whether under Paganism and Polytheism, or under Revelation and the doctrine of the Unity, he professes to give the NATURAL HISTORY.

And here let me observe it to his honour, that, though he be not yet got to THEISM, he is however on the advance and approaching to the borders of it; having been in the dregs of Atheism when he wrote his Epicurean arguments against the being of a God. Sometime or other he may come to his senses. A few animadversions on the *Essay* before us may help him forwards. The thing is full of curiosities: And the very *title-page*, as I observed, demands our attention. It is called,

THE NATURAL HISTORY OF RELIGION.

You ask, why he chuses to give it this title. Would not the *Moral history of Meteors* be full as sensible as the *Natural History of Religion*? Without doubt. Indeed had he given the history of what he himself would pass upon us for the only true Religion, namely, NATURALISM, or the belief of a God, the Creator and Physical Preserver, but not moral Governor of the world, the title of *Natural* would have fitted it well, because all *Morality* is excluded from the Idea.

But this great Philosopher is never without his Reasons. It is to insinuate, that what the world calls Religion, of which he undertakes to give the history, is not founded in the JUDGMENT, but in the PASSIONS only. However the expression labours miserably, as it does through all his profound Lucubrations. And where is the wonder that he who disdains to think in the mode of common sense, should be unable to express himself in the proprieties of common language?

As every Inquiry which regards Religion (says that respectable Personage) *is of the utmost importance, there are two questions in particular which challenge our principal attention, to wit, that concerning its foundation in reason, and that concerning its* ORIGIN IN HUMAN NATURE[1].

Here we see, he aims at a distinction. And what he aims at is not hard to find. The question is, whether he has hit the mark. I am afraid, not. And then the discovery of his aim is only the detection of his ignorance. In a word, it is a distinction without a difference.

If man be rightly defined a *rational animal*, then his Nature, or what our Philosopher calls *human Nature*, must be a *rational* Nature. But if so, a FOUNDATION IN REASON and an ORIGIN IN HUMAN NATURE are not too different predicates, but one and the same only in different expressions. Do I say, therefore, that our Philosopher had no meaning, because he was unable to express any? Far be that from the Reverence due to this Rectifier of Prejudices. My objection at present

---

[1] P. i. *Nat. Hist. of Religion.*

is not to his Theology but his Logic. By *Origin in human Nature* he meant, Origin in the fancy or the Passions. For that Religion, which has the origin, here designed, is what the world calls RELIGION; and this he resolves into *fanaticism* or *superstition*: As that Religion which has its *foundation in reason* is what the world calls NATURALISM, the Religion of Philosophers like himself, and which he endeavours in this Essay to establish.

But do not believe, I intend to meddle with this *Religion of Philosophers* any further than to expose it to the public contempt, as it deserves. Even I should be finely employed, not to say you, to enter into a formal confutation of Mr. David Hume's *Naturalism*. However I think it incumbent on me to prove, that this is indeed the Religion which this honest man means to recommend in his *Natural History*. For so heavy a charge ought never to be made without good evidence to support it.

In his third Section, at the 16th page, he makes UNKNOWN CAUSES the origin of what men call *Religion*, that Religion which his History pretends to investigate.

> "These UNKNOWN CAUSES, says He, become the constant object of our hope and fear; and while the passions are kept in perpetual alarm by an anxious expectation of the events, the imagination is equally employed in forming ideas of those powers, on which we have so entire a dependance."

He then goes on to acquaint us with the original of these UNKNOWN CAUSES.

> "Could men anatomize Nature, according to the most probable, at least the most intelligible philosophy, they would find, that these *Causes* are nothing but the particular fabric and structure of the MINUTE PARTS OF THEIR OWN BODIES AND OF EXTERNAL OBJECTS; and that, by a regular and constant machinery, all the events are produced, about which they are so much concerned. But this Philosophy exceeds the comprehension of the ignorant multitude".[2]

Here we see, the original of these *unknown Causes* is nothing but the result of MATTER and MOTION. And again,

---

[2] Page 17.

"The Vulgar, that is, indeed, ALL MANKIND, a few excepted, being ignorant and uninstructed, never elevate their contemplation to the Heavens, or penetrate by their disquisitions into the SECRET STRUCTURE OF VEGETABLE OR ANIMAL BODIES; so as to discover a supreme mind or original providence, which bestowed order on every part of Nature. They consider these admirable works in a more confined and selfish view; and finding their own happiness and misery to depend on the secret influence and unforeseen concurrence of external objects, they regard with perpetual attention, the UNKNOWN CAUSES, which govern all these natural events, and distribute pleasure and pain, good and ill, by their powerful, but silent operation. The UNKNOWN CAUSES are still appealed to, at every emergence; and in this general appearance or confused image, are the perpetual objects of human hopes and fears, wishes and apprehensions. By degrees, the active imagination of men, uneasy in this abstract conception of objects, about which it is incessantly employed, begins to render them more particular, and to clothe them in shapes more suitable to its natural comprehension. It represents them to be sensible, intelligent beings, like mankind; actuated by love and hatred, and flexible by gifts and entreaties, by prayers and sacrifices. HENCE THE ORIGIN OF RELIGION: *And hence the origin of idolatry or Polytheism*[3]."

The *few excepted* out of the *whole race of mankind* are, we see, our Philosopher and his gang, with their Pedler's ware of *matter* and *motion, who penetrate by their disquisitions into the secret structure of vegetable and animal bodies*, to extract, like the Naturalist in Gulliver, *Sunbeams out of Cucumbers*; just as wise a Project as this of raising Religion out of the intrigues of *matter and motion*.

All this shews how desirous our Essayist was of not being misunderstood: as meaning any thing else than Naturalism (or the belief of a Creator and Physical Preserver, but not Moral Governor) by the Religion he would recommend in the place of that Phantom, whose physical, or rather metaphysical, history he is writing. For this Phantom of a Religion, which acknowledges a *moral Governor*, arises, he

---

[3] Page 54–5.

tells us, from our ignorance of the result of *matter* and *motion*, caballing *in the minute parts of vegetable and animal bodies.*

The sum then of all he teaches is this; That that Religion, of which he professes himself a follower, and which has *its foundation in Reason*, is NATURALISM: and, That that Religion which *all mankind* follow, *a few excepted*, and of which he undertakes to give a *natural history*, is nothing but *Superstition* and *Fanaticism*, having *its origin in human Nature*; that is, in the imagination and the passions only.

REMARKS ON DR. DAVID HUME'S ESSAY ON THE NATURAL HISTORY OF RELIGION (1778)

William Warburton

Remark I

THE purpose of this ESSAY is to establish NATURALISM on the ruins of RELIGION; of which, whether under Paganism and Polytheism, or under Revelation and the doctrine of the Unity, Mr. HUME professes to give the NATURAL HISTORY.

And here let me observe it to his honour, that, though he be not yet got to THEISM, he is however on the advance and approaching to the borders of it; having been in the dregs of Atheism when he wrote his Epicurean arguments against the being of a God. Sometime or other he may come to his senses. A few animadversions on the *Essay* before us may help him forwards. The thing is full of curiosities: And the very *title-page*, as I observed, demands our attention. It is called,

THE NATURAL HISTORY OF RELIGION.

You ask, why he chuses to give it this title. Would not the *Moral history of Meteors* be full as sensible as the *Natural History of Religion?* Without doubt. Indeed had he given the history of what he himself would pass upon us for the only true Religion, namely, NATURALISM, or the belief of a God, the Creator and Physical Preserver, but not moral Governor of the world, the title of *Natural* would have fitted it well, because all *Morality* is excluded from the Idea.

But this great Philosopher is never without his Reasons. It is to insinuate, that what the world calls Religion, of which he undertakes to give the history, is not founded in the JUDGMENT, but in the PASSIONS only. However the expression labours miserably, as it does through all his profound Lucubrations. And where is the wonder that he, who disdains to think in the mode of common sense, should be unable to express himself in the proprieties of common language?

As every Inquiry which regards Religion (says that respectable Personage) *is of the utmost importance, there are two questions in particular which challenge our principal attention, to wit, that concerning foundation in reason, and that concerning its* ORIGIN IN HUMAN NATURE[1].

Here, we see, he aims at a distinction. And what he aims at is not hard to find. The question is, whether he has hit the mark. I am afraid, not. And then the discovery of his aim is only the detection of his ignorance. In a word, it is a distinction without a difference.

If man be rightly defined a *rational animal*, then his Nature, or what our Philosopher calls *human Nature*, must be a *rational* Nature. But if so, a FOUNDATION IN REASON and an ORIGIN IN HUMAN NATURE are not two different predicates, but one and the same only in different expressions. Do I say, therefore, that our Philosopher had no meaning, because he was unable to express any? Far be that from the Reverence due to this Rectifier of Prejudices. My objection at present is not to his Theology but his Logic. By *Origin in human Nature* he meant, Origin in the fancy or the Passions. For that Religion, which has the origin, here designed, is what the world calls RELIGION; and this he resolves into *fanaticism* or *superstition*: As that Religion which has its *foundation in reason* is what the world calls NATURALISM, the Religion of Philosophers like himself, and which he endeavours in this Essay to establish.

In his third Section, at the 16th page, he makes UNKNOWN CAUSES the origin of what men call *Religion*, that Religion which his History pretends to investigate.

"These UNKNOWN CAUSES," He says, "become the constant object of our hope and fear; and while the passions are kept in perpetual alarm by an anxious expectation of the events, the imagination is equally employed in forming ideas of those powers, on which we have so entire a dependance."

He then goes on to acquaint us with the original of these UNKNOWN CAUSES.

[1] P. 1. Nat. Hist. of Religion.

"Could men anatomize Nature, according to the most probable, at least the most intelligible, philosophy, they would
find, that these *Causes* are nothing but the particular fabric
and structure of the MINUTE PARTS OF THEIR OWN BODIES
AND OF EXTERNAL OBJECTS; and that, by a regular and
constant machinery, all the events are produced, about
which they are so much concerned. But this Philosophy
exceeds the comprehension of the ignorant multitude[2]."

Here we see the original of these *unknown Causes* is nothing
but the result of MATTER and MOTION. And again,

"The Vulgar, that is, indeed, ALL MANKIND, a few excepted,
being ignorant and uninstructed, never elevate their contemplation to the Heavens, or penetrate by their disquisitions into the SECRET STRUCTURE OF VEGETABLE OR
ANIMAL BODIES; so as to discover a supreme mind or original providence, which bestowed order on every part of
Nature. They consider these admirable works in a more
confined and selfish view; and finding their own happiness
and misery to depend on the secret influence and unforeseen
concurrence of external objects, they regard with perpetual
attention the UNKNOWN CAUSES, which govern all these
natural events, and distribute pleasure and pain, good and
ill, by their powerful, but silent operation. The UNKNOWN
CAUSES are still appealed to, at every emergence; and in this
general appearance or confused image, are the perpetual
objects of human hopes and fears, wishes and apprehensions. By degrees, the active imagination of men, uneasy
in this abstract conception of objects, about which it is
incessantly employed, begins to render them more particular, and to clothe them in shapes more suitable to its natural
comprehension. It represents them to be sensible, intelligent
beings, like mankind; actuated by love and hatred, and
flexible by gifts and entreaties, by prayers and sacrifices.
HENCE THE ORIGIN OF RELIGION: *And hence the origin of
idolatry or Polytheism*[3]."

The *few excepted* out of the *whole race of mankind* are, we
see, our Philosopher and his gang, with their Pedler's ware

[2] Page 17.

[3] Page 54, 55.

of *matter* and *motion, who penetrate by their disquisitions into the secret structure of vegetable and animal bodies,* to extract like the Naturalist in Gulliver, *Sunbeams out of Cucumbers;* just as wise a Project as this of raising Religion out of the intrigues of *matter and motion.*

All this shews how desirous our Essayist was of not being misunderstood: as meaning any thing else than Naturalism (or the belief of a Creator and Physical Preserver, but not Moral Governor) by the Religion he would recommend in the place of that Phantom, whose physical, or rather metaphysical, history, he is writing. For this Phantom of a Religion, which acknowledges a *moral Governor,* arises, he tells us, from our ignorance of the result of *matter* and *motion,* caballing *in the minute parts of vegetable and animal bodies.*

The sum then of all he teaches is this; That that Religion, of which he professes himself a follower, and which has *its foundation in Reason,* is NATURALISM; and, That that Religion which *all mankind* follow, *a few excepted,* and of which he undertakes to give a *natural history,* is nothing but *Superstition* and *Fanaticism,* having *its origin in human Nature;* that is, in the imagination and the passions only.

Remark III

But from his *Civil* let us return to his *Natural History;* and see how he supports his Thesis. He does it by something between history and argument. He calls it both: And some perhaps will think it neither.

The belief of one God, the physical preserver but not moral Governor of the Universe, is, what we have shewn our Philosopher dignifies with the title of *the primary principles of genuine Theism* and *Religion.* Now, if the belief of one God, a moral Governor, was prior in time to Polytheism, it will follow, that NATURALISM or the belief of one God, a Physical preserver only, is not *genuine Theism and Religion.* Because in his endeavour to prove Polytheism the first in time, he has shewn the inability of mere uninstructed man to rise up to this knowledge, on the first Essay of his Reason; the consequence of which is, that if the infant world had this knowledge, it must have been taught them by Revelation, and whatsoever is so taught, must be *true.*

But it is become the general opinion (which, though it has

been a long while a growing, our philosopher hopes very speedily to eradicate), that a belief of one God, the moral Governor, was the first Religion; induced thereto by the express assertion of an antient book confessedly of as good authority as any other record of very remote antiquity.

Our Philosopher's business therefore is to disprove the Fact. And how do you think he sets about it? You see there are but two ways. Either to prove *à priori*, and from the nature of things, that Polytheism must be before Theism; and then indeed he may reject history and record: Or else *à posteriori*, and from antient testimony; in which case, it will be incumbent on him to refute and set aside that celebrated record which expressly tells us, Theism was the first. Our honest Philosopher does neither. He insists chiefly on antient testimony, but is as silent concerning the Bible as if no such book had ever been written.

Lord Bolingbroke before him had employed this very medium of the priority of Polytheism to Theism, to inforce the same conclusion, namely, NATURALISM; but knowing better how to reason, and being perhaps at that moment less disposed to insult common sense in so profligate a manner, he labours all he can to depreciate the authority of the Bible. But our North British Philosopher despises his reader too much to stand upon Punctilios with him; he roundly affirms that all antiquity is on his side; and, as if Moses had no human authority because he allows him no divine, he will not condescend so much as to do him the honour, he has done Sanchoniathon, of quoting him, though it was in order to confute him. But you shall hear his own words, because his egregious dishonesty has led him into as ridiculous an absurdity.

As far as writing or history teaches, mankind, in antient times, appear universally to have been Polytheists. Shall we assert, that, in more antient times, before the knowledge of letters, or the discovery of any art or science, men entertained the principles of pure Theism: That is, while they were ignorant and barbarous, they discovered truth: But fell into error, as soon as they acquired learning and politeness[4]."

Shall we assert, that, says he. Why, no body ever asserted that Theism was before Polytheism but those who gave credit to their Bible. And those who did so can easily evade his

[4] Page 4.

difficulty, *that it is not natural to think that before the knowledge of letters, or the discovery of any art or science, men entertained the principles of pure Theism*; because this Bible tells us, that the first man did not gain the principles of pure Theism by *a knowledge of letters or the discovery of any art or science*, but by REVELATION. But this man, who had run into unlucky mistakes before concerning the state of Religion in South Britain, believed in good earnest that we had burnt our Bibles, and that therefore it would be less generous to insult its ashes, than to bury them in silence. This, I think, can only account for that virtuous assurance where he says, that AS FAR AS WRITING OR HISTORY REACHES, MANKIND IN ANTIENT TIMES APPEAR UNIVERSALLY TO HAVE BEEN POLYTHEISTS. And what system do you think it is, of the *origin of mankind*, which he espouses, instead of the Mosaic, to prove that Polytheism was the first Religion? No other, I will assure you, than the old Egyptian nonsense, which attempts to teach that men first started up like Mushrooms. In a word, the men, on whose principles this wonderful Logician argues, never questioned the truth of his Thesis. To them therefore all this bustle of a discovery is ridiculous and impertinent. And those who dispute the fact with him, the Religionists, he leaves in possession of all their arguments. So they laugh at it as an idle dream, raised on the absurdest of the Atheistic principles, the Epicurean.

To this ridicule the reader sees, our Philosopher exposes himself, even if we believe him to be here speaking of *pure Theism*, in the proper sense of the words; that is, of the belief of a God, the *moral Governor of the World*. But *Ridicule* may not be all which this mighty *Theist* deserves. For what, if our Philosopher should mean by his *pure and genuine Theism*, to which he denies a priority of being, his favourite NATURALISM? I should not be surprised, if he did: It is but running his *usual* philosophic course, from knavery to nonsense.

The reader, as he goes along, will see abundant reason for this charge. An Essay, then, so devoid of all manly sense, and even plausibility of reasoning, can afford a Remarker no other opportunity of entertaining the Public with him, than that of drawing the picture of some of his characteristic features, some of the predominant qualities, of which he is made up. I shall therefore present the Public with a few specimens of his philosophical virtues, his Reasoning, his

Consistency, his Candour, and his Modesty; and all these promiscuously, as they rise in the natural disorder of his *Essay*.

Remark XXI

I have given a specimen of his philosophic virtues, his reasoning, his consistency, his knowledge, his truth, his candour, and his modesty, as they promiscuously appear in the NATURAL HISTORY OF RELIGION. I have hunted him from track to track. And now what thick cover, do You suppose, has he chosen to skreen himself from the public contempt? He takes shelter in the dark umbrage of SCEPTICISM. These are his concluding words.

> "The whole is a riddle, an ænigma, an inexplicable mystery. Doubt, uncertainty, suspence of judgment, appear the only result of our most accurate scrutiny, concerning this subject. But such is the frailty of human reason, and such the irresistible contagion of opinion, that even this deliberate doubt could scarce be upheld; did we not enlarge our view, and opposing one species of superstition to another, set them a quarrelling; while we ourselves, during their fury and contention, happily make our escape, into THE CALM, THOUGH OBSCURE, REGIONS OF PHILOSOPHY."

Thus, we see, his last effort is to defend his *dogmatical* nonsense with *scepticism* still more nonsensical. Nor to this, neither, dares he trust himself; but presently meditates an *escape*, as he calls it, by setting the *Religionists a quarrelling*: without which, he frankly owns, that *deliberate doubt could scarce be upheld*. For the sake of this beloved object, DELIBERATE DOUBT, there is no mischief he is not ready to commit, even to the unhinging the national Religion, and unloosing all the hold it has on the minds of the people. And all this for the selfish and unnatural lust of *escaping* from right reason and common sense, *into the calm, though obscure, regions of philosophy*. But here we have earthed him; rolled up in the Scoria of a *dogmatist* and *Sceptic*, run down together. He has been long taken for a Philosopher: and so perhaps he may be found – like Aristotle's statue in the block,

> "Then take him to develop, if you can,
> And hew the block off, and get out the Man."

A BRIEF VIEW OF HUME'S THEORY
OF RELIGION
Henry O'Connor, Esq.

HE who has never read Hume's Essays knows not what arguments may be advanced against religion; and whoever has
attentively studied the writings of that philosopher, can learn
nothing new in infidelity. To him no doubts will bear an
aspect of unprecedented extravagance, and no determined
rejection of evidence, admitted to be insuperable, will indicate
a degree of obstinacy too absurd to exist in the mind of a
rational being. Among the licentious productions of the
last century, which were the less contemptible because they
possessed a hypocritical affectation of decency not even
assumed by the vulgar latitudinarians of the present times,
there was no work, written by any other author, which was
so ably calculated to unloose all moral obligations, and to
promote universal irreligion and disorder, as the two volumes
of *Essays*, by David Hume; yet these are pious effusions, –
they are divine, – compared with his "*Dialogues upon
Natural Religion*," in which that author has exceeded himself.
The young metaphysician, being duly prepared in the philosophy of those Treatises, has completed his diabolical education. He can plunge no deeper into the abyss of scepticism,
and can encounter no antagonist more acute or insinuating,
for, from the rare example as well as the astucious arguments
of Hume, he must admit, that, to be an infidel, implies neither
mediocrity of genius, nor any deficiency in learning, nor want
of virtue. Yet, of all Deists, this very Hume was the most
profane and incorrigible. He approached nearer to atheism
than perhaps any one ever did, who had heard of a God. He
really entertained, as the deliberate conviction of his mind,
such a resolute contempt of established opinions, and such a
rooted scorn of all venerable institutions, and of every sacred
system, especially of the Christian, (feelings which he neither
gloried in, nor disguised,) that the most impious scoffer

cannot invent or imagine any blasphemies, which the disciples of this formidable sceptic have not been instructed to approve.

The serious Christian has a right to inquire, for what purpose these alarming concessions are granted? Is it intended to represent impiety as a trifling failing, into which the best of men may fall? I confess, that, after the foregoing expressions, it behoves me to obviate any possible imputation of being little better than an infidel myself.

Impiety, even in thought, is a vice, into which no sensible man is likely to be betrayed. Still more is open profaneness detestable to every person of ordinary taste, of common politeness, or of decent morals. How then, it may be asked, did it happen, that, during a long life devoted to literary and philosophic pursuits, a philosopher possessing such excellent abilities, and of so amiable a disposition, persevered, with unshaken hardihood, in a system of opinions not many steps removed from atheism; to the propagation of which he omitted no argument, because it was too daring, and no sarcastic jest, because it might involve the most terrible insults to his Creator? This is a startling question; for, it is impossible to avoid being in some degree influenced by the opinions of others, nor, indeed, would it be unreasonable to receive, with equal readiness, doctrines which the learned have doubted, or denied, and those which have gained universal assent. The fact, therefore, of such a man as Hume being a sceptic and scoffer at religion, supplies, undoubtedly, a *prima facie* presumption against its truth; and the statement of that fact by me without comment or explanation, might accordingly be alleged in evidence, that I was undermining the cause which I have professed to support. It will be proper, therefore, for the credit of religion, that this ensnaring question should receive a satisfactory answer; and necessary, in my own defence, that such an answer to it should here be rendered by me. Now, it were a poor explanation, to affirm, that this philosopher's impiety arose from his neglecting to "search the Scriptures," in the manner which some have absurdly recommended, namely, with *faith*, and prayers for *grace* to believe them; since he, who could ever dream of so commencing his investigations, must either be incapable of the simplest reasonings, or already possessed with a most irrational conviction of that upon which he laments his incredulity, and

which he labours so fantastically to believe. Nor would it
avail to urge, that Hume "wanted a meek and humble spirit;"
for, the arrogant and conceited have believed, the meek sometimes demurred, – and, at any rate, overweening vanity does
not appear to have entered into the character of our sceptic.
The truth is, he split upon that rock, which must be dangerous
to all, and has ever been most fatal to the most enterprising
spirits. He neglected the general sense and opinions of mankind; he professedly abandoned the universal method of
reasoning from facts;[1] and, – not at all pretending to disprove
or annul the evidences of the Christian faith, an attempt
which had been often tried before him, and which had
invariably terminated in the most shameful discomfiture, –
he left the beaten track of practical, every day argument, to
pursue an airy, fantastic course, and, as must ever be the case
with those whose better genius recalls them not from such
distracting, visionary speculations, to nature, to their senses,
and to earth, he hurried on from doubt to doubt, from one
metaphysical uncertainty to another, till, like the fiends of
Milton, who, from their compeers

> " – apart,
> Sat on a hill retired, and reasoned high
> Of fate, free will, fore knowledge absolute,
> And found no end,"

he, at last, in a kind of delirium, actually *congratulates* himself upon his "happy escape" into those "obscure regions,"
where, he informs us, "bewilderment is the result of our most
accurate scrutiny," and where nothing is to be found but
"doubt, uncertainty, and suspense of judgment."[2]

It is my intention, in the present tract, to review very briefly
the THEORY OF RELIGION, which this subtle sceptic has
devised; and, for this purpose, I shall here quote the whole

---

[1] The *Essay on Miracles*, it will be remembered, makes no account of
particular testimony, but was framed for the purpose of refuting all such
evidence, – no matter how forcible and convincing it might be. Its object
was, not, to impugn the credibility of the Christian narrative, by directly
assailing the evidence by which it is sustained, but, as Mr. HUME himself
states, to be, in spite of evidence, an "*everlasting* remedy" against the belief
of miracles, and an infallible antidote, therefore, against the force of truth.
See p. 159–160, *ante*, and HUME's *Essays*, vol. ii. p. 117.

[2] See *Nat. Hist. of Religion*, concluding paragraph.

of his introduction to that treatise, in which he professes to write its natural history. The reader will then have as clear and distinct a summary, as can be sketched, of that metaphysical system, which betrayed its penetrating projector into "doubt, uncertainty, and suspense of judgment."

"As every inquiry" (says he) "which regards religion, is of the utmost importance, there are two questions in particular, which challenge our attention, to wit, that concerning its foundation in reason, and that concerning its origin in human nature. Happily, the first question, which is the most important, admits of the most obvious, at least the clearest solution. The whole frame of nature bespeaks an intelligent author, and no rational inquirer can, after serious reflection, suspend his belief a moment, with regard to the primary principles of genuine theism and religion.[3] But, the other question, concerning the origin of religion in human nature, is exposed to some more difficulty. The belief of invisible, intelligent power, has been very generally diffused over the human race, in all places, and in all ages; but it has neither, perhaps, been so universal as to admit of no exception, nor has it been in any degree uniform, in the ideas which it has suggested. Some nations have been discovered who entertained no sentiments of religion, if travellers and historians may be credited; and no two nations, scarce any two men, have ever agreed precisely in the same sentiments. It would appear, therefore, that this preconception springs not from an original instinct, or primary impression of nature, such as gives rise to self love, affection between the sexes, love of progeny, gratitude, resentment, &c.; since every instinct of this kind has been found absolutely universal in all nations and ages, and has always a precise determinate object, which it inflexibly pursues. The first religious principles must be secondary; such as may easily be perverted by various accidents and causes, and whose operation, too, in some cases, may, by an extraordinary concurrence of circumstances, be altogether prevented. What those principles are, which give rise to the original belief, and what those antecedents and causes are, which direct its operation, is the subject of our present inquiry."

This is a very deep and dangerous theory, but, for the most

---

[3] This opinion is greatly modified in his posthumous *Dialogues.*

part, correct. The distinction between religion as it is founded "in reason," and that which has its origin "in human nature," seems very just and accurate, notwithstanding the minute verbal criticism of Doctor Warburton.[4] In the voluminous works of that zealous controversialist is now printed an irregular pamphlet, entitled "Remarks upon Mr. *David Hume's* Essay, by a *Gentleman of Cambridge*," and, although originally published under a fictitious signature, the tract possessed so many undoubted characteristics of its dignified and politic author, so much universal erudition, so much tact and intemperance in debate, together with so many personal scurrilities, and was withal rendered so remarkable by its peculiarly vehement and unpolished wit, that nothing less than the extreme duplicity of precaution, used to prevent detection, could have saved it from being immediately recognized for the workmanship of that "foul mouthed critic," who was supposed to be the "*most impudent man* alive."[5] From the account, given by Hurd, of the rise and progress of this curious production, it appears to have been most elaborately complotted and prepared by Dr. Warburton and himself, the former "beating out the mass," the other undertaking to "give it a POLISH."[6] It was slyly concerted between these two distinguished prelates, to pass it off upon the public, as the juvenile trifle of some raw college youth; a device, which, however prudent in the anticipation of defeat, was equally unsuited to the awful solemnity and importance of the subject, and unbecoming to the dignity of the persons concerned. Every honest mind must therefore rejoice, that, in a great measure, the deception failed.   Dr. Warburton, indeed, escaped, leaving his friend in the scrape, who, from perhaps a conscientious reflection upon the superior injury which the cause of religion would receive by the demonstrator of the *Divine Legation* being discovered as a principal actor, – at least until the object of attack had been sufficiently decried, and Hume's popularity, then rising into brightness, had declined, – and, probably, concerned lest irresolute believers might imagine,

---

[4] Note (34.)

[5] A letter from BOLINGBROKE to this prelate is said to have actually borne for its superscription, "*To the* MOST IMPUDENT MAN ALIVE."

[6] WARBURTON's *works*, edited by BISHOP HURD; vol. i. p. 67.

"Si Pergama dextrâ defendi possunt
Etiam hâc defensa fuissent,"

considerately allowed his name to pass as the sole author of
a tract, which, as his accomplice had premonished him before
its publication, "was not the thing it should be."[7] The reasoning, indeed, or rather the ribaldry, of the pamphlet, was
utterly ineffective for the confutation of that "wretched man,"
whom the pamphleteer affected to despise. That formidable
antagonist must, doubtless, have keenly felt the unmeasured
severity of insolence, with which he was assailed, but, perceiving that, however his arguments might have been misrepresented, or mistaken, and his character maligned, neither he
was proved guilty, nor they were refuted, he wisely pocketed
the affronts, and took no notice of the "*Gentleman of Cambridge.*"

Here we also must leave him, and his "remarks," since, to
drag them from their classic retirement could have no other
effect, than to gratify the spleen of critics, or satiate the malice
of the enemies of religion.

That the belief of invisible, intelligent power is, as Mr.
Hume says, universal, cannot be denied. That this opinion
has manifested itself in a variety of forms, is equally unquestionable. That, upon the hypothetical credit of certain travellers, some nations are supposed to have entertained no
sentiments of religion, and that no two nations, scarcely
indeed any two men, have ever agreed precisely in the same
sentiments, are very correct assertions; nor was it less correct
reasoning for our philosopher to reject from his system those
doubtful exceptions, which, he informs us, were "not worth
mentioning."[8] "Were a traveller," says he, "to transport himself into any unknown region, if he found the inhabitants
ignorant and barbarous he might beforehand declare them
idolaters; and there is scarcely a possibility of his being mistaken." All this is unobjectionable. In short, there is but one
branch of this finely wrought system, from which it is
expected that the reader will withhold his assent; and, after
the reasonings already suggested in this volume, it is appre-

[7] Ibid.

[8] Note (13,) referred to *ante.*

hended, that the question, upon which issue is now joined, may be decided in few words.

The point to be determined is, whether the sentiment of religion springs from an original instinct, or primary impression of nature, such as gives rise to self-love, affection between the sexes, love of progeny, gratitude, resentment, &c.; or, whether the first religious principles are only a secondary species of instincts. Mr. Hume rejects the former of these alternatives.

Now, it will be observed, that, like most of Hume's theories, the present one is, in some degree, enveloped in *a negation*. Upon the threshold of the argument, it exemplifies what the religious sentiments are *not*, and alludes to a class of instincts, to which he affirms that they do *not* belong; and thus it assumes the form of an objection, at the root of one principal division of the most important Essay in the present volume.[9]

The grounds, however, of his distinction between the religious instincts, and those which are the "original and primary impressions of nature," consist in a mistake which has already been adverted to.[10] Instincts of the latter sort have *not* been found "universal in all nations and ages;" nor do they "pursue inflexibly a precise determinate object." On the contrary, it would be difficult to exemplify, in any single instance, the truth of that description. Indeed, its inaccuracy has, I think, been fully manifested in the Essay which has been just now referred to; but it may be satisfactory to examine here the particular illustrations, which Mr. Hume has adduced, of "invariable, universal, and determinate instincts."

First, then, of SELF-LOVE: this, doubtless, is altogether universal; for, in an accurate philosophical sense, it is not so properly termed an *instinct*, as a necessary property of every thinking being. The imagination cannot conceive a creature to be indifferent respecting its own happiness, any more than an inanimate mass can be supposed to hold together by the repulsion of its particles. The word "self-love," therefore, signifying, in the common acceptation of the terms of which it is compounded, a *love of self*, i.e. a *desire of happiness*, or *pleasure in being pleased*, – cannot, without manifest trifling, be employed to denote an instinct, or quality of mind. To

[9] P. 110–117 *ante*.

[10] P. 9–10, also 26, *ante*.

say that one man is fond of exercise, another of rest, that this man loves his children, that man his bottle, are assertions which may communicate knowledge, though it should be remarked, that, in some of these instances, the word *love*, or its synonyme, has different meanings; but, to assert that a person is fond of, or loves himself, – in the sense in which that proposition has been stated as an analysis of human passion, namely, to signify that such a person is desirous of pleasure, and averse to pain, – appears to me to be no more than filling the ear with sounds, which leave the understanding empty. Moreover, *love* implies a relation of objects, (viz. that of the person loving to the thing beloved,) and relation excludes the idea of absolute unity between the correlatives; but what that relation may be, which is stated to subsist between an individual object and itself, is surely difficult to conceive. Hence it seems, that the compound word "self-love" is not only, as I have just endeavoured to shew, insignificant as the subject of any proposition, but a gross impropriety in the use of terms, which, however allowable in a poem or in a work of imagination, cannot be tolerated from a philosophical writer. Self-love is sometimes used in the sense of *selfishness*, or the want of benevolence, when it expresses, indeed, a very intelligible character; but then no moral mode, no religious sentiment, admits of greater difference in degree, than this very passion of selfishness, which is exhibited in all varieties, of greater and less, from the noblest philanthropy, and most disinterested goodness, of which the human mind is capable, to the most unsocial, and sordid, indifference to the feelings of others. It is unnecessary to enlarge further upon this first example.

In the next place, AFFECTION BETWEEN THE SEXES does *not*, even among brutes, "always pursue the same determinate object." Even among such animals as are governed entirely by instinct, there are monstrous productions, arising from no less monstrous attachments. Of the human species, all individuals have *not* "inflexibly pursued the precise object," which nature intended for the right gratification of this faculty. Whole nations have misdirected it; and philosophers, (some even of late years,) it is said, have advocated principles more or less abominable, and totally irreconcileable with the purposes of nature. Different regulations for the government of this principle are established, and adhered to, in different countries; some persons have never felt its influence; and certain nations, which are also represented as destitute of religion,[11] are said to be very deficient in this instinct. The more refined and elegant passion is, in its nature and operation, so vague and variable, so "easily perverted" by fancy or fashion, and so often "altogether prevented by various circumstances," that it may not be amiss to warn the youthful sceptic against those errors of too great sensibility, or obduracy, into which he is so liable to be conducted by this, his primary and unerring instinct.

Neither GRATITUDE nor RESENTMENT is always excited by the same class of objects. Injuries of the deepest die, and most calculated to provoke anger, are, by the true Christian, despised and *heartily* forgiven; and sometimes, benefits, conferred upon us by those whom we hate, add coals of fire to our resentment. Both of these sentiments are also found to exist in many different degrees; in some persons they can hardly be said to exist at all; and either of them, according as it is wisely or ill directed, may become a virtue or a vice.

The LOVE OF OFFSPRING, although it is by far the most invariable of all those natural tendencies which Mr. Hume has enumerated, does yet fall far short of its definition. Birds are universally oviparous, and, as they often also feed on eggs, they not unusually eat their own offspring. Dogs and cats have been known, frequently, and without suffering under the pressure of extraordinary hunger, to eat their young. Most women of fashion (if we may venture to make *them* the subjects of respectful investigation) will be found to resemble those exceptions, in committing, to the care of hirelings, the chief concern of their existence; and it has also been observed by the curious in such matters, that, for a great deal of the care which infants receive from their mammas, they are not more indebted to the sacred principle of parental affection, than to that feminine instinct, in consequence of which the junior members of the sex conceive a fondness for dolls, and unmarried females of a certain age, (whose parental instincts have, unhappily, been denied their proper objects,) naturally fall into the formation of similar attachments

[11] Note (13,) referred to *ante.*

toward the young and helpless, insomuch as sometimes to admit monkeys and kittens to a share of their affections.[12]

These subjects, it may be said, ought not to be satirically dealt with; but, the question is, who is the author of the satire? Definitions are of little use, if they cannot bear an application; and, however ridiculous the consequences may be, to which they lead, I do not see that there is any reason for complaint, because they are brought unceremoniously to their proper test, and estimated at their true value. It is one thing, to treat with levity important subjects, to encumber them with ridiculous principles, or introduce ludicrous topics among them; it is another, and a very different thing, to detect, and stigmatize the ridicule, which is brought upon these subjects, by the false principles, and erroneous reasonings, of others. If, indeed, ridicule in argument, *ridentem dicere verum*, be in any case allowable, (a concession, the propriety of which may well be doubted,) we should admit it for reasons, and with restrictions, very different from those which the proposers of that test are wont to assign, who affirm, that nothing, which is not truly itself absurd, can, by any ingenuity, be represented in a ludicrous point of view.[13] Upon this supposition, being manifestly opposed to facts, the propriety of ridicule, as a test of truth, can never be maintained. But, when we distinguish between the subject and the reasoning, when we employ not satire against, and instead of, argument, but, by argument, unveil the naked absurdity of sophism, and when the absurdity is, not in a caricature drawn by ourselves, but, in the original itself, then, doubtless, (although the privilege be liable to abuse,) it may be allowable, that, in rejecting nonsense, our argument should be enforced with a lash of satire, which, in that case, cannot be so truly said to be applied by us, as by the hand of the guilty lictor upon himself. And he, surely, seems to be in this situation, and to be the author of all the ridicule, which, assuredly, upon the subject of morals might better have been avoided, who systematically reckons up the most disgusting

---

[12] MONTAIGNE quotes with approbation a saying of PLUTARCH, that "those, who are delighted with dogs and monkeys, generally esteem them in consequence of a law of our nature, that the soul discharges herself upon improper objects, when the true are wanting."

[13] Note (35.)

perversion of some instincts, and the most absurd misapplication of others, among the operation of those primary and determinate impressions of nature "which are universal in all ages and nations, and have always a precise object inflexibly pursued." Having discovered with what liberal allowances these conditions must be interpreted, it will be easy to decide, how far the religious principles are entitled to be classed among those, which Mr. Hume has enumerated as examples of the primary and original instincts of nature; – whether the former, with all their diversity, have been oftener perverted than these have been; and whether their operations have been more signally prevented, by any, the most extraordinary, concurrence of circumstances.

But, even supposing that the religious sentiments were only a secondary species of instincts, it will be difficult to show, upon what account, they, any more than the primary ones, should be considered an imperfect contrivance, or for what reason we should suppose, that a proper object has been denied to them. Nor shall I attempt to explain what meaning Mr. Hume may possibly have attached to the words "secondary instincts," as distinguished from those which are admitted by him to be *primary*, but which, it has been shown, do not imply entire conformity in operation, or universality of existence. The only intelligible sense, which these words seem capable of conveying, was not, I think, the sense in which he understood or applied them, namely, to mean such tendencies as are entirely artificial, and owing to the excess of various passions; for these could not have extended their influence over the world, nor have existed in all ages and nations, but would have been confined to particular countries or districts, like other accidental opinions, and local customs. But, whatever might have been this philosopher's meaning, it seems to be a *petitio principii* directed against all that can compel assent, to suppose, that any instinct, whether religious or animal, original or secondary, clearly existing in the human mind, should be without a proper object.

When Mr. Hume ventured to assert, that "the first religious instincts must be secondary," he appears to have had in view the establishment of the old and short-sighted argument, that religion is owing to nothing else than the ordinary passion of fear: –

"Primos in orbe deos timor fecit."

Thus, our philosopher, following the steps of Lucretius, labours to bring religion into contempt, by tracing its descent from a passion, the name of which, being in general applied only to its excess, and even its least excess being ranked among the most infamous of human frailties, has been associated in our imagination with nothing but what is vile and disgraceful, and has become, of all epithets, the term of utmost contumely and reproach. Nevertheless, even had he succeeded to show that religion *was* derived from Fear, it would not thence follow, that its origin might not be a primary instinct. A brave man is prepared to encounter danger or death, provided his duty to his God, or to his country, his allegiance to a temporal sovereign, or even his character requires: –

"Non ille, pro caris amicis
Aut patriâ, timidus perire;"

but madness or ebriety, alone, can produce that "dull forgetfulness" and apathy of life, which not even the most ferocious of wild beasts exhibit. This sort or degree of fear, without which the species would quickly become extinct, is as universal as any other instinct whatsoever. It is *natural* to contemplate, with some concern and alarm, the destruction of our mortal frame, and, accordingly, we shall find, that those apprehensions are not without their proper use; it is equally *natural*, and therefore, according to the analogy of nature, it must be equally reasonable, to have the fear of God before our eyes.

Such must be the conclusion of the followers of Lucretius, and I heartily wish them joy of a more comfortable theory than their (most gloomy of all) imaginations could suggest; although it be an immediate and inevitable corollary from their own tenets. It is, therefore, almost unnecessary to advert to the fallacy of those tenets, which do not materially affect the truth of religion; however, it is so easy to refute them, that a single hint or two may be excused, which will dissipate the whole fabric of this enormous conceit.

It has been shown, that neither the credibility nor the dignity of religion can be lessened, by ascribing its origin to that fear, which is a salutary principle, and which implies no cowardice or infirmity. The libel would be innoxious, if it failed to assert, or imply, that piety could only be the result of weakness. Now, this impotent calumny, which is oftener insinuated than distinctly averred, happily admits of a summary refutation.

It must be admitted, indeed, that extreme cowardice often magnifies real terrors, and sometimes even creates imaginary ones. We can conceive a person so deficient in the most ordinary courage, as to start at his own shadow, to tremble upon the approach of a child, to fancy every arm prepared to strike, and every man he meets to be an assassin; but the veriest slave never so far imposed upon himself the delusions of fancy, as to permit chimerical, and imaginary beings, to disturb his peace. The wayfarer who sinks with the apprehension of a single highwayman, or at the barking of a cur, need not, and will not, imagine himself beset by an infinite host of giants, by fiery serpents, and enchanted dragons. He will not people the air with malignant genii, nor the earth with fearful prodigies. How, then, is it made to appear, that the same passion, which, in the common affairs of life, has sample scope, and which, in these, only exaggerates real dangers, or affixes that idea to harmless objects, should, as if marred of its power, or of the opportunity, to operate upon the things of sense, seek out for itself a new sphere of exertion, and should there so change its nature, and assume to itself a task so different from its ordinary operations, that it seems to be no longer fear alone, but with some other imaginative, and creative principle superadded, which, not only enervates and dastardizes the mind, but, gathers around it a world of fictions and chimeras.

Again, to bring this theory to the test of facts, it is known to every schoolboy, that the most renowned ornaments, of ancient, and modern chivalry, have been Christians. As is notorious to all, who have studied to any purpose the *natural history of religion,* – if only in the country to which Mr. Hume owed his birth, – many an undaunted spirit has derived, from the principles and assurances of the Gospel, greater and calmer resolution in the perilous hour, than even the soldier's doctrine of predestination, the ferocious creed of Mahomet, could have inspired. Indeed, it may be submitted to the most obstinate disciple of Lucretius, to declare, if he really believed, or, from experience, ever remarked piety, to be a cause, or the companion of cowardice. It will, perhaps, be argued, that this *fear* which hath created imaginary objects, and hath supplied them with worshippers among the brave, is of a *peculiar kind*; that it is a *particular superstitious panic differing from ordinary cowardice*: and this is just the inference which I have been advocating, and which chiefly crowns my argument with success.

Lord Shaftesbury seems, better than Mr. Hume, to have understood this subject. He takes a pride in having compelled from the arguments of Lucretius an unwilling admission, that there is in mankind a natural disposition to religion.

"It was a sign," says he, in his *Letter concerning Enthusiasm*, sect. 6th, "the Latin poet believed there was a good stock of *visionary spirit* originally in human nature. He was satisfied that men were inclined to see visions. Notwithstanding he denied the principles of religion to be *natural*, he was forced tacitly to allow there was a wondrous disposition in mankind towards *supernatural* objects, and that, if these ideas were vain, they were yet in a manner *innate*, or such as men were really born to, and could hardly by any means avoid. From which concession," he adds, in that rambling and superficial manner which was his lordship's fatal defect in philosophizing, as it was the chief error of his style, "a divine, *methinks*, might raise a good argument against him, for the truth as well as the usefulness of religion."

Thus our noble author runs on, without seeming to think his own inferences worthy of a moment's regard; but his more considerate reader will probably stop to reflect, that it had been no inapt conjecture for his lordship to have added, in the same random way, "*methinks*, it must be unreasonable, to reject, as an impossibility which no evidence can encounter,[14] the most credible of all those systems, for the TRUTH, as well as for the *usefulness* of which, in general, GOOD *arguments* may, it seems, even according to the admission of sceptics, be derived from the very objections which are raised against them."

With this observation, founded, as all the foregoing have been, upon sceptical principles, I here conclude my inferences from those subtle reasonings, by which the studies, and the minds of so many, have been distracted; not, however, with-

---

[14] P. 108; 135–136 *ante*; and HUME's *Essays*, vol. ii. p. 135–136.

out some most gratifying, and, I trust, not altogether vain expectations, that these Essays, if they shall fail to deter speculative enthusiasts from wisely venturing within the fascinating regions of metaphysics, will, at least, point out the perils, and expose the dreary hopelessness, of such pursuits; or, perhaps, assist the inexperienced inquirer out of some perplexities, and relieve the wavering Christian from the more dangerous doubts, which have bewildered, and misled so many votaries, of that sublime, but most unprofitable science.

IV. Immortality of the Soul and of a Future State

LETTER II. A VIEW OF THE PRINCIPAL
DEISTICAL WRITERS OF THE LAST AND
PRESENT CENTURY
John Leland

Letter II

Observations on Mr. Hume's essay concerning a particular providence and a future state. His attempt to shew that we cannot justly argue from the course of nature to a particular intelligent cause, because the subject lies entirely beyond the reach of human experience, and because God is a singular cause, and the universe a singular effect, and therefore we cannot argue by a comparison with any other cause, or any other effect. His argument examined, whereby he pretends to prove, that since we know God only by the effects in the works of nature, we can judge of his proceedings no farther than we now see of them, and therefore cannot infer any rewards or punishments beyond what is already known by experience and observation. The usefulness of believing future retributions acknowledged by Mr. Hume, and that the contrary doctrine is inconsistent with good policy.

Sir,

IT appears from what was observed in my former letter, that few writers have carried scepticism in philosophy to a greater height than Mr. Hume. I now proceed to consider those things in his writings that seem to be more directly and immediately designed against religion. Some part of what he calls his PHILOSOPHICAL ESSAYS *concerning Human Understanding*, manifestly tends to subvert the very foundations of natural religion, or its most important principles. Another part of them is particularly level'd against the proofs and evidences of the christian revelation.

The former is what I shall first consider, and shall therefore examine the eleventh of those essays, the title of which is, *concerning a particular providence and a future state.* Mr. Hume introduces what he offers in this essay as sceptical paradoxes advanced by a friend, and pretends by no means to approve of them. He proposes some objections as from himself, to his friend's way of arguing; but takes care to do it in such a manner, as to give his friend a superiority in the argument. And some of the worst parts of this essay are directly proposed in his own person. The essay may be considered as consisting of two parts. The one seems to be designed against the existence of God, or of one supreme intelligent cause of the universe: The other, which appears to be the main intention of the essay, is particularly level'd against the doctrine of a future state of rewards and punishments.

I shall begin with the former, because it comes first in order to be considered, though it is not particularly mentioned till towards the conclusion of the essay. He observes in the person of his Epicurean friend, that

> "while we argue from the course of nature, and infer a particular intelligent cause, which at first bestowed, and still preserves order in the universe, we embrace a principle which is both uncertain and useless. The reason he gives why it is uncertain is, because the subject lies entirely beyond the reach of human experience[1]."

This is a specimen of the use our author would make of the principles he had laid down in the preceding essays. He had represented Experience as the only foundation of our knowledge with respect to matters of fact, and the existence of objects: that it is by experience alone that we know the relation of cause and effect; and he had also asserted, that not so much a probable argument can be drawn from experience to lay a foundation for our reasoning from cause to effect, or from effect to cause. I shall not add any thing here to what was offered in my former letter to shew the absurdity, the confusion, and inconsistency of these principles. I shall only observe, that this very writer, who had represented all arguments drawn from experience, with relation to cause and effect, as absolutely uncertain, yet makes it an objection against the argument from the course of nature

---

[1] Hume's Philosophical Essays, p. 224.

to an intelligent cause, that *the subject lies entirely beyond the reach of human experience.* What is the meaning of this is not easy to apprehend. It will be readily allowed, that we do not know by experience the whole course of nature; yet enough of it falls within the reach even of human observation and experience, to lay a reasonable foundation for inferring from it a supreme intelligent cause. In that part of the universe which cometh under our notice and observation, we may behold such illustrious characters of wisdom, power, and goodness, as determine us by the most natural way of reasoning in the world, to acknowledge a most wise, and powerful, and benign author and cause of the universe. The inference is not beyond the reach of our faculties, but is one of the most obvious that offereth to the human mind. But perhaps what the author intends by observing that *this subject lies entirely beyond the reach of human experience,* is this, That notwithstanding the admirable marks of wisdom and design which we behold in the course of nature, and order of things, we cannot argue from thence to prove a wise and intelligent cause of the universe, or that there was any wisdom employed in the formation of it, because neither we, nor any of the human race, were present at the making of it, or saw how it was made.

This must be owned to be a very extraordinary way of reasoning, and I believe you will easily excuse me if I do not attempt a confutation of it.

Mr. Hume, after having argued thus in the person of his Epicurean friend, comes in the conclusion of this essay to propose another argument as from himself.

"I much doubt, saith he, whether it be possible for a cause to be known only by its effect, or to be of so singular and particular a nature as to have no parallel, and no similarity with any other cause or object, that has ever fallen under our observation. 'Tis only when two species of objects are found to be constantly conjoin'd, that we can infer the one from the other. And were an effect presented which was entirely singular, and could not be comprehended under any known species, I do not see that we could form any conjecture or inference at all concerning its cause. If experience, and observation, and analogy be, indeed, the only guides we can reasonably follow in inferences of this nature:

> Both the effect and cause must bear a similarity and resem-
> blance to other effects and causes which we know, and
> which we have found in many instances to be conjoin'd
> with each other[2]."

Mr. *Hume* leaves it to his friend's reflections to *prosecute the
consequences of this Principle*, which he had hinted before,
might lead *into Reasonings of too nice and delicate a nature*
to be insisted on. The argument, as he hath managed it, is
indeed sufficiently obscure and perplexed. But the general
intention of it seems to be this, that all our arguings from
cause to effect, or from effect to cause proceed upon analogy,
or the comparing similar causes with similar effects. Where
therefore there is supposed to be a singular cause to which
there is no parallel (though he much doubts whether there
can be cause of so singular a nature) and a singular effect,
there can be no arguing from the one to the other: Because
in that case we cannot argue by a comparison with any other
cause, or any other effect. Except therefore we can find
another world to compare this with, and an intelligent cause
of that world, we cannot argue from the effects in this present
world to an intelligent cause: *i.e.* We cannot be sure there is
one God, except we can prove there is one other God at
least; or that this world was formed and produced by a wise
intelligent cause, unless we know of another world like this,
which was also formed by a wise intelligent cause, and perhaps, not then neither: For he seems to insist upon it, that
there should be *many instances* of such causes and effects
being *conjoined with each other*, in order to lay a proper
foundation for *observation, experience,* and *analogy, the only
guides we can reasonably follow in inferences of this nature.*
He immediately after observes, that "according to the antagonists of *Epicurus*, the universe, an effect quite singular and
unparallel'd, is always supposed to be the proof of a Deity,
a cause no less singular and unparallel'd." If by calling the
universe a singular and unparallel'd effect, he intends to signify that no other universe has come under our observation,
it is very true: But it by no means follows, that we cannot
argue from the evident marks of wisdom and design which
we may observe in this universe that we do know, because we

---

[2] Hume's Philosophical Essays, p. 232, 233.

do not know any thing of any other universe. This grand universal system, and even that small part of it that we are more particularly acquainted with, comprehendeth such an amazing variety of phenomena, all which exhibit the most incontestable proofs of admirable wisdom, power, and diffusive goodness, so that one would think it scarce possible for a reasonable mind to resist the evidence. But such is this subtil metaphysical gentleman's way of arguing in a matter of the highest consequence, the absurdity of which is obvious to any man of plain understanding. It is of a piece with what he had advanced before, that there is no such thing as cause or effect at all, nor can any probable inference be drawn from the one to the other, than which, as hath been already shewn, nothing can be more inconsistent with common sense, and the reason of all mankind.

The other thing observable in this essay, and which seems to be the principal intention of it, relateth to the proof of a Providence and a Future State. He introduces his friend as putting himself in the place of *Epicurus*, and making an harangue to the people of *Athens*, to prove that the principles of his philosophy were as innocent and salutary as those of any other philosophers. The course of his reasoning or declamation is this. That

> "the chief or sole argument brought by philosophers for a divine Existence is derived from the order of nature; where there appear such marks of intelligence and design, that they think it extravagant to assign for its cause, either chance, or the blind unguided force of matter. That this is an argument drawn from effects to causes; and that when we infer any particular cause from an effect, we must proportion the one to the other, and can never be allowed to ascribe to the cause any qualities, but what are exactly sufficient to produce the effect. And if we ascribe to it farther qualities, or affirm it capable of producing any other effect, we only indulge the licence of conjecture without reason or authority."[3] That therefore "allowing God to be the author of the existence or order of the Universe, it follows, that he possesses that precise degree of power, intelligence, and benevolence, which appears in his work-

---

[3] Hume's Philosophical Essays, p. 215

manship, but nothing farther can ever be proved."[4] Those therefore are vain reasoners, and reverse the order of nature, who instead of regarding this present life, and the present scene of things as the sole object of their contemplation, render it a passage to something farther. The Divinity may indeed possibly possess attributes, which we have never seen exerted, and may be governed by principles of action, which we cannot discover to be satisfied: But we can never have reason to infer any attributes, or any principles of action in him, but so far as we know them to be exerted or satisfied."

He asks, "are there any marks of distributive justice in the world"? And if it be said, that the "justice of God exerts itself in part, but not in its full extent," he answers,

"that we have no reason to give it any particular extent, but only so far as we see it at present[5] exert itself." That "indeed, when we find that any work has proceeded from the skill and industry of man, who is a being whom we know by experience, and whose nature we are acquainted with, we can draw a hundred inferences concerning what may be expected from him, and these inferences will all be founded on experience and observation. But since the Deity is known to us only by his productions, and is a single being in the Universe, not comprehended under any species or genus, from whose experienced attributes or qualities we can by analogy infer any attribute or quality in him, we can only infer such attributes or perfections, and such a degree of those attributes, as is precisely adapted to the effect we examine. But farther attributes or farther degrees of those attributes, we can never be authorized to infer or suppose by any rules of just reasoning."

He adds, that

"The great source of our mistakes on this subject is this. We tacitly consider ourselves as in the place of the Supreme Being, and conclude, that he will on every occasion observe the same conduct, which we ourselves in his situation would have embraced as reasonable and eligible. Whereas it must

[4] Hume's *Philosophical Essays*, p. 220.
[5] *Ib.* p. 203.

evidently appear contrary to all rules of analogy to reason from the intentions and projects of men to those of a Being so different, and so much superior – so remote and incomprehensible, who bears less analogy to any other being in the universe, that the sun to a waxen taper."

He concludes therefore,

> "that no new fact can ever be infer'd from the religious Hypothesis: no reward or punishment expected or dreaded beyond what is already known by practice and observation[6]."

This is a faithful extract of the argument in this essay, drawn together as closely as I could, without the repetitions with which it aboundeth.

I shall now make a few remarks upon it.

The whole of his reasoning depends upon this maxim, that when once we have traced an effect up to its cause, we can never ascribe any thing to the cause but what is precisely proportioned to the effect, and what we ourselves discern to be so: nor can we infer any thing farther concerning the cause, than what the effect, or the present appearance of it necessarily leads to. He had to the same purpose observed in a former essay; that "it is allowed by all philosophers, that the effect is the measure of the power."[7] But this is far from being universally true. For we in many instances clearly perceive, that a cause can produce an effect which it doth not actually produce, or a greater effect than it hath actually produced. This gentleman's whole reasoning proceeds upon confounding necessary and free causes, and indeed he seems not willing to allow any distinction between them, or that there are any other but necessary and material causes[8]. A necessary cause acts up to the utmost of its power, and therefore the effect must be exactly proportioned to it. But the case is manifestly different as to free and voluntary causes. They may have a power of producing effects, which they do not actually produce. And as they act from discernment and choice, we may, in many cases, reasonably ascribe to them

[6] Hume's Philosophical Essays, p. 230, 231.

[7] *Ib.* p. 125.

[8] *Ib.* p. 131, 132, 141, 151.

farther views than we discern or discover in their present course of action. This author himself owns, that this may be reasonably done with respect to man whom we know by experience, and whose nature and conduct we are acquainted with; but denies that the same way of arguing will hold with respect to the Deity. But surely when once we come from the consideration of his works to the knowledge of a self-existent and absolutely perfect Being, we may from the nature of that self-existence and absolutely perfect cause reasonably conclude, that He is able to produce certain effects beyond what actually come under our present notice and observation, and indeed that He can do whatsoever doth not imply a contradiction. This Universe is a vast, a glorious, and amazing system, comprehending an infinite variety of parts. And it is but a small part of it that comes under our own more immediate notice. But we know enough to be convinced, that it demonstrateth a wisdom as well as power beyond all imagination great and wonderful. And we may justly conclude the same concerning those parts of the Universe that we are not acquainted with. And for any man to say, that we cannot reasonably ascribe any degree of wisdom or power to God but what is exactly proportioned to that part of the universal frame which comes under our own particular observation, is a very strange way of arguing. The proofs of the wisdom and power of God, as appearing in our part of the system, are so striking, that it is hard to conceive, how any man that is not under the influence of the most obstinate prejudice, can refuse to submit to their force. And yet there are many phænomena, the reasons and ends of which we are not at present able to assign. The proper conduct in such a case, is to believe there are most wise reasons for these things, though we do not now discern those reasons, and to argue from the uncontested characters of wisdom in things that we do know, that this most wise and powerful agent, the author of nature, hath also acted with admirable wisdom in those things, the designs and ends of which we do not know. It would be wrong therefore to confine the measures of his wisdom precisely to what appeareth to our narrow apprehensions in that part of his works, which falleth under our immediate inspection. This was the great fault of the *Epicureans*, and other atheistical philosophers, who judging by their own narrow views, urged several things as proofs of the want of wisdom and contrivance, which upon a fuller knowledge of the works of nature, furnish farther convincing proofs of the wisdom of the great Former of all things.

In like manner with respect to his goodness, there are numberless things in this present constitution, which lead us to regard him as a most benign and benevolent Being. And therefore it is highly reasonable, that when we meet with any phænomena, which we cannot reconcile with our ideas of the divine goodness, we should conclude, that it is only for want of having the whole of things before us, and considering them in their connexion and harmony, that they appear to us with a disorderly aspect. And it is very just in such a case to make use of any reasonable hypothesis, which tendeth to set the goodness of God in a fair and consistent light.

The same way of reasoning holds with regard to the justice and righteousness of God as the great Governor of the world. We may reasonably conclude from the intimate sense we have of the excellency of such a character, and the great evil and deformity of injustice and unrighteousness, which sense is implanted in us by the author of our beings, and from the natural rewards of virtue, and punishment of vice even in the present constitution of things; that he is a lover of righteousness and virtue, and an enemy to vice and wickedness. Our author himself makes his *Epicurean* friend acknowledge, that in the present order of things, virtue is attended with more peace of mind, and with many other advantages above vice.[9] And yet it cannot be denied, that there are many instances obvious to common observation, in which vice seemeth to flourish and prosper, and virtue to be exposed to great evils and calamities. What is to be concluded from this? Is it that because the justice of God here sheweth itself only *in part*, and not *in its full extent* (to use our author's expression) therefore righteousness as in God is imperfect in its degree, and that he doth not possess it in the full extent of that perfection, nor will ever exert it any farther than we see him exert it in this present state? This were an unreasonable conclusion concerning a being of such admirable perfection, whose righteousness as well as wisdom must be supposed to be infinitely superior to ours. It is natural there-

[9] Hume's Philosophical Essays, p. 221.

fore to think that this present life is only a part of the divine scheme, which shall be compleated in a future state.

But he urgeth, that the great source of our mistakes on this subject is, that

> "we tacitly consider ourselves as in the place of the supreme Being, and conclude that he will on every occasion observe the same conduct, which we ourselves in his situation would have embraced as reasonable and eligible. Whereas it must evidently appear contrary to all rules of analogy, to reason from the intentions and purposes of men to those of a Being so different and so much superior, so remote and incomprehensible.[10]"

But though it were the highest absurdity to pretend to tie down the infinite incomprehensible Being to our scanty model, and measures of acting, and to assume that he will *on every occasion*, for so our author is pleased to put the case, observe the same conduct that we should judge eligible: since there may be innumerable things concerning which we are unable to form any proper judgment, for want of having the same comprehensive view of things that he hath: yet on the other hand, there are some cases so manifest that we may safely pronounce concerning them, as worthy or unworthy of the divine perfections. And as our own natures are the work of God, we may reasonably argue from the traces of excellencies in ourselves to the infinitely superior perfections in the great Author of the Universe, still taking care to remove all those limitations and defects with which those qualities are attended in us. Since therefore we cannot possibly help regarding goodness and benevolence, justice and righteousness, as necessary ingredients in a worthy and excellent character, and as among the noblest excellencies of an intellectual Being, we are unavoidably led to conclude, that they are to be found in the highest possible degree of eminency in the absolutely perfect Being, the Author and Governor of the world. These are not mere arbitrary suppositions, but are evidently founded in nature and reason. And though in many particular instances we through the narrowness of our views cannot be proper judges of the grounds and reasons of the divine administrations, yet in general we

[10] Hume's Philosophical Essays, p. 230.

have reason to conclude, that if there be such a thing as goodness and righteousness in God, or any perfection in him correspondent to what is called goodness and righteousness in us, he will order it so that in the final issue of things a remarkable difference shall be made between the righteous and the wicked: that at one time or other, and taking in the whole of existence, virtue, though now for a time it may be greatly afflicted and oppressed, shall meet with its due reward; and vice and wickedness, though now it may seem to prosper and triumph, shall receive its proper punishment. Since therefore, by the observation of all ages, it hath often happened, that in the present course of human affairs, good and excellent persons have been unhappy, and exposed to many evils and sufferings; and bad and vicious men have been in very prosperous circumstances, and have had a large affluence of all worldly enjoyments even to the end of their lives; and that, as this gentleman himself elsewhere expresseth it, "such is the confusion and disorder of human affairs, that no perfect œconomy or regular distribution of happiness or misery, is in this life ever to be expected[11]." It seems reasonable to conclude, that there shall be a future state or existence, in which these apparent irregularities shall be set right, and there shall be a more perfect distribution of rewards and punishments to men according to their moral conduct. There is nothing in this way of arguing but what is conformable to the soundest principles of reason, and to the natural feelings of the human heart. But though a future state of retributions in general be probable, yet as many doubts might still be apt to arise in our minds concerning it, an express revelation from God assuring us of it in his name, and more distinctly pointing out the nature and certainty of those retributions, would be of the most signal advantage.

I shall have occasion to resume this subject, when I come to consider what lord *Bolingbroke* hath more largely offered in relation to it. At present it is proper to observe that though Mr. *Hume* seems to allow his *Epicurean* friend's reasoning to be just, yet he owns, that

"in fact men do not reason after that manner; and that they draw many consequences from the belief of a divine exist-

---

[11] Hume's Moral Political Essays, p. 244, 245.

ence, and suppose that the Diety will inflict punishments on vice, and bestow rewards on virtue, beyond what appears in the ordinary course of nature. Whether this reasoning of theirs (adds he) be just or not, is no matter; its influence on their life and conduct must still be the same. And those who attempt to disabuse them of such prejudices, may for aught I know be good reasoners, but I cannot allow them to be good citizens and politicians: since they free men from one restraint upon their passions; and make the infringement of the laws of equity and society in one respect more easy and secure[12]."

I think it follows from this by his own account, that he did not act a wise or good part, the part of a friend to the public or to mankind, in publishing this Essay, the manifest design of which is to persuade men, that there is no just foundation in reason for expecting a future state of rewards and punishments at all. Nor is the concession he here makes very favourable to what he addeth in the next page, concerning the universal liberty to be allowed by the state to all kinds of philosophy. According to his own way of representing it, *Epicurus* must have been cast, if he had pleaded his cause before the people; and the principal design of this Essay, which seems to be to shew not only the reasonableness, but harmlessness of that philosophy, is lost. For if the spreading of those principles and reasonings is contrary to the rules of good policy; and the character of good citizens, if they have a tendency to free them from a strong *restraint upon their passions*, and to make the *infringement of the laws of equity and society more easy and secure*; then such principles and reasonings, according to his way of representing the matter, ought in good policy to be restrain'd, as having a bad influence on the community.

There is one passage more in this essay, which may deserve some notice. It is in page 230, where he observes that

"God discovers himself by some faint traces or out-lines, beyond which we have no authority to ascribe to him any attribute or perfection. What we imagine to be a superior perfection may really be a defect. Or, were it ever so much a perfection, the ascribing it to the supreme Being, where

[12] Hume's Philosophical Essays, p. 231.

it appears not to have been really exerted to the full in his works, favours more of flattery and panegyric, than of just reasoning and sound philosophy."

The course of his arguing seems to be this. That it would favour of *flattery*, not of *sound reasoning*, to ascribe any attribute or perfection to God, which *appears not to have been exerted to the full in his works*. And he had observed before, That "it is impossible for us to know any thing of the cause, but what we have antecedently, not infer'd, but *discover'd to the full* in the effect[13]." It is plain therefore, that according to him we ought not to ascribe any perfection to God, but what is not merely *infer'd*, but *discover'd to the full* in his works. It is also manifest, that according to him there is no attribute or perfection of the Deity exerted or discovered to the full in his works. For he had said just before, that he *discovers himself only by some faint traces or outlines*. The natural conclusion from these premises taken together is plainly this. That it would be flattery and presumption in us to ascribe any attribute or perfection to God at all. And now I leave it to you to judge of the obligations the world is under to this writer. In one part of this Essay he makes an attempt to subvert the proof of the existence of God, or a supreme intelligent cause of the universe. And here he insinuateth, that it would be wrong to ascribe any perfection or attribute to him at all. And the main design of the whole Essay is to shew, that no argument can be drawn from any of his perfections, to make it probable that there shall be rewards and punishments in a future state, though he acknowledgeth that it is of great advantage to mankind to believe them.

You will not wonder after this, that this gentleman, who hath endeavoured to shake the foundations of natural religion, should use his utmost efforts to subvert the evidences of the christian revelation. What he hath offered this way will be the subject of some future letters.

---

[13] Hume's Philosophical Essays, p. 222.

LETTER X. AN EXAMINATION OF MR. HUME'S ESSAY ON A PARTICULAR PROVIDENCE, AND A FUTURE STATE

Joseph Priestley

Dear Sir

You tell me you have been a good deal staggered with the eleventh of Mr. Hume's *Philosophical Essays*, on a *particular providence* and *a future state*, thinking his reasoning, if not conclusive, yet so plausible, as to be well intitled to a particular reply; I shall, therefore, give it as much consideration as I flatter myself, after what I have already advanced on the same subject, you will think sufficient.

In the character of an Epicurean philosopher, addressing an Athenian audience, he says, p. 216,

"Allowing the gods to be the authors of the existence, or order, of the universe, it follows, that they possess that precise degree of power, intelligence, and benevolence, which appear in their workmanship. But nothing farther can be proved, except we call in the assistance of exaggeration and flattery, to supply the place of argument and reason."

He farther says, p. 223,

"You have no reason to give distributive justice any particular extent, but only so far as you see it at present extend itself."

This is the sum of his argument, which he has only repeated in his posthumous Dialogues, and the reasoning of which you will find obviated in the preceding letters. He himself makes a friend, whom he introduces as discussing the question with him, reply to it, that intelligence once proved, from our own experience and observation, we are necessarily carried beyond what we have observed, to such unseen consequences, as we naturally expect from such intelligence, in similar cases.

"If you saw," says he, p. 225, "a half finished building, surrounded with heaps of bricks, and stones, and mortar, and all the instruments of masonry, could you not infer from the effect, that it was a work of design and contrivance; and could you not return again from this inferred cause, to infer new additions to the effect, and conclude that the building would soon be finished, and receive all the farther improvements that art could bestow upon it? Why then do you refuse to admit the same mode of reasoning with regard to the order of nature?" &c.

This reply appears to me to be satisfactory. But Mr. Hume refuses to acquiesce in it, on account of a supposed total *dissimilarity* between the Divine Being and other intelligent agents, and of our more perfect knowledge of man than of God. The substance of his answer is, that we know man from various of his productions, and, therefore, from this experience of his conduct can foretell what will be the result of those of his works of which we see only a part. "Whereas the deity," he says, p. 227,

"is known to us only by his productions, and is a single being in the universe, not comprehended under any species or genus, from whose experienced attributes or qualities we can, by analogy, infer any attribute or quality in him. As the universe shews wisdom and goodness, we infer wisdom and goodness. As it shows a particular degree of these perfections, we infer a particular degree of them, precisely adapted to the effects we examine. But farther attributes, and farther degrees of the same attributes, we can never be authorised to infer, or suppose, by any rules of just reasoning."

He therefore says, p. 230,

"No new fact can be inferred from the religious hypothesis, no event foreseen or foretold, no reward or punishment expected or dreaded, beyond what is already known by practice and observation."

But if the deity be an intelligent and designing cause (of which the universe furnishes abundant evidence) he is not, in Mr.

Hume's sense, an *unique*, of a genus or species by himself; but is to be placed in the general *class of intelligent and designing agents*, though infinitely superior to all others of that kind; so that, by Mr. Hume's own concession, we are not without some *clue* to guide us in our inquiries concerning the probable tendencies and issues of what we see.

Besides, admitting the deity to be an *unique* with respect to intelligence, it is not with *one* of his productions only that we are acquainted. We see innumerable of them; and as far as our experience goes, we see that all of them advance to some state of perfection. Properly speaking, nothing is left *unfinished*. It is true that particular plants and animals perish before they arrive at this state, but this is not the case with the *species*; and all individuals perish in consequence of some *general laws*, calculated for the good of the whole species, that is, of the greater part of the individuals of which it consists. Consequently, without regard to the productions of other intelligent agents, we are not destitute of *analogies*, from which to infer a future better state of things, in which there may be a fuller display of the divine attributes, both of justice and benevolence.

On the whole, therefore, if we see things to be in a progress to a better state, we may reasonably conclude that the melioration will continue to proceed, and, either equably or accelerated, as we have hitherto observed it. Whatever be the *final object* of a work of design, yet, from what we know of such works, we can generally form a tolerable guess whether they be *finished* or *unfinished*, and whether any scheme be near its beginning, its middle, or its termination. We are, therefore, by no means precluded from all reasoning concerning a future state of things by the consideration of the infinite superiority of the author of the system of the universe to all other intelligent beings. Notwithstanding his superiority to any of them, he may be said to be *one of them*, and, without any information from the scriptures, we might have discovered that in this sense, at least, *in the image of God has he made man*. Or, though God should not be considered as of the same class with any of his creatures, his productions, having the same author, supply abundance of analogies among themselves.

In the same manner, the benevolence of the deity (which, in this place, Mr. Hume does not deny, but suppose) being simply admitted, we are at liberty to reason concerning it, as well as concerning the benevolence of any other being whatever. And therefore if, in any nearly parallel case, we can see no reason why benevolence should be limited, or why a *less* and not a *greater* degree of good should be intended, it must appear probable to us, that the greatest is intended; though, for sufficient, but unknown reasons, it cannot take place at present. Just as, if we are once satisfied that any particular *parent* has a just affection for his child, we conclude that, though he does not put him into immediate possession of every thing that he has in his power to bestow upon him, it is because he is persuaded that, for the present, it would not be for his advantage; but that, in due time (of which we also naturally presume the parent himself to be the best judge) he will do much more for him, even all that his knowledge and ability can enable him to do. And though we may presume envy and jealousy to prevent this in natural parents, we cannot possibly suppose any thing of this kind to affect the *universal parent*, because we cannot imagine any interference of interest between this parent and his offspring.

We always argue in the same manner concerning the conduct of a *governor*. If we are once fully satisfied with respect to his *love of justice*, and have also no doubt of his *wisdom* and *power*, we immediately conclude, that every incorrigible criminal in his dominions will be properly punished; and though, for the present, many criminals walk at large, we conclude that their conduct is duly attended to, and that their future treatment will be made to correspond to it.

In like manner, if the present state of things bear the aspect of a scene of *distributive justice*, it may reasonably be considered as only the beginning of a scheme of more exact and impartial administration; so that, in due time, virtue will be more adequately rewarded, and vice more exemplarily punished, than we now see it to be. Every thing, therefore, that I have advanced on this subject in the preceding *Letters* may be perfectly well founded, notwithstanding this particular objection of Mr. Hume, and notwithstanding the great stress he lays upon it, both in this work, and in his *posthumous Dialogues*.

I am,
Dear Sir, &c.

ESSAYS ON SUICIDE, AND THE IMMORTALITY OF THE SOUL, ASCRIBED TO THE LATE DAVID HUME, ESQ.

Anonymous

Source: The Monthly Review, vol. 70, 1784

IN a short preface to these *essays* we are told, that they are generally attributed to the late Mr. Hume, though not published in any edition of his works; that the celebrity of the author's name renders them, in some degree, objects of great curiosity; that, owing to this circumstance, a few copies have been clandestinely circulated, for some time, at a large price, but without any comment; that the present publication possesses very superior advantages; and that the *notes* annexed are intended to expose the sophistry contained in the original essays.

The Writer of this article knows that the essays here mentioned were written by Mr. Hume. That almost thirty years ago they made part of a volume, which was publicly advertised to be sold by Mr. Millar; that, before the day fixed for publication, several copies were delivered to some of the Author's friends, who were impatient to see whatever came from his pen; that a noble Lord, still living, threatened to prosecute Mr. Millar, if he published the essays now before us; that the Author, like a bold veteran in the cause of infidelity, was not in the least intimidated by this menace, but that the poor bookseller was terribly frightened, to such a degree, indeed, that he called in all the copies he had delivered, cancelled the two essays, and, with some difficulty, prevailed upon Mr. Hume to substitute some other pieces in the room of those objected to by the noble Lord; that by some means or other, however, a few copies got abroad, and have been clandestinely circulated, at a large price, as already mentioned.

In regard to the present Editor, though we are far from calling in question the uprightness and benevolence of his intentions, yet we cannot applaud his judgment, or think it equal to his zeal. He does not consider, that while he spreads the antidote, he disseminates the poison at the same time, and seems to resemble a physician, who should take great pains to propagate a distemper, in order to have the credit and advantage arising from the cure. There was, indeed, little, very little danger of the essays doing much mischief. The warmest of Mr. Hume's admirers think them unworthy of him, and every competent judge will, we are fully persuaded, be of opinion that they carry their own confutation along with them. A few examples will be sufficient to shew this.

Mr. Hume affirms, that it is as clear as any purpose of nature can be, that the whole scope and intention of man's creation is limited to the present life, and that those who inculcate the doctrine of a future state, have no other motive but to gain a livelihood, and to acquire power and riches in this world. – He tells us that, were one to go round the world with an intention of giving a good supper to the righteous, and a sound drubbing to the wicked, he would frequently be embarrassed in his choice, and would find that the merits and the demerits of most men and women scarcely amount to the value of either. – The life of a man, he says, is of no greater importance to the universe than that of an oyster. – It would be no crime, we are told, in any man, to divert the Nile or Danube from their courses, were he able to effect such purposes. Where then is the crime, Mr. Hume asks, of turning a few ounces of blood from their natural channel? –

Were a drunken libertine to throw out such nauseous stuff in the presence of his bacchanalian companions, there might be some excuse for him; but were any man to advance such doctrines in the company of sober citizens, men of plain sense and decent manners, no person, we apprehend, would think him entitled to a serious reply, but would hear him with silent contempt.

To combat such opinions requires no great abilities; it is but justice to the Editor, however, to acknowledge that his notes contain some pertinent and judicious reflections.

ESSAYS ON SUICIDE, AND THE IMMORTALITY OF THE SOUL, ASCRIBED TO THE LATE DAVID HUME, ESQ.

Anonymous

Source: The Gentleman's Magazine, vol. 56, 1784

These Essays, it is well known, were printed and advertised by Mr. Millar, with some others by Mr. Hume, near thirty years ago; but before the day of publication, being intimidated by threats of a prosecution, the bookseller called in some copies that he had dispersed, cancelled the two Essays, and (with difficulty) prevailed on Mr. Hume to substitute some others less obnoxious. Some copies, however, escaped this proscription, and have since been privately sold at a large price. As needy authors evade the patent by writing, or pretending to write, notes on the Bible, the present editor seems to think himself safe from prosecution by supplying this code of infidelity with what he calls "a comment" or "an antidote." A poor evasion, and which, we apprehend, would no more justify the vender of poison of any kind *in foro legis*, than *in foro conscientiæ*; as many, who swallow the poison, will not apply the antidote, even were it much stronger than that here administered. And, by adding Rousseau's Letters, the design is obvious. Sophistical and fallacious as are the arguments, we will not, by retailing them, be guilty of a practice that we condemn; but, as a much better antidote than any here prescribed, will recommend the small tract reviewed in our next article, which is supposed to be by the Dean of Canterbury.

AN ESSAY ON THE IMMORTALITY
OF THE SOUL
Anonymous

MR. HUME divides his Essay on the Immortality of the Soul, into Metaphysical, Moral, and Physical arguments, by which he very fallaciously, and very vainly, endeavours to prove, on the ground of natural philosophy, not the Immortality, but the MORTALITY of the Soul. It is on the same ground, of mere natural philosophy, that I shall undertake to prove the reverse.

I shall not tire my Readers with a refutation of every one of his arguments. The whole string of them must appear to every person who has the least tincture of logic, to be no more than a concatenation of sophisms, in support of scepticism. The three or four last of his physical arguments will afford me sufficient ground for shewing the fallacy of the sophistry, from whence he draws his conclusive inference, which is in substance, though differently and obliquely expressed, *that the doctrine of the immortality of the soul is disproved by natural philosophy; and that, therefore, it requires an implicit faith in Divine Revelation, as a doctrine which not only surpasses, but contradicts our comprehension, full as much as if we were to believe that Existence and Non-existence are synonymous terms.*

I intend to shew, not only the fallacy, but the malignity, (I hope, no intentional one) of Mr. Hume's performance.

To do *this,* I am very glad to find that I need not give myself the trouble of discussing and controverting any other of Mr. Hume's sophistical arguments, than those very few of his physical ones, which lead him *so exultingly* to his conclusion, as if they were truly decisive of the controversy.

To facilitate to my readers, as well as to myself, the scrutiny of them, in the course of my refutation, the following is a literal transcript of them; and also of the inference he draws from them, and with which he concludes his performance:

"Were our horrors of annihilation an original passion, not the effect of our general love of happiness, it would rather prove the mortality of the soul: for, as nature does nothing in vain, she would never give us a horror against an impossible event. She may give us a horror against an unavoidable event, provided our endeavours, as in the present case, may often remove it to some distance. Death is in the end unavoidable; yet the human species could not be preserved, had not nature inspired us with an aversion towards it. All doctrines are to be suspected, which are favoured by the passions; and the hopes and fears which gave rise to this doctrine,[1] are very obvious.

'Tis an infinite advantage, in every controversy, to defend the negative. If the question be out of the common experienced course of nature, this circumstance is almost, if not altogether decisive. By what arguments or analogies can we prove any state of existence, which no one ever saw, and which no way resembles any that every was seen? Who will repose such trust in any pretended philosophy, as to admit, upon its testimony, the reality of so marvellous a scene? Some new species of logic is requisite for that purpose, and some new faculties of the mind, that may enable us to comprehend that logic.

Nothing could set in a fuller light the infinite obligations which mankind have to Divine Revelation, since we find that no other medium could ascertain this great and important truth."

Without deviating in the least from that infinite obligation, which I confess (and probably with more sincerity than Mr. Hume) to have in common with all mankind to the Divine Revelation, I shall not only undertake to disprove his pretended Philosophical Demonstration, *of there being no other medium than Divine Revelation, to ascertain the immortality of the soul*: But I shall undertake to prove to the contrary, (as it has been done in different shapes, and even in the remotest ages, by mere natural philosophers, before any christian ones existed) *that this great and important truth is ascertained by mere natural philosophy*: But before I enter upon this important task, I shall revert to that malignity

---

[1] He means the doctrine of the Immortality of the Soul, which he ought to have expressed.

in Mr. Hume's performance, which I have had already in contemplation, and promised to expose.

If our abhorrence of annihilation was an original passion, (as Mr. Hume insinuates it possible to be) and consequently common to us all; and that Mr. Hume, or any other man, had found means to convince all those of the human race, who either are not blessed with the light of the Gospel, or have no *implicit* faith in Revelation, that they are to be annihilated by death, he would have had the diabolical art, of making his own species, the most miserable of all beings on the face of our globe, wherever his doctrine should happen to be promulgated and adopted.

The truth of this assertion could be illustrated many ways. I shall confine myself to a comparative one; which is, The miserable condition in which the numerous crew of a very large ship, would find themselves, if at any period of their voyage, they were made *conscious* that their fate would be *this*, That it should be put out of their power, by an Invisible Agent, to alter their course; and that, at the end of it, every one of them should perish in the harbour they were bound to; except a very trifling number amongst them, who should have acquired the extraordinary art of diving and swimming under water, to reach the shore. With what courage and glee the rest, and consequently the generality of them, would work the ship; and with what stomachs they would sit down to their mess, can easily be imagined.

Very happily for mankind, such an original passion does not exist, nor our annihilation; which, since nature does nothing in vain, (as Mr. Hume himself allows) would be necessarily the object of it.

The truth is, that our abhorence of annihilation is no more than a derivative passion: it draws its origin, together with its imaginary object, from that truly original and general one, OUR LOVE FOR HAPPINESS. And since Mr. Hume allows, that Nature (*a divine or religious man would say the Author of it*) does nothing in vain, it follows, that true happiness (for I hope that Mr. Hume would also allow, that Nature (or its Author) did not intend it to be a delusive and fleeting object, no more than an ideal one) must be obtainable by some means, and at some period, or other; and since we find that it is not to be obtained in our present state of existence, it follows, also, that there must be a future one.

I am well convinced, that this, and every other argument of mine, must be similar to some of those which have been so often and so convincingly employed, in this important controversy, by many ancient and modern authors, eminently superior to myself: But since Mr. Hume has endeavoured to obliterate such arguments in the memory of his readers, by his fascinating sophistry; it is necessary for me to employ those which occur to my own mind, in order to destroy the charm, by the help of which he administers his poison.

I shall now proceed to expose the fallacy and malignity of his next sophistical argument, and of those with which he so *exultingly* imagines to crown the whole of his labour.

If Nature (as Mr. Hume is here pleased to say) had given us a horror against death, she would not only have done something *ultimately* in vain, but something *wantonly* cruel; and consequently still more unworthy of her. She would have joined to our love for happiness, a horror against an event, not only unavoidable, but which, by our endeavours to remove it at a distance, we should be obliged to have frequently in contemplation; and to which, after all our cares to avoid, and retard it, we should at last be forced to submit, with all the painful sensations and struggles of such a horror.

If this were true, she would have given us, instead of one, two original passions; of which the one would prove at last to have been a delusive, and the other a horrible, painful one; by which she would have made us doubly unhappy: unless some such other ingenious sceptic as the late celebrated Mr. Hume, could make us believe, that a fictitious object of love, and a real one of horror, are necessary ingredients in the composition of happiness.

I must here beg leave to observe, by way of illustration, how unnaturally cruel *that* mother would be, who, by some magical art and malice, should inspire one of her daughters with an insuperable desire of remaining single; and with a consciousness of this being her only means to be happy; and, moreover, with a horror against a man, to whom she should already have promised her; and given the power to lay, sometime or other, violent hands on her, in order to make her the victim, both of *his* violence, and of *her* horror against him. The application is obvious.

Very happily for us, this *horror* does likewise not exist, and is no more than what, soon after, Mr. Hume himself condescends to call it, *an aversion*: for there is no nation under the sun, of which a great number of its individuals, and sometimes their collective bodies, do not only conquer this (so artfully) supposed horror, but boldly encounter, and even sometimes covet death, either in the pursuit, or in the despair of happiness. Examples of this kind are too numerous, to leave this assertion in want of any other proof.

Why such an eminent scholar as the late Mr. Hume, could lower himself so much as to make horror and aversion original passions, and their denominations synonymous terms, can easily be conceived. His sophistry required it.

The truth is, that they are both, in common with all their brethren, derivative passions, which draw their origin from that truly, and only original one, our love of happiness. But aversion and horror differ very much in strength, and are therefore distinguished by different names. Our reason can over-power the one; but not the other. We have an aversion for many things, which we either voluntarily submit to, or reluctantly undergo, to obtain some good, or to avoid some evil: such, for example, among the lesser ones, as *sea-sickness*, or *the drawing of a tooth*; and among those that require a greater fortitude of mind, *the torture*, to avoid an ignominious death, or the guilt and shame of betraying confederates; and, *death* itself, from different motives, as I have already shewn. Instead of which, horror overpowers our reason to a superlative degree. A person who only abhors a toad, or even a spider, would stand a very bad chance of his life, or his senses, if a number of those animals were forcibly applied to his bosom, and his eyes kept fixed upon them. And what would become of a weak and delicate woman, who faints away at the mere effluvia of a cat, which she does not see, if this animal was thrown into, and tied to her lap? The answer is obvious; she would rave, or faint away.

In short, death can be dreaded, and reluctantly submitted to, but not abhorred, except by those unhappy persons who believe the mortality of the soul, and, consequently, their annihilation; or, by those, who believing its immortality, dread the consequences of its future existence; or are so fondly attached to their imperfect, fluctuating, and perishing state of happiness in this life, that they cannot find, nor promote within themselves, any relish for a perfect, steady, and permanent happiness in a future one.

As to Mr. Hume's remark, *that all doctrines are to be suspected which are favoured by our passions*, it is full as applicable to the false doctrine of the soul's mortality, as to the true one of its immortality. Our dread of being unhappy in a future state of existence, can favour the one, full as much as our hope of the reverse can favour the other. The one can arise from a bad, and the other from a good conscience.

As to the advantage in *any* controversy (as Mr. Hume says) of defending the negative, it can only take place where the affirmative is deficient in proof; which is not the case in *this* controversy. I have already shewn, and will still further shew, that the doctrine of the soul's immortality, is proved on Mr. Hume's own ground, from this axiom in natural philosophy, *That Nature does nothing in vain*: an axiom on which natural philosophy itself is established, since, without admitting and adherring to it, all reasoning on the process of nature, would be idle and nefarious; and which axiom therefore, Mr. Hume himself has been forced to adopt, in spite of his scepticism; without perceiving (at least not avowedly) that this very scepticism, this nefarious doctrine, this darling of his, which has induced, and seduced him to call in question the sacred doctrine of the soul's immortality, is totally destroyed by it. But, supposing for a moment, as fallaciously and as falsely as Mr. Hume has done, that this doctrine was destitute of such a proof, the advantage of defending the negative in this controversy, would be then as great in denying the mortality, as in denying the immortality of the soul: for, (to retort on Mr. Hume, his own manner of arguing, where he confounds the soul's future *state* of existence, with the existence itself) by what arguments or analogies could we then prove the mortality, any more than the immortality of a being, which no one ever saw, and no way resembles any that ever was seen? – Who would, in that case, repose such a trust in any pretended philosophy, as to admit, upon its bare testimony, the mortality, or immortality of such a being? Some new species of logic would be required for this purpose; and some new faculties of the mind, to comprehend such logic.

Nothing less, I hope, will be required, to destroy the force of the following arguments, with which I shall conclude and corroborate my preceding ones.

Since all systematical philosophers, and even such sceptical ones as the late Mr. Hume, are forced to adopt this axiom in natural philosophy, *That Nature does nothing in vain*, I shall proceed to prove on this very ground, as the only one on which we can reason coherently on the process of nature. That the dictates of reason, of natural philosophy, and of natural religion, concur in establishing the doctrine of our soul's immortality.

REASON alone, if properly exerted, without the assistance of any scholastic philosophy, teaches us,

That since Nature does nothing in vain, she would not have given us an unbounded love of happiness, together with ideas of all kinds and degrees of happiness, if such kinds and degrees of happiness did not exist.

That amongst these ideas of happiness, we have one of a perfect and permanent happiness, together with an adequate love of it; of which we shall be easily convinced, if we only consider, that we always strive to perfectionate and perpetuate, as much and as far as we can, those imperfect and transitory situations in which we think and feel ourselves happy; and consequently, that if it were in our power, we would convert the state of happiness we then enjoy, into a perfect and permanent one; which proves, that (whether we consider it or not) we have an idea, and a love adequate to this idea, of a perfect and permanent happiness; and that, since Nature does nothing in vain, this most valuable kind and degree of happiness must also exist.

That all kinds and degrees of happiness, which we have any idea of, are obtainable (whether pursued or not) in our present state of existence, except this perfect and permanent happiness.

That since Nature does nothing in vain, this perfect and permanent happiness must also be obtainable, whether pursued or not.

That since it is not obtainable in our present state of existence, Nature must have prepared us a future one: and that to pass from our present to that future state of existence, we must be immortal; otherwise Nature would have done something in vain, which it is evident, from the common experienced course of nature, to be impossible.

That therefore, since our body is mortal, our soul, which at present animates our body, must be essentially ourself, and immortal.

NATURAL PHILOSOPHY, which is reason improved by knowledge, teaches us,

That since Nature does nothing in vain, she does not give us passions without suitable objects, no more than eyes without visible ones.

That we have two sorts of passions; instinctive ones, which are similar to those which we discover in the brutes; and mental ones, which are inherent in our soul, and only discoverable in our own species.

That amongst these mental passions, we have an original one, which is an unbounded love of happiness; from which all our other mental passions derive, such as a love of truth, of knowledge, &c. and which, together with our mental faculties, characterizes our soul, and distinguishes it from that which animates the brutes.

That from thence we acquire ideas of all kinds and degrees of happiness; which kinds and degrees of happiness are the objects of our love of happiness; and which, therefore, from Nature's doing nothing in vain, must necessarily exist, and be obtainable.

That amongst these objects, a perfect and permanent happiness is the most desirable one.

That all these objects are attainable (whether pursued or not) in our present state of existence; except this most desirable one, a perfect and permanent happiness.

That since Nature does nothing in vain, this most desirable object of our love of happiness must also be obtainable, whether pursued or not.

That, since it is not obtainable in our present state of existence, and that our body is mortal; Nature, to have done nothing in vain, must have made our soul immortal.

This proof, though of itself sufficient, is still corroborated by the following one:

That it is our soul, in which this mental passion of an unbounded love of happiness originates, and is inherent, together with a mental faculty of forming ideas of all kinds and degrees of happiness, and consequently of a perfect and permanent happiness; and of thereby acquiring an adequate love, together with a sense of the want, and of the value of it; and that therefore our soul, since Nature does nothing in vain, must necessarily continue to exist, when the organized matter which it animates in its present state of existence, is worn out and separated from it by a natural, or torn from it by a premature or accidental dissolution.

NATURAL RELIGION, which arises from natural philosophy, discovers the existence of God, in the infinite power, wisdom, and goodness which are displayed in the formation and preservation of the universe; and therefore attributes, very justly, Nature's doing nothing in vain, to the infinite wisdom and goodness of God, as being the author of it.

On this improved ground, it teaches us,

That God, who from his infinite wisdom and goodness, does nothing in vain, has not given us an unbounded love of happiness, together with the power of forming ideas of all kinds and degrees of happiness, and consequently of a perfect and permanent happiness, without having given us the power of pursuing, and the means of obtaining such happiness.

That this power implies a free-agency, since no power can be exerted without it.

That God has given this power and free-agency to our soul, since it is this spiritual being within us, which is possessed of faculties and passions which are inherent in it; and which not only distinguish it from that soul which animates the brutes, but enable it to govern those instinctive faculties and passions which we have in common with them.

That it is our soul's exertion of this power over our instinctive faculties and passions, in making them subservient to its own, which constitutes *virtue*; and that our soul's indulging the former to such a degree as to make its own subservient to them, constitutes *vice*.

That all kinds and degrees of happiness, are the result and reward of virtue; and all kinds and degrees of misery, the result and punishment of vice.

That, consequently, our soul's constant practice of virtue, must terminate in all kinds and degrees of happiness, and ultimately, in a perfect and permanent happiness; and that its constant indulgence of vice, must terminate in all kinds and degrees of misery, and ultimately, in a perfect and permanent misery.

That since God, in his infinite wisdom, does nothing in vain; and that this ultimate termination of our soul's good or bad use of the power he has given it, does not take place in its present state of existence; it implies the necessity of its continuing to exist, when the matter it animates is separated from it, which proves its immortality.

I shall now draw, from the whole of what I hope to have stated coherently and convincingly, a conclusive inference. But, I must first beg leave to expose the incongruity and malignity of that insidious one, which Mr. Hume has drawn from his sceptical sophistry. He infers from the whole of it, That we have infinite obligations to Divine Revelation, for revealing to us the immortality of our soul; which he pretends *only* to have shewn, that no other medium could ascertain.

I wish, for his sake, that he may himself have felt those infinite obligations which we have to Divine Revelation; and that his delusive scepticism may have induced him to express them erroneously, and not sneeringly, nor, consequently, blasphemously. Of *this*, however, he gives reason to be suspected, when we consider, that according to his conclusive inference, we should be infinitely obliged to Divine Revelation for telling us a lye, since the whole of his performance, from whence he draws this inference, tends to prove (thanks to God! very fallaciously) by moral, as well as physical and metaphysical arguments, that not only Nature, but God himself, as the author of Nature, has made our soul full as mortal as our body, by having connected them together in such a manner, that the one must perish with the other.

I shall leave it to my readers, to judge of the sincerity and coherency of such an inference; and I flatter myself, that they will do justice to the decisive coherency and energy of my own; which is,

That the dictates of Reason, Natural Philosophy, and Natural Religion, establish the doctrine of our soul's immortality, independently of, though consistently with, the dictates of Divine Revelation; and, consequently,

That it is not true, what Mr. Hume asserts,

"That no other medium than Divine Revelation could ascertain this great and important truth:"

nor,

That Divine Revelation requires from us, for our conviction of this great and important truth, an implicit faith, at the expence of our understanding.

AFTER having thus completed my little Essay on the Immortality of the Soul, I must now beg leave to observe,

That we have certainly those infinite obligations to Divine Revelation, which Mr. Hume, in spite of his real or pretended acknowledgement, has endeavoured, either wickedly or unwisely, to annihilate; and which obligations, to the best of my conception, are,

First, For having illustrated and corroborated all such truths as we were already enabled to ascertain ourselves, or to be convinced of by others, by the means of those mental faculties, which God, in his infinite wisdom and goodness, had originally endowed us with.

Secondly, – For those sacred Records, whereby we are informed of the source of that hereditary corruption of our nature, which militates so forcibly against that power and free-agency, by the exertion of which, God had originally enabled our first Parent to make himself and his progeny perfectly and permanently happy.

Thirdly, – For that infinite comfort, which we receive from our faith in the Gospel, through the knowledge we acquire by it, of those means, whereby God, in his infinite mercy, has redeemed us from the misery which our inheritance of that corruption had entailed on us. And,

Finally, for teaching us the means we are ourselves to employ, to receive the benefits of this Redemption, in our present and future state of existence,

To prove what sort of faith is the free gift of God, or what sort of human faith Divine Revelation requires from us in general; or in particular, with respect to the origin and the future *state* of our soul's existence, is one of the duties of all those who are called to expound those sacred records, whereby Divine Revelation has been conveyed to us: a task, of which I do not doubt but many of them do still acquit themselves occasionally; and of which, an infinite number of their predecessors, from the time of our Saviour's suffering to the present one inclusively, have acquitted themselves with the greatest success, to the blessed satisfaction and edification of all persons open to conviction.

The task I undertook in this little Essay, was no more than to expose the fallacy and malignity of Mr. Hume's scepticism; and to prove on his own ground, in the shortest and plainest manner, not the soul's future *state* of existence, (into which he had so sophistically metamorphosed the question) but barely the soul's future existence; which is, in other words, its IMMORTALITY.

Of this task, I have acquitted myself to the best of my small abilities. If my arguments carry conviction, and that, nevertheless, they should be attacked, derided, or cavilled at, by such ingenious sceptical authors as the late Mr. Hume; or other writing geniuses of an inferior and worse stamp; I must hope, that much abler pens than mine, will not disdain, nor fail to defend and support them, by more corroborating, and illustrating arguments of their own; or by exposing the fallacy of every one of those of Mr. Hume, of which the few last have *alone* furnished me the means to prove his conclusive inference to be a false one, without *a minute discussion of the whole of his fallacious and malignant performance:* a task, which my avocations, and situation in life; the narrowness of my circumstances; and consequential want of literary assistance, do not permit me to undertake.

INTRODUCTION
George Giles Vincent

BESIDES Science, the purpose announced in the Title-page, has been the object aimed at by me to accomplish in my earliest works, namely, that of finding out, and showing, some system in our nature, by which, as human beings, we are all mainly directed, and as the purpose of a thinking, reflecting, and reasoning being; in which all mankind might be brought to agree by their common nature, on that being explained to them, as beings upon earth, and harmonise in their associations, and promote universal good.

I have always thought some more explanation was required than the world, meaning men, appeared to be in possession of, as to the powers, and properties of those powers, moving in man as a moral, and as such, a reasonable being, as I have noticed in my former works; and I would refer particularly to what I have said in the introduction to my work of the Moral System, as the purpose of my labours.

In pursuing my inquiries on the law moving in the human being, and constituting man a moral being, I have so far accomplished my expectations of being able to show a system in human nature, and a law constituted in it, directing us; and what is of more importance, I have been enabled by it to show, by the evidence drawn from that nature, the Higher Objects the human being can, and does, raise himself to in his imagination of the Supreme Being, and of a Futurity. And that the Power of his Imagination, founded upon the law of human nature, of reason, is an assurance, and confirmatory, of the evidence in human nature of such Higher Objects, through which contemplations the purpose proposed is to be effected.

Such has been the course, the consideration of the nature of the human being has led me to; and which I hope to have so far happily explained, that it shall be seen, and shall be of use, and acceptable to all my readers.

Thus far is the introduction of the first Edition of this work, which I have revised, condensed some parts, and added fresh and elucidatory matter throughout; and especially in the Fourth Chapter; which has been reconstructed, and much addition made to it, for the purpose proposed, by showing that human laws, or compulsory means of enforcement of religion, are not required to be made by man, and pointing out the idea that it did require such means, is a mistake, and showing how that erroneous view may have arisen. But that moral direction and precepts may, and do, require in many cases the aid and coercion of human laws; and which there can be little doubt has led men into the mistake, that religion required such means to enforce that likewise.

The adoption of and obedience to the precepts and rules of which latter is by the consciences of men, their good will and opinion, and the compulsion is not to be sought by human means, as that is otherwise provided for, and reserved to the Supreme Being, by the knowledge given to man of futurity; for obtaining of life again or existence in which, we can alone look to the Almighty Power who has given the human being existence in the creation, and to obtain whose grace, man can reasonably only consider may be by obedience to the law his Creator hath constituted in man, given to him for direction, of his reason; for it could not be supposed, that by a man's disobedience of that law, favour of the Almighty Being who created man, could be hoped for or expected.

I wish further to notice that I have made a small alteration in the headings of the Chapters IV. and V. This of itself is a matter of no moment to mention; but it may be useful to confine the attention, more directly to the main subjects of them, under discussion.

In the revision of this work it has appeared to me, that it may be very useful to prepare the reader for the fair and unprejudiced reception into his mind of those two most important subjects that concern mankind, namely, a Supreme Being, a Creator, and God as that being, and a future state. On which subjects endeavours have been made by some writers on philosophy to withdraw the attention of man by certain philosophical speculations.

It is a measure of precaution before we proceed in the work of the science of the moral nature, in which these subjects are necessarily matters of principal consideration, that the error should be shown of these speculations.

Mr. David Hume, in certain of his Essays, which would appear to be opposed to the science of the moral nature, which shows these subjects are raised to the knowledge of the human being, my endeavour will be, to point out the error in Mr. Hume's writings; which I think has arisen from a mistake on his part, and so palpable, that were he living he would not dispute it himself; but it is proper on the present occasion to come to the consideration of the subjects in a plain and truthful way, in which they can be comprehended by the human understanding, and therefore I am desirous to dispel all taint of scepticism from the minds of philosophers, and men of letters, in calling the attention to the science of the Moral Nature.

The matters I advert to in Mr. Hume's Essays are, I apprehend, considered as subjects of metaphysics by Mr. Hume himself, and possibly may be so considered by other writers, who have commented on, or considered them.

I do not think so myself with respect to the first subject, namely, that "Of the idea of necessary connection," whatever the other may be, namely, "Of a particular Providence and of a Future State."[1]

Certainly, Mr. Hume in the way he has treated the subject first named, makes it a matter of positive, external, visible, and sensible effect, by the way he endeavours to exemplify his case and argument, by referring to an actual visible cause and effect; "of one billiard ball striking another;" taking, as it appears to me, the subject out of the category of metaphysics; and proving, by the instance or exemplification he gives, the fact or point which he denies, and contradicts himself in his attempt to justify his doctrine.

What is meant under the head of the idea of necessary connection? On the difficulty, or, rather, according to Mr. Hume, the impossibility, of seeing or determining which, he appears to build a theory or argument to sustain these points, namely, that there is no means of establishing or showing cause is precursor, or connected with effect, and thence it is to be supposed he means we cannot be sure of, or prove, a future, as instanced in the influences of the will over the body.

---

[1] "Of the Idea of Necessary Connection," sect. vii. part 1, p. 65, vol. ii. The other is, that "Of a particular Providence and of a Future State," sect. xi. p. 141, vol. ii.

He says, this can be known only by experience, but never can be seen by any apparent power in the cause which connects it with effect, and renders the one an infallible consequence of the other. Mr. Hume has before said,[2]

> "When we look about us towards external objects and consider the operation of causes, we are never able in a single instance to discover any power or necessary connection; any quality which binds the effect to the cause, and renders the one an infallible consequence of the other. We only find the one does actually, in fact, follow the other. Impulse of one billiard ball is attended with motion in the second. This is the whole that appears to the outward senses. The mind feels no sentiment or inward impression from this succession of objects: consequently, there is not in any single particular instance of cause and effect, anything which can suggest the idea of power or necessary connection."

It appears to me scarcely possible, perhaps the term impossible is better than scarcely possible, to make out or understand Mr. Hume's meaning or object in this Essay and others of his of a like kind.

If it is meant applicable to moral science, I would say at the outset he appears to me to mistake his subject, especially in making any comparison between the mathematical and the moral sciences.

They do not appear in the least similar, or have anything alike, except that both are subjects of human knowledge; so are earth and air, fire and water, but the things themselves have no similitude nor any connection.

Mathematics are certain rules, as lines, figures, forms, and numbers defined, by which you determine a fact, applicable to quantity, measure, weight, and, in some respects, power and force, and so far applicable to motion.

Morals are the effects of human action or power of human action in relation to the human being.

The former is capable of certainty in quantity, measure, and weight, and as to motion in velocity and time.

The latter is of no immediate certainty of effect, until it

---

[2] Hume, 2nd vol., "Enquiry Concerning Human Understanding," sect. vii., "Of the Idea of Necessary Connection." New edition, p. 68, &c.

takes place, being affected by circumstances; but for which, laws and rules are or may be found, that shall or may be for the good, and avoid and prevent the harm, of the human being; the great objects with such being.

The two subjects, however, are as different, and wide from likeness and similitude, as it is possible for any two things or subjects to be, as human contrivance or mechanism, and electric or galvanic force.

It has been a favorite theme with many philosophers to suppose that laws and rules may be given for morals, that shall render them as certain or as definite in kind and degree, as subjects of weight, size, and measure, and as exact as a mathematical problem.

It appears to me that Mr. Hume has mistaken, or had no idea, or definite idea of, the subjects he was descanting upon under the head of necessary connection; but had mixed up the two subjects, and other matters considered with them, and consequently can come to no conclusion intelligible in moral philosophy, which especially has reference to human meaning, intention, actions, and capability, and which it would appear is his object or purpose in what he has written upon, but laboured under some mistake.

I am not sure that my views adequately reach Mr. Hume's meanings or hypothesis, but I suspect it is no fault with me, for what can be meant in the instance (satisfactory, no doubt, it was to him,) given as the billiard ball? "The impulse of one billiard ball," &c. To my conceptions, the reasoning and argument are just the reverse of that for which Mr. Hume makes use of them, namely, that one thing striking another moving it, produces no inward impression on the senses or the mind: he might with equal justness say, a flash of lightning and clap of thunder produced no internal impression. Now, physiologically speaking, we are instructed that the outward senses are nothing but internal impressions, that is, the outward perception is felt only to be known internally in the mind, the sense, I would say impression, internally there; which sense of the mind is expressed by consciousness. How have we learnt, but from experience, that fire burns? Having learnt this, does a man put his fingers into the flames? We have learnt from the outward sense of the burning the internal impression made, and do not wantonly do the same act again, or burn our fingers.

I cannot understand Mr. Hume's argument, if such I suppose it is meant, for this is the construction to be put upon the paragraph cited: – That the outward senses, the mind does not feel, or that there results no sentiment or inward impression from this succession of objects. As the impulse of one billiard ball is attended with motion in the second, this, the whole that appears to the outward senses, the mind feels no sentiment or inward impression from this succession of objects. Consequently there is not in any instances of cause and effect anything which can suggest this idea of power or necessary connection.

The inference I suppose that is to be adduced, is that we cannot have any idea of succession from present things, or facts, and realities, that are present, that there will or can be a succession, or consequence, and that therefore we cannot know of the future in time, and necessarily cannot have a knowledge of futurity. At least it is this position, to which the argument is applicable; and in some other portions of the Essays, I think I have met with the express assertion, that therefore, we cannot show or prove a futurity.

My own feeling is, that there is no necessity of following up the insufficiency of the Essay on the subject it professes to consider, and certainly of the conclusion; I have supposed it may be intended for, or is directed to, while we have a basis in the certain facts in nature, which are stated, such as a law in our nature; the power and means of idea, and its application, and the authority we have in it, to carry out, and support what the science of our moral nature teaches us. Which basis does not appear to have been considered, or, if it has, has not had the proper view or application of it that it should have had, and the force of which properly seen is of the greatest use in clearing to our minds the subject of the future, and of the greatest benefit to mankind, as the subjects of it.

But it appears, the view taken in the science has been lost sight of, if seen, or if seen, never has been noticed, to the effect it is capable of being applied, and is the legitimate application of it, that is, logically or reasonably; and can be and is maintained by the only reasonable sense or view we can apply it, or that can be taken of the human being, his actions, and his final purpose, or object of his creation, namely, that of an intellectual being with mind and reason being placed upon the earth, is in relation to futurity.

The human being, a creature with mind and reason, is wholly distinguished by such peculiar nature; and his actions and purposes are proceeding from his eminent and distinguishing faculties. Seeking for the mode and way in which they guide or direct him, they raise to him idea, which is a power, or property, or quality in his nature, through these peculiar powers of his nature of his mind and reason. Which power of idea, is the means or source, guided by his reason, of all that he does, or can do prospectively; and is, in fact, the power within him, through his nature, of proceeding forward in life, and doing or accomplishing everything of which he has any previous knowledge (which is idea), and all that is requisite for him, sustaining life by his own act, preservation of it by care; and every object and work required is, in truth, only accomplished by this power, originating everything proceeding from man by his will with knowledge, the previous knowledge given him by idea, by which he knows beforehand what his wishes, wants, and requirements are, and has certainty to some degree of accomplishing.

Such a common and palpable matter, subject, or property, of the human mind, as idea is, always using it and acting as his power, and means of knowing what he does, or he is acting for, in life, and that in fact he can do nothing of his previous knowledge without it, – that the nature and importance of this power should not have drawn more attention of the human being, to have considered it more than he has, is to be attributed to the impression in the mind of subjects, matters, and *ideas*, the multiplicity of things to retain, which are ever increasing and multiplying, as he gains knowledge, has fresh thoughts or inductions of reasoning, to infinity; and until he has weighed and studied his moral nature, he makes no sufficient distinction in the multiplicity, and all things appear blended together, and in confusion, till by study and attention he learns to separate the power and properties of different matters and subjects in his mind, and give to each subject what they embrace, apply to, and the particular qualities and powers applicable to each. And which, as to this, idea, we see it is a power or property in our mind that brings before us the subject in regard to which we act, and direct all our attention. We cannot refuse an assent to this quality, power, or property we have in our mind; and we must see that it is a power the human being possesses, by which he is to act, and can only act, as a conscious and reasonable being, in whatever he does with knowledge.

It is by idea we have the knowledge of the Supreme Being, and of a future state; and shall we say, because it is only an action or power of the mind, and we cannot shew or know the reality of these subjects directly, or immediately, they are not truths, and we should not adopt, and believe, and place our confidence and reliance on them? When we see this power of idea is the whole means of our acting, or proceeding in life, of which we have any knowledge, and is the only means by which we proceed forward in life, with knowledge of what we wish, or what we would do, or obtain, or accomplish.

We shall bring such tests of the reasonableness of the ideas we have of a Supreme Being, and of a future state, as we think all must see and understand, and give their acceptance of; and with respect to futurity, we shall give such test or proof, that, although it cannot be known otherwise than in idea, the fact itself, though unseen but in image of the mind, shall be acknowledged by all, and shall be incapable of being denied.

These subjects are those of metaphysics, that is, formed in, and existing in the mind by the powers or laws of the nature of the mind to raise subjects in image, or by representation, but sensible of, nevertheless, by its internal perception, that we cannot doubt the idea or image raised, and that it represents that which must be a truth although not present, and which the reasonable powers attesting, the truth to our mind's judgment must be received, and be believed, by the reasonable being.

In a subsequent section of Mr. Hume's Essays "Of a Particular Providence and of a Future State," I find nothing that affects the doctrine of a future state as considered in the science of the moral nature, but rather the points or positions of the argument (it is presumed to be meant) to oppose such idea unconsciously most signally maintain my argument in asserting it; possibly not so intended, but, on the contrary, introduced to prove the very opposite, viz. that we can have no knowledge of futurity, and that it cannot be; consequently, a future state is an anomaly, and is nothing more than chimera or illusion of the imagination, or imaginary powers of the brain.

Premising, before I proceed further in my observations, that although I may come under the designation there referred to of a religious philosopher, I am not a philosopher who may be trying to establish religion upon the principles of reason.

On this point, what I say is, that reason constitutes man naturally a religious being. But I interfere with no religion, for that is not the purpose of the science of the moral nature, nor of my works, or labours, but to shew the knowledge we can obtain in the moral nature, and what that nature consists in, and its powers and properties; and to shew, that by it we learn or gain a knowledge of those two great subjects of the Supreme Being, and of a future state; that these ideas agree with every religion, and if possible, through the agency of such knowledge, harmonise all men of whatever religion, and however different such may be, and that their strifes, their hostility, and hatred of each other on account of religion, shall cease or be neutralized.

Proceeding in his argument, which Mr. Hume introduces as a disputation between his friend as representing Epicurus and himself as the opposer representing the Athenian people, a preliminary stipulation of rules for the argument is laid down.

"That the accusers have acknowledged that the chief or sole argument for a divine existence (which I never questioned) is derived from the order of nature. Where there appear such marks of intelligence and design, that you think it extravagant to assign for its cause either chance or the blind and unguided force of matter, you allow, this is an argument drawn from effects to causes. From the order of the work, you infer there must have been project, and forethought, in the workman. If you cannot make out this point, you allow that your conclusion fails; and you pretend not to establish the conclusion in a greater latitude than the phenomena of nature will justify."

A rule is thus laid down, that when we infer cause from effect, we must proportion the one to the other, and can never be allowed to ascribe to the cause any qualities but what are exactly sufficient to produce the effect.

As it is tiresome to proceed upon all the premises, I think

we can proceed very well on what has been stated, though the premises perhaps admit of some comment and some exception.

The argument of limiting the cause precisely to the effect, considering the infinite number and variety of effects, is scarcely intelligible in meaning, and appears to cramp or tie up and fix the opposer, which, however proper in a subject of positive limit, does not appear quite fair in a subject of unlimited power and nature, as far as we can see, and must admit; but we think we shall avoid the necessity of any objection here, because, as the effect is unlimited, is, in truth and fact, infinite, the power or cause must be the same.

The effect upon which I have drawn the idea of cause is nature. It is a necessary inference, and a legitimate argument on the ground or limit taken, that the cause shall be equal to the effect and no more, that the cause shall be equal to creation, which is the effect of that nature we seek for or look up to of cause for that; it follows, of necessity, that the cause we form or raise in idea, can raise into creation or being.

We can see no limit to this power or cause, and the creature once raised into being, with power of reproduction, is in itself infinite in nature, and the power to create or form that which shall be and is infinite, necessarily is as great as the effect, from which we raise the idea, and the power of that cause drawn from the effect is alike infinite, and therefore is the power seen in the cause raised by the effect of nature that it is infinite. *The cause* raised and become known to man in idea from the effect of nature too, is infinite, and power to create, and with power creative, such cause can raise into being or renate the creature of nature, man, who by his nature has knowledge given him of futurity, into a state of life or being in futurity, when his life on earth shall have ceased in death.

This appears to me to dispose of Mr. Hume's argument, if it be meant, because we cannot fairly in reason suppose greater power to cause raised from effect, than is required for the effect, when considered we do find power, or give attribute of power, in the cause raised of creation, we do suppose or recognise power in that cause or attribute equal to the effect, viz. of creation. To create again, or renate, the effect in that nature, which raises the idea, and in that the knowledge of futurity; as in the case of the human being who has in his nature the effect of the power of idea, and in that of the means of knowledge, and which he does raise by that means, namely, by idea of futurity.

I think it very questionable what is intended, and what is supposed to be shewn in the hypothetical discourse or argument, in fact, it is no more than an hypothesis; and as I have adverted to the case, that it appears to me by the position of the argument, Mr. Hume by it unconsciously proves the opposite of that intended, which was meant to defeat the possibility in reason of there being a future state for man, which the basis of the reasoning, or argument, that the cause drawn from effects shall be no greater than the effect was intended, that, that effect in human nature by the powers possessed or given to man in that his nature, is to raise or produce the effect, that by idea man does raise the knowledge of futurity, and in the cause conceived or drawn from such effect, it is requisite that the power or attribute of that cause should be equal to the effect, that effect being a knowledge of futurity, and in that futurity, a future state for the human being, which by the power of creation, in reason it must be inferred, that cause raised being infinite, must be able to do.

It perhaps was not necessary to have entered into the speculations of Mr. Hume, or those of any other writer upon the subject of moral philosophy, treating the subject in the way I have done, as a matter of science grounded on the facts of human nature, and its powers, and tracing the conclusions at which I arrive. But Mr. Hume was so celebrated a writer, and his philosophical dissertations have a certain estimation with moralists and philosophers, especially upon the subject of moral philosophy, and its necessary adjunct of religious subjects, that I have been tempted to say what I have on these points mentioned; and where I think a few notices all that is required to place the subjects in a clear light, before those who may devote their attention to the consideration of moral philosophy, and at the same time shew the greater necessity for bringing before the world the subject as a matter, or in the form, of science.

For this purpose I have taken this opportunity of introducing these observations in the introduction to the revised edition of my work on the "Science of the Moral Nature."

I would further observe, that we are drawn, in the consideration of the moral nature as a science, to that subject which is of the greatest import of the means man has of directing himself of his mind, as a moral and as such a reasonable being, and the purpose and object he has in life, or in this state or being of a creature as an animal upon the earth, with the power of mind and reason and self-internal consciousness or perception of his own being, and of his own nature in a measure, and of learning knowledge not only of himself, but of all other things apparent to him upon earth, and in the universe.

These powers in human nature develope themselves in various ways, but there is one uniform mode or way in which they act, by which they are known as one character, or form, in which they are recognised, as constituting the same being, namely, man.

It is this nature we are studying in the science of the moral nature, and we find a power open to us on enquiry, which leads us all to act independent of all objects around us, and presenting themselves to us in nature, from our own internal action of our minds, raising up to us or giving us a knowledge of any or every subject upon which we bring the powers of our minds, of thought, reflection, and reason, and other powers and properties of our minds to bear upon, and by which we proceed to act, to do, and accomplish all the purposes and objects of our lives, or contemplated, desired, or required by us.

Among these we find those things, matters, or subjects raised and formed in our minds, or imaginations, and which before we act are represented to us there, but which nowhere exist to us in our possession, or accomplishment, but in our minds, from the impulse of which internal sense we do act, and accomplish, that desired or required.

This power enabling us to move and act as we wish or propose doing and required, is that we call idea. It is a power within us of representing everything we know, or raised in imagination, and to which all our previously known actions or intentions refer and from which they proceed, and so confiding in them are we, that where reasonable we proceed without any hesitation, or scruple, within ourselves, of their attainment or accomplishment.

So common and familiar to us is this power, that we do nothing, and cannot do anything with previous knowledge, without this power and means, in our nature; and we never seem to think of it, nor regard it as the great motive power of human nature, as a moral and reasonable being, as idea certainly is.

Idea, however, is not a thing or matter self-existent, within us, but that which is acquired by means of, or the powers in our nature to recognise our perceptions, be these caused either by outward or external things, or those formed within us by the internal power and action of the mind, operating within itself, on what it has acquired and knows.

It is by this extraordinary power or quality of the mind, of idea, that we conceive to exist, or become acquainted with those highest and greatest subjects, and most important of all others to man, thinking and reflecting upon all nature, and himself especially as part, and reasoning on that he forms and raises the internal idea of cause, and thus obtains a knowledge of the Supreme Being, and as one universal and prime, or first power, God.

Once raised, the idea is so prompt, and is brought before him by the presence of all nature, that his knowledge never fails him of the Being, a knowledge of WHOM is thus raised to man by his nature.

A knowledge of the Supreme Being is thus raised to man by his nature, and to man is manifestly designed and intended in the conformation of his nature, by that Supreme Being who is power creative, and who in His creation has so constituted the creature man.

It is, therefore, we see, by this means man has in his own nature, he can and does obtain a knowledge of God. This knowledge, so obtained, it is most important to him to see is raised to him by the powers in his own nature, because he sees that so given to him it is clearly the intendment of that Supreme Being who is the author of creation and of man's being upon earth; and thus seen, he feels within himself the means by which he has a knowledge of God.

This knowledge so derived is obtained by the means or powers by which he directs his acts, and is the source of everything he does, and of every act and proceeding of his life, and of which he is in a degree or measure dependent for every good and benefit resting on himself, by those powers, by the grace and goodness of God towards him, with which he is blessed, of his mind and reason.

That man is to rely on this means for his direction is evident, for if he did not he would be wanting in everything that is resting with or dependent on himself, as he cannot do anything, accept, or receive anything, without the idea of its use, its service, or necessity; which being so, he acts accordingly, by the idea he has of that he does being so.

Considerately, then, seeing this, man must be sensible that power of idea, given to him in his nature, is that power and authority given to him, and intended he should act by, rely upon, and place every trust and confidence in, guided in what he does as a reasonable being, by what is reasonable, as he can see and judge that to be wherein he has to act, and place reliance upon or confidence in.

Besides the idea and knowledge by that of God, man learns the future in time, which is endless, and is futurity; and with the knowledge of the Supreme Being and Creator, as such Being is, man looks on himself as the being to whom such knowledge is given as the creature of a future state, which it is in the power of the Almighty Being to give or raise him to, when he shall have ceased to exist in this life or world by death.

These are the great purposes to which the mental powers, the moral nature, raise up in man, and lead him to look forward to, and as the object of his being an intellectual creature with mind and reason placed upon the earth.

Before finishing these observations on the two essays I have selected from David Hume, I wish to make a suggestion, but not as assuming any authority from my own views or opinion on the subject, for the consideration of philosophers, men of letters, and others, who may have given their attention to, or considered the subject of metaphysics.

Whether we may not designate metaphysics those subject matters the mind raises or forms by inference or induction of reason from the existence of all nature, and the several subjects, matters, and things seen to exist we refer to as nature. Which subject matters themselves raised, are not seen or perceptible in the natural bodies themselves, but which are required, or necessary, for their being or existence; and which subject matters we are justified in forming or raising by our knowledge and experience. As we may instance in the subjects we are here concerned with, of the Supreme Being as cause, or power creative, and primeval, and originative; and the attributes; and time, and the future in that, and extended to endless continuity, futurity.

I will take the first to instance my meaning of that designated as metaphysics, referring to beings abstracted from all matter.

The mind raises or forms the idea that there must be cause for all that it witnesses in nature; as the heavens, the stars in the etherial expanse, the sun, the moon, and the earth. By which cause we mean the same as God, who created all.

This Cause is in no way appearing to us, or recognisable by us in itself in nature, in form, materiality, or appearance; but the powers of the mind by reason infer the existence; and that Cause inferred, is the idea raised and perceived by the mind, and inferred or raised by the induction of reason, but which Cause itself is nowhere seen in any matter or in nature.

But then it is clearly shown that the mind raises the Supreme Being in idea, by its powers of thought, reflection, imagination, and reasoning. And that the human being by the powers of his nature has the means given to him to raise the idea of the Supreme Being. And that the urgencies of his mind, and we might perhaps add, that the requirements of his nature, are not provided for or satisfied without reference to and recognition of such Power or Being; and are necessary for the good sustentation of life, and greater happiness of man, by the confidence given to him of the endurance of nature.

It is on this nature of man to raise idea that I found my argument that he has the knowledge of God given to him; and that it is that knowledge intended to be given to man by his being provided with the means of having such in his nature; and that he can and ought to rely on and confide in it; and that it is quite sufficient, and all that it was intended he should have, through his own powers in this state of being or life; and that this should be unfolded to him by time, and his own labours and exertions, by inquiry, for his better acquaintance and use, in the progression of time. His nature at the same time in the very rudest state of man, raising the idea of the most high and ulterior Power.

It appears to me that the Supreme Being considered to exist, but abstracted from all matter, and the idea raised from nature by the mind of the Supreme Being, not Himself visible or perceptible in nature, are one and the same. Both are abstracted from all matter; that is, are not seen or recognisable as anything material, but yet exist to the mind.

We may then say, the knowledge we have of God is raised to us by the metaphysical power in our nature of our mind, forming or raising us up to, or carrying us, by idea to be credited and relied upon, beyond that which can be seen in nature, but drawn from nature by the inference or induction of reason.

But there is this question to be satisfied. If the existence, or imagined existence, of the Supreme Being is abstracted from all matter, how can we say we have, or can have, any knowledge of that not recognisable to us in any matter, form, substance, or appearance? And to be abstracted from all matter is the same as to say that exists which cannot be seen or perceived in itself. But here it is I refer to the extraordinary power given to the human being in his moral nature, which enables us to form and raise a Being in existence to our minds, which reasonable we can receive and adopt, constantly rely upon, and act on, and find the subject thus raised or known to us only in idea to be true, right, and correct.

As the endurance or continuation of the system of the universe, the earth, the sun, the moon, and stars, we only know that they will endure by idea raised and formed by the inference and induction of our reason; that raised by and dependent on the Supreme Power and Will, from their apparent nature, as we can see and learn, we find by experience that the idea raised of time enduring is correct, and that they will endure into all future time is consistent with all reasonable inference.

And the subject raised to us in idea by reasonable inference or induction justifies and sanctions the reasonable being to believe, rely upon, and confide in the idea raised and formed. And that as reasonable beings we are sanctioned by having the same confiding faith in the knowledge we obtain by idea of the Supreme Being, raised by reasonable inference and induction, as we have of those things prospective in the future, as we rest on and confide in for the purposes of our lives and existences in the future of this life; but which are only known to us by idea, until they come to pass.

If the case is as I have suggested, that the ideas raised, that we refer to as metaphysics, are as one and the same as the idea we raise and form in reference to the Supreme Being, we must all see that metaphysics are not that obscure and difficult subject as has been supposed for us to comprehend, which they have been generally held to be, and proceed from the nature of the human being. In point of fact it would appear that those subjects we term or mean as metaphysics, as the idea and knowledge of the Supreme Being and futurity, are derived from or raise subjects in idea, beyond that which is directly or immediately of itself apparent in nature; but which subjects, nevertheless, appear absolutely required for that which is witnessed in nature, and being reasonable, we have the authority of the law of our nature directing us, of reason, to receive and adopt.

It is certain that we have this power of knowledge of the Supreme Being and futurity; and given to us in the powers constituted in human nature in the creation, by that Power who formed creation; and it is reasonable to infer that it was intended by that Power that created the human being, that he should have this knowledge; and that intended, it is sufficient to satisfy our inquiring and reasoning minds, by the means within ourselves, of the existence of the Supreme Being and of a futurity.

The subjects themselves of the Supreme Being and Futurity, form the matters of discussion, observation, notice, and application of the following work. We shall, therefore, say no more here than we refer to them in general terms of our knowledge or recognition of them, and as the subjects become matter for our observation, consideration, and discussion on them; but in no way intended as a dissertation on metaphysics, but as subjects of themselves (however metaphysical) as they relate to or concern us as human beings for our welfare and happiness in life, and for the higher objects and purposes of a future state, we can only conceive, and most truly believe, that man, blessed with the extraordinary powers of his moral nature, is destined in the ordinations of God Who created him.

It may be useful further to observe that difficulty may be experienced by some when they first enter on the consideration of the position I have brought forward, and have endeavoured to explain, that the human being in his peculiar nature has a law directing to what is morally right. And that this law is in reason, and is perfectly plain and discoverable when that power or property of human nature is properly studied, examined, and considered.

Men will naturally see that by their mind and reason they are directed as moral and reasonable beings; and that, that which they do which is right, and as well as that they see and do which is wrong, and should correct themselves in and not do, proceeds from the same general power in their mind and its agency of reason. But they will not, perhaps, immediately see, or indeed will they be able, if labouring under prejudices and errors, to see and understand that in the power directing them there is a law exclusively the means of their direction to what is morally right.

The two senses or meanings that I have referred to of reason, most probably will not occur to those first adverting to or considering the subject of the direction they have by their mind as reasonable beings; and they may not, therefore, see or make any distinction between the power of their mind in reason, acting in its general capacity, or as a general agent, applicable to all matters and subjects; and in the particular use and application of reason to any given or particular subject; and they may not notice that the powers we possess of discrimination of what is right for the particular subject is that alone known as reason for that, and that being the moral subject or man is reason in a moral sense; and, therefore, that reason in a specific sense of meaning, or as applied to man the moral subject, is only known in what is morally right. While reason, as a general agent, and in a general sense, may or may not be known in what is morally right, and be opposed to the specific sense or meaning.

As where a man may be badly disposed or inclined, and contemplated fraud, theft, robbery, murder, or other wrong, he might or would apply his mind and reason as a general agent, the better to direct him in accomplishing these bad purposes. But this is not applying or using his reason in a specific sense, or to the moral subject or man; and a man using his reason as a general agent to accomplish these bad purposes, could not say his actions were right or reasonable in a specific sense, or in relation to the moral subject or the human beings he would defraud, rob, murder, or wrong.

It is, therefore, in these two senses we refer to or consider reason, namely, in a general sense, or as an agent or power of discernment generally applied in directing men, and in a specific sense, or as applied to any given or particular subject, and that being the moral subject or man, reason is only seen or recognised in what is morally right.

The man badly disposed, or inclined to do wrong, would use the powers of his mind and reason to aid and assist him in his base designs and acts of wrong; and it is in such cases, where in the general agency of the mind and reason such power may direct them otherwise than to that which is morally right. Men may have supposed that reason is not a direction to what is morally right, because it has aided or assisted the badly-disposed man in his base designs. But in such cases of delinquency reason is not used in the specific sense or meaning, or as applied to the particular subject, and that being the moral subject, it is seen and known only in what is morally right.

Those criminally disposed, in hoping their acts may not be seen, and at the same time using the power of the mind and reason to effect their base designs, and where the individual hopes to hide or conceal his intended acts which are wrong and criminal, at once shows he knew what he intended to do, and was committing, was wrong; and his hope in, and endeavour at concealment, is proof of his knowledge of right and wrong, and of his guilt in doing what was wrong.

Where he might have learnt this knowledge of right and wrong probably might be in his education and society, and in the laws of his country, and in the rules and precepts of his religion for his conduct and actions in life. This knowledge would be that he obtained from outward sources the opinions, sentiments, rules, and laws he had become acquainted with in his education and practical life.

But it is very possible he might never have thought of, or if thought of, he had not considered the law he had in his nature for his direction, or that he had any knowledge from within himself that he had a law for his direction within himself, when he inquired into, and learnt, and obtained a knowledge of that nature, and his direction by it was to that which was morally right, and, by that law a power in his nature directing him, he was as a reasonable being to do what was morally right, and abstain from and not commit what was wrong.

The knowledge of the nature and power of his reason as his direction within himself to that which was morally right, might or might not have been thought of or considered; but if he had not seen or known that he had this law of his direction from within himself, he would not have had that further aid of knowledge from within himself to direct him to what was morally right, and, to restrain him from doing what was morally wrong; and which, seeing was a law within himself, might be a control over him, the knowledge he had obtained from outward sources had not, or ceased to have when he ceased to regard the world, and the laws, and rules of society, and risked or braved the effects of its prohibitions, its displeasure, and the penalties awaiting the offence of his disregard of such.

It may not ordinarily be considered how a man learns the knowledge of the moral right, and where the criminal wrong. But I think myself it is a matter of very great importance, for the greater improvement of the condition of mankind, the means of more facile and correct knowledge of their moral nature, and showing to them the law they have in their nature, distinguishing them, of their reason, for their direction, and which law can be no other than that given to them in creation by the Creator; and, therefore, the science in the studying and philosophically obtaining a knowledge of the moral nature, they may see and learn the law in human nature which man has for his direction; and seeing this within himself, he can and will feel more certainly the law and the authority he has in that law derived from his nature constituted in it by his Creator, than by any other outward means communicating the like knowledge of the moral right and wrong.

The science of the moral nature would put man in possession of knowledge that could not be controverted by any unsound speculation or sophistry. And he has rendered to him, by his own internal means of knowledge by idea, the case or fact of futurity raised to him by the knowledge he has or obtains of time, and is as much assured of, as a necessary result in the endless continuation of time, as of that future we live in daily hope and expectancy prospectively in life, and as certain to us as the endurance of the system of the universe, of the earth, its satellite the moon, the sun, the stars, and planets.

In this knowledge of futurity the power is seen by which is reserved in the Supreme Being, for the compulsion of man, to regard and observe the law which He has given to him of his direction of reason, as man could hope for grace and favour in the Almighty Power, to raise him again into a future life or being, held out to the human being by the knowledge of futurity which he may hope for by his virtuous and good deeds, but could not have the same hope for by his omission, neglect, or disobedience of that law given by the Creator to him in his nature, for his direction.

This knowledge is brought home to man in himself by being shown to him in the science of the moral nature, which had only wanted to be inquired into to be seen and learnt.

THE SOUL: THE DOCTRINE OF IMMORTALITY
Thomas Huxley

DESCARTES taught that an absolute difference of kind separates matter, as that which possesses extension, from spirit, as that which thinks. They not only have no character in common, but it is inconceivable that they should have any. On the assumption, that the attributes of the two were wholly different, it appeared to be a necessary consequence that the hypothetical causes of these attributes – their respective substances – must be totally different. Notably, in the matter of divisibility, since that which has no extension cannot be divisible, it seemed that the *chose pensante*, the soul, must be an indivisible entity.

Later philosophers, accepting this notion of the soul, were naturally much perplexed to understand how, if matter and spirit had nothing in common, they could act and react on one another. All the changes of matter being modes of motion, the difficulty of understanding how a moving extended material body was to affect a thinking thing which had no dimension, was as great as that involved in solving the problem of how to hit a nominative case with a stick. Hence, the successors of Descartes either found themselves obliged, with the Occasionalists, to call in the aid of the Deity, who was supposed to be a sort of go-between betwixt matter and spirit; or they had recourse, with Leibnitz, to the doctrine of pre-established harmony, which denied any influence of the body on the soul, or *vice versâ*, and compared matter and spirit to two clocks so accurately regulated to keep time with one another, that the one struck when ever the other pointed to the hour; or, with Berkeley, they abolished the "substance" of matter altogether, as a superfluity, though they failed to see that the same arguments equally justified the abolition of soul as another superfluity, and the reduction of the universe to a series of events or phenomena; or, finally, with Spinoza, to whom Berkeley makes a perilously close approach, they asserted the existence of only one substance, with two chief attributes, the one, thought, and the other, extension.

There remained only one possible position, which, had it been taken up earlier, might have saved an immensity of trouble; and that was to affirm that we do not, and cannot, know anything about the "substance" either of the thinking thing, or of the extended thing. And Hume's sound common sense led him to defend this thesis, which Locke had already foreshadowed, with respect to the question of the substance of the soul. Hume enunciates two opinions. The first is that the question itself is unintelligible, and therefore cannot receive any answer; the second is that the popular doctrine respecting the immateriality, simplicity, and indivisibility of a thinking substance is a "true atheism, and will serve to justify all those sentiments for which Spinoza is so universally infamous."

In support of the first opinion, Hume points out that it is impossible to attach any definite meaning to the word "substance" when employed for the hypothetical substratum of soul and matter. For if we define substance as that which may exist by itself, the definition does not distinguish the soul from perceptions. It is perfectly easy to conceive that states of consciousness are self-subsistent. And, if the substance of the soul is defined as that in which perceptions inhere, what is meant by the inherence? Is such inherence conceivable? If conceivable, what evidence is there of it? And what is the use of a substratum to things which, for anything we know to the contrary, are capable of existing by themselves?

Moreover, it may be added, supposing the soul has a substance, how do we know that it is different from the substance, which, on like grounds, must be supposed to underlie the qualities of matter?

Again, if it be said that our personal identity requires the assumption of a substance which remains the same while the accidents of perception shift and change, the question arises what is meant by personal identity?

"For my part," says Hume, "when I enter most intimately into what I call *myself*, I always stumble on some particular perception or other, of heat or cold, light or shade, love or hatred, pain or pleasure. I never can catch *myself* at any time without a perception, and never can observe anything but the perception. When my perceptions are removed for any time, as by sound sleep, so long am I insensible of *myself*, and may be truly said not to exist. And were all my perceptions removed by death, and I could neither think, nor feel, nor see, nor love, nor hate, after the dissolution of my body, I should be entirely annihilated, nor do I conceive what is further requisite to make me a perfect nonentity.   If any one, upon serious and unprejudiced reflection, thinks he has a different notion of *himself*, I must confess I can reason no longer with him. All I can allow him is, that he may be in the right as well as I, and that we are essentially different in this particular. He may perhaps perceive something simple and continued which he calls *himself*, though I am certain there is no such principle in me.

But setting aside some metaphysicians of this kind, I may venture to affirm of the rest of mankind, that they are nothing but a bundle or collection of different perceptions, which succeed one another with an inconceivable rapidity, and are in a perpetual flux and movement . . . . The mind is a kind of theatre, where several perceptions successively make their appearance, pass, repass, glide away, and mingle in an infinite variety of postures and situations. There is properly no *simplicity* in it at one time, nor *identity* in different, whatever natural propension we may have to imagine that simplicity and identity. The comparison of the theatre must not mislead us. They are the successive perceptions only that constitute the mind; nor have we the most distant notion of the place where these scenes are represented, or of the materials of which it is composed.

What then gives so great a propension to ascribe an identity to these successive perceptions, and to suppose ourselves possessed of an invariable and uninterrupted existence through the whole course of our lives? In order to answer this question, we must distinguish between personal identity as it regards our thought and imagination, and as it regards our passions, or the concern we take in ourselves. The first is our present subject; and to explain it perfectly we must take the matter pretty deep, and account for that identity which we attribute to plants and animals; there being a great analogy betwixt it and the identity of a self or person." – (I. pp. 321, 322.)

Perfect identity is exhibited by an object which remains unchanged throughout a certain time; perfect diversity is seen in two or more objects which are separated by intervals of space and periods of time. But, in both these cases, there is no sharp line of demarcation between identity and diversity, and it is impossible to say when an object ceases to be one and becomes two.

When a sea-anemone multiplies by division, there is a time during which it is said to be one animal partially divided; but, after a while, it becomes two animals adherent together, and the limit between these conditions is purely arbitrary. So in mineralogy, a crystal of a definite chemical composition may have its substance replaced, particle by particle, by another chemical compound. When does it lose its primitive identity and become a new thing?

Again, a plant or an animal, in the course of its existence, from the condition of an egg or seed to the end of life, remains the same neither in form, nor in structure, nor in the matter of which it is composed: every attribute it possesses is constantly changing, and yet we say that it is always one and the same individual. And if, in this case, we attribute identity without supposing an indivisible immaterial something to underlie and condition that identity, why should we need the supposition in the case of that succession of changeful phenomena we call the mind!

In fact, we ascribe identity to an individual plant or animal, simply because there has been no moment of time at which we could observe any division of it into parts separated by time or space. Every experience we have of it is as one thing and not as two; and we sum up our experiences in the ascription of identity, although we know quite well that, strictly speaking, it has not been the same for any two moments.

So with the mind. Our perceptions flow in even succession; the impressions of the present moment are inextricably mixed up with the memories of yesterday and the expectations of to-morrow, and all are connected by the links of cause and effect.

" . . . as the same individual republic may not only change

its members, but also its laws and constitutions; in like manner the same person may vary his character and disposition, as well as his impressions and ideas, without losing his identity. Whatever changes he endures, his several parts are still connected by the relation of causation. And in this view our identity with regard to the passions serves to corroborate that with regard to the imagination, by the making our distant perceptions influence each other, and by giving us a present concern for our past or future pains or pleasures.

As memory alone acquaints us with the continuance and extent of this succession of perceptions, tis to be considered, upon that account chiefly, as the source of personal identity. Had we no memory we never should have any notion of causation, nor consequently of that chain of causes and effects which constitute our self or person. But having once acquired this notion of causation from the memory, we can extend the same chain of causes, and consequently the identity of our persons, beyond our memory, and can comprehend times, and circumstances, and actions, which we have entirely forgot, but suppose in general to have existed. For how few of our past actions are there of which we have any memory? Who can tell me, for instance, what were his thoughts and actions on the first of January, 1715, the eleventh of March, 1719, and the third of August, 1733? Or will he affirm, because he has entirely forgot the incidents of those days, that the present self is not the same person with the self of that time, and by that means overturn all the most established notions of personal identity? In this view, therefore, memory does not so much *produce* as *discover* personal identity, by showing us the relation of cause and effect among our different perceptions. 'Twill be incumbent on those who affirm that memory produces entirely our personal identity, to give a reason why we can thus extend our identity beyond our memory.

The whole of this doctrine leads us to a conclusion which is of great importance in the present affair, viz. that all the nice and subtle questions concerning personal identity can never possibly be decided, and are to be regarded rather as grammatical than as philosophical difficulties. Identity depends on the relations of ideas, and these relations produce identity by means of that easy transition they occasion.

But as the relations, and the easiness of the transition may diminish by insensible degrees, we have no just standard by which we can decide any dispute concerning the time when they acquire or lose a title to the name of identity. All the disputes concerning the identity of connected objects are merely verbal, except so far as the relation of parts gives rise to some fiction or imaginary principle of union, as we have already observed.

What I have said concerning the first origin and uncertainty of our notion of identity, as applied to the human mind may be extended, with little or no variation, to that of *simplicity*. An object, whose different co-existent parts are bound together by a close relation, operates upon the imagination after much the same manner as one perfectly simple and undivisible, and requires not a much greater stretch of thought in order to its conception. From this similarity of operation we attribute a simplicity to it, and feign a principle of union as the support of this simplicity, and the centre of all the different parts and qualities of the object." – (I. pp. 331–3.)

The final result of Hume's reasoning comes to this: As we use the name of body for the sum of the phenomena which make up our corporeal existence, so we employ the name of soul for the sum of the phenomena which constitute our mental existence; and we have no more reason, in the latter case, than in the former, to suppose that there is anything beyond the phenomena which answers to the name. In the case of the soul, as in that of the body, the idea of substance is a mere fiction of the imagination. This conclusion is nothing but a rigorous application of Berkeley's reasoning concerning matter to mind, and it is fully adopted by Kant.[1]

Having arrived at the conclusion that the conception of a soul, as a substantive thing, is a mere figment of the imagination; and that, whether it exists or not, we can by no possi-

---

[1] "Our internal intuition shows no permanent existence, for the Ego is only the consciousness of my thinking." "There is no means whatever by which we can learn anything respecting the constitution of the soul, so far as regards the possibility of its separate existence." – *Kritik von den Paralogismen der reinen Vernunft*.

bility know anything about it, the inquiry as to the durability of the soul may seem superfluous.

Nevertheless, there is still a sense in which, even under these conditions, such an inquiry is justifiable. Leaving aside the problem of the substance of the soul, and taking the word "soul" simply as a name for the series of mental phenomena which make up an individual mind; it remains open to us to ask, whether that series commenced with, or before, the series of phenomena which constitute the corresponding individual body; and whether it terminates with the end of the corporeal series, or goes on after the existence of the body has ended. And, in both cases, there arises the further question, whether the excess of duration of the mental series over that of the body, is finite or infinite.

Hume has discussed some of these questions in the remarkable essay *On the Immortality of the Soul*, which was not published till after his death, and which seems long to have remained but little known. Nevertheless, indeed, possibly, for that reason, its influence has been manifested in unexpected quarters, and its main arguments have been adduced by archiepiscopal and episcopal authority in evidence of the value of revelation. Dr. Whately,[2] sometime Archbishop of Dublin, paraphrases Hume, though he forgets to cite him; and Bishop Courtenay's elaborate work,[3] dedicated to the Archbishop, is a development of that prelate's version of Hume's essay.

This little paper occupies only some ten pages, but it is not wonderful that it attracted an acute logician like Whately, for it is a model of clear and vigorous statement. The argument hardly admits of condensation, so that I must let Hume speak for himself: –

"By the mere light of reason it seems difficult to prove the immortality of the soul; the arguments for it are commonly derived either from metaphysical topics, or moral, or physi-

---

[2] *Essays on Some of the Peculiarities of the Christian Religion*, (Essay I. Revelation of a Future State), by Richard Whately, D.D., Archbishop of Dublin. Fifth Edition, revised, 1846.

[3] *The Future States: their Evidences and Nature; considered on Principles Physical, Moral, and Scriptural, with the Design of showing the Value of the Gospel Revelation* by the Right Rev. Reginald Courtenay, D.D., Lord Bishop of Kingston (Jamaica), 1857.

cal. But in reality it is the gospel, and the gospel alone, that has brought *life and immortality* to light.[4]

1. Metaphysical topics suppose that the soul is immaterial, and that 'tis impossible for thought to belong to a material substance.[5] But just metaphysics teach us that the notion of substance is wholly confused and imperfect; and that we have no other idea of any substance, than as an aggregate of particular qualities inhering in an unknown something. Matter, therefore, and spirit, are at bottom equally unknown, and we cannot determine what qualities inhere in the one or in the other.[6] They likewise teach us, that nothing can be decided *a priori* concerning any cause or effect; and that experience, being the only source of our judgments of this nature, we cannot know from any other principle, whether matter, by its structure or arrangement, may not be the cause of thought. Abstract reasonings cannot decide any question of fact or existence. But admitting a spiritual substance to be dispersed throughout the universe, like the ethereal fire of the Stoics, and to be the only inherent subject of thought, we have reason to conclude from *analogy*, that nature uses it after the manner she does the other substance, *matter*. She employs it as a kind of paste or clay; modifies it into a variety of forms or existences; dissolves after a time each modification, and from its substance erects a new form. As the same material substance may successively compose the bodies of all animals, the same spiritual substance may compose their minds: Their consciousness, or that system of thought

---

[4] "Now that 'Jesus Christ brought life and immortality to light through the Gospel,' and that in the most literal sense, which implies that the revelation of the doctrine is *peculiar* to His Gospel, seems to be at least the most obvious meaning of the Scriptures of the New Testament." – Whately, *l.c.* p. 27.

[5] Compare, *Of the Immateriality of the Soul*, Section V. of Part IV., Book I., of the *Treatise*, in which Hume concludes (I. p. 319) that, whether it be material or immaterial, "in both cases the metaphysical arguments for the immortality of the soul are equally inconclusive; and in both cases the moral arguments and those derived from the analogy of nature are equally strong and convincing."

[6] "The question again respecting the materiality of the soul is one which I am at a loss to understand clearly, till it shall have been clearly determined *what matter is*. We know nothing of it, any more than of mind, except its attributes." – Whately, *l.c.* p. 66.

which they formed during life, may be continually dissolved by death, and nothing interests them in the new modification. The most positive assertors of the mortality of the soul never denied the immortality of its substance; and that an immaterial substance, as well as a material, may lose its memory or consciousness, appears in part from experience, if the soul be immaterial. Reasoning from the common course of nature, and without supposing any new interposition of the Supreme Cause, which ought always to be excluded from philosophy, *what is incorruptible must also be ingenerable.* The soul, therefore, if immortal, existed before our birth, and if the former existence noways concerned us, neither will the latter. Animals undoubtedly feel, think, love, hate, will, and even reason, though in a more imperfect manner than men: Are their souls also immaterial and immortal?"[7]

Hume next proceeds to consider the moral arguments, and chiefly

"... those derived from the justice of God, which is supposed to be further interested in the future punishment of the vicious and reward of the virtuous."

But if by the justice of God we mean the same attribute which we call justice in ourselves, then why should either reward or punishment be extended beyond this life?[8] Our sole means of knowing anything is the reasoning faculty which God has given us; and that reasoning faculty not only denies us any conception of a future state, but fails to furnish a single valid argument in favour of the belief that the mind will endure after the dissolution of the body.

[7] "None of those who contend for the natural immortality of the soul ... have been able to extricate themselves from one difficulty, viz. that all their arguments apply, with exactly the same force, to prove an immortality, not only of *brutes*, but even of *plants*; though in such a conclusion as this they are never willing to acquiesce." – Whately, *l.c.* p. 67.

[8] "Nor are we therefore authorised to infer *à priori*, independent of Revelation, a future state of retribution, from the irregularities prevailing in the present life, since that future state does not account fully for these irregularities. It may explain, indeed, how present evil may be conducive to future good, but not why the good could not be attained without the evil; it may reconcile with our notions of the divine justice the present prosperity of the wicked, but it does not account for the existence of the wicked." – Whately, *l.c.* pp. 69, 70.

" . . . If any purpose of nature be clear, we may affirm that the whole scope and intention of man's creation, so far as we can judge by natural reason, is limited to the present life."

To the argument that the powers of man are so much greater than the needs of this life require, that they suggest a future scene in which they can be employed, Hume replies: –

"If the reason of man gives him great superiority above other animals, his necessities are proportionably multiplied upon him; his whole time, his whole capacity, activity, courage, and passion, find sufficient employment in fencing against the miseries of his present condition; and frequently, nay, almost always, are too slender for the business assigned them. A pair of shoes, perhaps, was never yet wrought to the highest degree of perfection that commodity is capable of attaining; yet it is necessary, at least very useful, that there should be some politicians and moralists, even some geometers, poets and philosophers, among mankind. The powers of men are no more superior to their wants, considered merely in this life, than those of foxes and hares are, compared to *their* wants and to their period of existence. The inference from parity of reason is therefore obvious."

In short, Hume argues that, if the faculties with which we are endowed are unable to discover a future state, and if the most attentive consideration of their nature serves to show that they are adapted to this life and nothing more, it is surely inconsistent with any conception of justice that we should be dealt with, as if we had all along had a clear knowledge of the fact thus carefully concealed from us. What should we think of the justice of a father, who gave his son every reason to suppose that a trivial fault would only be visited by a box on the ear; and then, years afterwards, put him on the rack for a week for the same fault?

Again, the suggestion arises, if God is the cause of all things, he is responsible for evil as well as for good; and it appears utterly irreconcilable with our notions of justice that he should punish another for that which he has, in fact, done himself. Moreover, just punishment bears a proportion to the offence, while suffering which is infinite is *ipso facto* disproportionate to any finite deed.

"Why then eternal punishment for the temporary offences of so frail a creature as man? Can any one approve of Alexander's rage, who intended to exterminate a whole nation because they had seized his favourite horse Bucephalus?

Heaven and hell suppose two distinct species of men, the good and the bad; but the greatest part of mankind float betwixt vice and virtue. Were one to go round the world with the intention of giving a good supper to the righteous and a sound drubbing to the wicked, he would frequently be embarrassed in his choice, and would find the merits and demerits of most men and women scarcely amount to the value of either."[9]

One can but admire the broad humanity and the insight into the springs of action manifest in this passage. *Comprendre est à moitié pardonner.* The more one knows of the real conditions which determine men's acts the less one finds either to praise or blame. For kindly David Hume, "the damnation of one man is an infinitely greater evil in the universe than the subversion of a thousand million of kingdoms." And he would have felt with his countryman Burns, that even "auld Nickie Ben" should "hae a chance."

As against those who reason for the necessity of a future state, in order that the justice of the Deity may be satisfied, Hume's argumentation appears unanswerable. For if the justice of God resembles what we mean by justice, the bestowal of infinite happiness for finite well-doing and infinite misery for finite ill-doing, it is in no sense just. And, if the justice of God does not resemble what we mean by justice, it is an abuse of language to employ the name of justice for the attribute described by it. But, as against those who choose

---

[9] "So reason also shows, that for man to expect to earn for himself by the practice of virtue, and claim, as his just right, an immortality of exalted happiness, is a most extravagant and groundless pretension." – Whately, *l.c.* p. 101. On the other hand, however, the Archbishop sees no unreasonableness in a man's earning for himself an immortality of intense unhappiness by the practice of vice. So that life is, naturally, a venture in which you may lose all, but can earn nothing. It may be thought somewhat hard upon mankind if they are pushed into a speculation of this sort, willynilly.

to argue that there is nothing in what is known to us of the attributes of the Deity inconsistent with a future state of rewards and punishments, Hume's pleadings have no force. Bishop Butler's argument that, inasmuch as the visitation of our acts by rewards and punishments takes place in this life, rewards and punishments must be consistent with the attributes of the Deity, and therefore may go on as long as the mind endures, is unanswerable. Whatever exists is, by the hypothesis, existent by the will of God; and, therefore, the pains and pleasures which exist now may go on existing for all eternity, either increasing, diminishing, or being endlessly varied in their intensity, as they are now.

It is remarkable that Hume does not refer to the sentimental arguments for the immortality of the soul which are so much in vogue at the present day; and which are based upon our desire for a longer conscious existence than that which nature appears to have allotted to us. Perhaps he did not think them worth notice. For indeed it is not a little strange, that our strong desire that a certain occurrence should happen should be put forward as evidence that it will happen. If my intense desire to see the friend, from whom I have parted, does not bring him from the other side of the world, or take me thither; if the mother's agonised prayer that her child should live has not prevented him from dying; experience certainly affords no presumption that the strong desire to be alive after death, which we call the aspiration after immortality, is any more likely to be gratified. As Hume truly says, "All doctrines are to be suspected which are favoured by our passions;" and the doctrine, that we are immortal because we should extremely like to be so, contains the quintessence of suspiciousness.

In respect of the existence and attributes of the soul, as of those of the Deity, then, logic is powerless and reason silent. At the most we can get no further than the conclusion of Kant:–

"After we have satisfied ourselves of the vanity of all the ambitious attempts of reason to fly beyond the bounds of experience, enough remains of practical value to content us. It is true that no one may boast that he *knows* that God and a future life exist; for, if he possesses such knowledge, he is just the man for whom I have long been seeking. All knowledge (touching an object of mere reason) can be communicated, and therefore I might hope to see my own knowledge increased to this prodigious extent, by his instruction. No; our conviction in these matters is not *logical*, but *moral* certainty; and, inasmuch as it rests upon subjective grounds, (of moral disposition) I must not even say: *it is* morally certain that there is a God, and so on; but, *I am* morally certain, and so on. That is to say: the belief in a God and in another world is so interwoven with my moral nature, that the former can no more vanish, than the latter can ever be torn from me.

The only point to be remarked here is that this act of faith of the intellect (*Vernunftglaube*) assumes the existence of moral dispositions. If we leave them aside, and suppose a mind quite indifferent to moral laws, the inquiry started by reason becomes merely a subject for speculation; and [the conclusion attained] may then indeed be supported by strong arguments from analogy, but not by such as are competent to overcome persistent scepticism.

There is no one, however, who can fail to be interested in these questions. For, although he may be excluded from moral influences by the want of a good disposition, yet, even in this case, enough remains to lead him to fear a divine existence and a future state. To this end, no more is necessary than that he can at least have no certainty that there is no such being, and no future life; for, to make this conclusion demonstratively certain, he must be able to prove the impossibility of both; and this assuredly no rational man can undertake to do. This negative belief, indeed, cannot produce either morality or good dispositions, but can operate in an analogous fashion, by powerfully repressing the outbreak of evil tendencies.

But it will be said, is this all that Pure Reason can do when it gazes out beyond the bounds of experience? Nothing more than two articles of faith? Common sense could achieve as much without calling the philosophers to its counsels!

I will not here speak of the service which philosophy has rendered to human reason by the laborious efforts of its criticism, granting that the outcome proves to be merely negative: about that matter something is to be said in the following section. But do you then ask, that the knowledge which interests all men shall transcend the common understanding and be discovered for you only by philosophers? The very thing which you make a reproach, is the best confirmation of the justice of the previous conclusions, since it shows that which could not, at first, have been anticipated; namely, that in those matters which concern all men alike, nature is not guilty of distributing her gifts with partiality; and that the highest philosophy, in dealing with the most important concerns of humanity, is able to take us no further than the guidance which she affords to the commonest understanding."[10]

In short, nothing can be proved or disproved, respecting either the distinct existence, the substance, or the durability of the soul. So far, Kant is at one with Hume. But Kant adds, as you cannot disprove the immortality of the soul, and as the belief therein is very useful for moral purposes, you may assume it. To which, had Hume lived half a century later, he would probably have replied, that, if morality has no better foundation than an assumption, it is not likely to bear much strain; and, if it has a better foundation, the assumption rather weakens than strengthens it.

As has been already said, Hume is not content with denying that we know anything about the existence or the nature of the soul; but he carries the war into the enemy's camp, and accuses those who affirm the immateriality, simplicity, and indivisibility of the thinking substance, of atheism and Spinozism, which are assumed to be convertible terms.

The method of attack is ingenious. Observation appears to acquaint us with two different systems of beings, and both Spinoza and orthodox philosophers agree, that the necessary substratum of each of these is a substance, in which the phenomena adhere, or of which they are attributes or modes.

"I observe first the universe of objects or of body; the sun, moon, and stars; the earth, seas, plants, animals, men, ships, houses, and other productions either of art or of nature. Here Spinoza appears, and tells me that these are only modifications and that the subject in which they inhere is simple, uncompounded, and indivisible. After this I consider the other system of beings, viz. the universe of thought, or my impressions and ideas. Then I observe

[10] *Kritik der reinen Vernunft.* Ed. Hartenstein, p. 547.

another sun, moon, and stars; an earth and seas, covered and inhabited by plants and animals, towns, houses, mountains, rivers; and, in short, everything I can discover or conceive in the first system. Upon my inquiring concerning these, theologians present themselves, and tell me that these also are modifications, and modifications of one simple, uncompounded, and indivisible substance. Immediately upon which I am deafened with the noise of a hundred voices, that treat the first hypothesis with detestation and scorn, and the second with applause and veneration. I turn my attention to these hypotheses to see what may be the reason of so great a partiality; and find that they have the same fault of being unintelligible, and that, as far as we can understand them, they are so much alike, that 'tis impossible to discover any absurdity in one, which is not common to both of them." – (I. p. 309.)

For the manner in which Hume makes his case good, I must refer to the original. Plain people may rest satisfied that both hypotheses are unintelligible, without plunging any further among syllogisms, the premisses of which convey no meaning, while the conclusions carry no conviction.